The Big Book of Crochet Stitches

Fabulous Fans, Pretty Picots, Clever Clusters, and a Whole Lot More

Jean Leinhauser and Rita Weiss

Martingale®
Create with Confidence

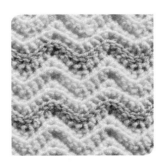

The Big Book of Crochet Stitches: Fabulous Fans,
Pretty Picots, Clever Clusters, and a Whole Lot More
© 2014 by Jean Leinhauser and Rita Weiss

Create with Confidence

Martingale®
19021 120th Ave. NE, Ste. 102
Bothell, WA 98011-9511 USA
ShopMartingale.com

Printed in China
19 18 17 16 15   8 7 6 5 4 3

**Library of Congress Cataloging-in-Publication Data is
available upon request.**

ISBN: 978-1-60468-450-6

Mission Statement

Dedicated to providing quality products
and service to inspire creativity.

Credits

President and CEO • Tom Wierzbicki
Editor in Chief • Mary V. Green
Design Director • Paul Schlosser
Managing Editor • Karen Costello Soltys
Copy Editor • Sheila Chapman Ryan
Production Manager • Regina Girard
Cover and Text Designer • Regina Girard
Photographer • Brent Kane
Samples Coordinator • Kimberly Britt

Contents

Introduction

My coauthor and late friend, Jean Leinhauser, loved everything about crochet, but most of all—I think—she loved the stitches that were used to create her projects. She collected crochet stitches like some collectors covet antiques.

Whenever she saw a photograph of a crocheted project—especially those designed overseas—she was more fascinated with the *stitches* used than the design itself. It didn't take her long before she had completely figured out how to make the stitch.

Other crocheters may have notebooks filled with photos of completed crocheted projects. Jean's notebooks, however, were filled with stitches, and she loved the idea that others could share her collection. Jean died before she could see *The Big Book of Crochet Stitches* completed, but the stitches have all come from her vast collection. This book includes some of her favorite stitches for you to use in many different ways: for afghans, sweaters, baby items—anything you would like to crochet.

What you *won't* find here is any mention of the word "gauge." That's because the stitches in this book can be worked with any type of yarn you choose, from a bulky weight to the finest lace thread.

What you *will* find here are the words "chain multiple." A multiple is the number of chains you will need to work one complete unit of the pattern. See "Multiples" on page 5 for more details.

Have fun making swatches of these patterns. Pick your favorites and begin creating your projects. You may discover, however, that the most difficult job is choosing which stitches to use.

—Rita Weiss

The patterns will look different depending on the yarn you choose to use. Experiment and have fun!

Multiples

Each stitch pattern starts with a "multiple" given like this:

Chain multiple: 6 + 4

A multiple is the number of chain stitches needed to work one complete unit of a pattern. To work the pattern in the example (6 + 4), you need to chain any number of stitches which can be divided evenly by 6: 12, 18, 24, 36, etc. To this number, you need to add 4 more chains, giving a total of 16, 22, 28, 40, etc. The "+" number is added just once.

Abbreviations, Symbols, and Glossary

Crochet patterns are written using special shorthand so that the instructions don't take up too much space. The abbreviations sometimes seem confusing, but once you learn them, you'll have no trouble following them.

Abbreviations

beg	begin(ning)
ch(s)	chain(s)
cont	continue(ing)
dc	double crochet
dec	decrease(ing)
dtr	double triple crochet
hdc	half double crochet
inc	Increase(ing)
lp(s)	loop(s)
patt	pattern
prev	previous
rem	remain(ing)
rep	repeat
RS	right side
sc	single crochet
sk	skip
sl st	slip stitch
sp(s)	space(s)
st(s)	stitch(es)
tog	together
tr	triple crochet
trtr	triple triple crochet
WS	wrong side
YO	yarn over

Symbols

* An asterisk or † dagger in a pattern row indicates a portion of instructions to be repeated. For instance, "rep from * 3 times" means that after working the instructions once, you must work them again 3 times, for a total of 4 times in all.

** Double asterisks can also be used to indicate a place in the instructions to stop a repeat before it is completed, such as "rep from * across, ending last rep at **."

( ) Parentheses enclose instructions which are to be worked the number of times indicated after the parentheses. For instance, "(ch 1, sc, ch 1) 3 times" means that you will chain 1, work 1 single crochet, and then chain 1 again 3 times for a total of 6 chains and 3 single crochets. Parentheses can also set off or clarify a group of stitches to be worked into the same space or stitch. For instance, "(dc, ch 2, dc) in corner sp."

[ ] Brackets and ( ) parentheses are also used to give you additional information.

Glossary

Join. This means to join with a slip stitch unless another stitch is specified.

Finish off. This means to end your piece by pulling the cut yarn end through the last loop remaining on the hook. This will prevent the work from unraveling.

These patterns have been written using the crochet terminology that is used in the United States. Terms which may have different equivalents in other parts of the world are listed below.

United States	International
Double crochet	Treble crochet
Gauge	Tension
Single crochet	Double crochet
Skip	Miss
Slip stitch	Single crochet

Bubbles

Chain multiple: 3 + 2

Stitch Guide

Cluster (CL): (YO, insert hook in specified st, YO and draw up a lp to height of a dc, YO and draw through 2 lps on hook) 5 times, YO and draw through 6 lps on hook: CL made.

Instructions

Row 1: Sc in 2nd ch from hook and in each rem ch; ch 1, turn.

Row 2 (RS): Sc in first sc; *CL in next sc, sc in next 2 sc; rep from * across; ch 1, turn.

Row 3: Sc in each st across; ch 1, turn.

Row 4: Sc in first 2 sc, CL in next sc; *sc in next 2 sc, CL in next sc; rep from * across, sc in last sc; ch 1, turn.

Row 5: Sc in each st across; ch 1, turn.

Rep rows 2–5 for patt.

Baby Bobbles

Chain multiple: 2 + 1

Instructions

Work all sl sts loosely.

Row 1: Sl st in 3rd ch from hook; *hdc in next ch, sl st in next ch; rep from * across; ch 2, turn.

Row 2 (RS): Sk first sl st; *sl st in next hdc, hdc in next sl st; rep from * across, sl st in top of turning ch; ch 2, turn.

Rep row 2 for patt.

Bobblin' Along

Chain multiple: 4 + 3

Stitch Guide

Bobble (BB): YO, insert hook in specified st and draw up a lp to height of a dc; YO and draw through 2 lps; (YO, insert hook in same st and draw up a lp, YO and draw through 2 lps) 4 times; YO and draw through all 6 lps on hook, ch 1: BB made.

Instructions

Row 1 (RS): Dc in 4th ch from hook and in each rem ch; ch 1, turn.

Row 2: Sc in each of first 2 sts; *BB in next st, sc in each of next 3 sts; rep from * to last 3 sts, BB in next st, sc in each of last 2 sts; ch 3, turn.

Row 3: Dc in each st across, sk turning ch; ch 1, turn.

Row 4: Sc in each of first 4 sts; *BB in next st, sc in each of next 3 sts; rep from * across, ending with sc in top of turning ch; ch 3, turn.

Row 5: Rep row 3.

Rep rows 2–5 for patt.

Why Bobble

Chain multiple: 4 + 2

Stitch Guide

Bobble (BB): *YO, insert hook in specified st and draw up a lp to height of dc; rep from * once more in same st or sp; YO and draw through all 5 lps on hook: BB made.

Y-stitch (Y-st): Tr in specified st, ch 1, dc in center of post (vertical bar) of tr just made: Y-st made.

Instructions

Row 1: Sc in 2nd ch from hook; *ch 4, work Y-st in top of last sc made, sk next 3 chs, sc in next ch; rep from * across; ch 6, turn.

Row 2 (RS): BB in first sc, sc in next ch-4 sp; *(BB, ch 3, BB) in next sc, sc in next ch-4 lp; rep from * across to last sc; (BB, ch 1, tr) in last sc; ch 1, turn.

Row 3: Sc in first tr; *ch 4, work Y-st in top of last sc made, sc in next ch-3 sp; rep from * across, working last sc in turning ch-6 sp; ch 6, turn.

Rep rows 2 and 3 for patt.

Fancy Floral

Chain multiple: 10 + 2

Stitch Guide

Bobble (BB): *YO twice, insert hook in specified st or sp and draw up a lp, (YO and draw through 2 lps on hook) twice; rep from * once in same st or sp; YO and draw through all 3 lps on hook: BB made.

Shell: Work (BB, ch 3, BB) in specified ch or st: shell made.

Bobble cluster (BBCL): *YO twice, insert hook in top of last dc (or in 3rd ch of turning ch-6) and draw up a lp, (YO and draw through 2 lps on hook) twice; rep from * once in top of same dc (or in same ch); **YO twice, insert hook in next ch-sp and draw up a lp, (YO and draw through 2 lps on hook) twice; rep from ** once in same ch-sp***; rep from ** to *** once in next ch-sp; YO and draw through all 7 lps on hook, ch 1: BBCL made.

Instructions

Row 1: Work shell in 7th ch from hook; *ch 2, sk next 2 chs, dc in next ch, ch 3, sk next 2 chs, sc in next ch, ch 3, sk next 2 chs, dc in next ch, ch 2, sk next 2 chs, work shell in next ch; rep from * across to last 3 chs, sk next 2 chs, dc in last ch; ch 6 (counts as dc and ch-3 sp throughout), turn.

Row 2: *Sc in next ch-sp, ch 3**; dc in next ch-sp, ch 3, work BBCL, ch 3, BB in top of last BBCL, dc in next ch-sp, ch 3; rep from * across, ending final rep at **; sk next BB, dc in next ch; ch 6, turn.

Row 3: *Sc in next sc, ch 3**; dc in next dc, ch 2, work shell in top of next BBCL, ch 2, dc in next dc, ch 3; rep from * across, ending final rep at **; dc in 3rd ch of turning ch-6; ch 6, turn.

Row 4: *Work BBCL, ch 3, BB in top of last BBCL**; dc in next ch-sp, ch 3, sc in next ch-sp, ch 3, dc in next ch-sp, ch 3; rep from * across, ending final rep at **; dc in 3rd ch of turning ch-6; ch 3 (counts as dc of next row), turn.

Row 5: *Work shell in top of next BBCL**; ch 2, dc in next dc, ch 3, sc in next sc, ch 3, dc in next dc, ch 2; rep from * across, ending final rep at **; dc in 3rd ch of turning ch-6; ch 6, turn.

Rep rows 2–5 for patt.

Shell Ripple

Chain multiple: 11 + 3

Stitch Guide

Cluster (CL): Keeping last lp of each dc on hook, dc in specified 3 sts, YO and draw through all 4 lps on hook: CL made.

Shell: (3 dc, ch 3, 3 dc) in specified st or sp.

Instructions

Row 1 (RS): Dc in 3rd ch from hook, ch 1, sk next ch, dc in next ch; ch 1, sk next ch, 3 dc in next ch; ch 3, 3 dc in next ch; ch 1, sk next ch, dc in next ch, ch 1; *sk next ch, CL over next 3 chs; ch 1, sk next ch, dc in next ch, ch 1; sk next ch, 3 dc in next ch; ch 3, 3 dc in next ch, ch 1, sk next ch, dc in next ch, ch 1; rep from * to last 4 chs; (sk next ch, dc in next ch) twice; ch 2, turn.

Row 2: Sk first 2 dc, (dc in next dc, ch 1) twice; sk next 2 dc, shell in next ch-3 sp; ch 1, sk next 2 dc, dc in next dc, ch 1; *CL over next dc, next CL, and next dc; ch 1, dc in next dc, ch 1, sk next 2 dc; shell in next ch-3 sp; ch 1, sk next 2 dc, dc in next dc, ch 1; rep from * to last 2 dc; dc in last 2 dc; ch 2, turn.

Row 3: Sk first 2 dc, (dc in next dc, ch 1) twice; sk next 2 dc, shell in next ch-3 sp, ch 1, sk next 2 dc, dc in next dc, ch 1; *CL over next dc, next CL, and next dc; ch 1, dc in next dc, ch 1, sk next 2 dc, shell in next ch-3 sp; ch 1, sk next 2 dc, dc in next dc, ch 1; rep from * to last 2 dc; dc in last 2 dc; ch 2, turn, leaving turning ch unworked.

Rep row 3 for patt.

Textured Ripple

Chain multiple: 9 + 3
Two colors: color A and color B

Instructions

Work beg ch with color A.

Row 1 (WS): Sc in 2nd ch from hook and in next 4 chs, 3 sc in next ch; *sc in next 3 chs, sk next 2 chs, sc in next 3 chs, 3 sc in next ch; rep from * across to last 5 chs, sc in last 5 chs; ch 1, turn.

Row 2 (RS): Working in back lps only, dec over first 2 sts (to work dec: draw up lp in each of 2 sts indicated, YO and draw through all 3 lps on hook: dec made); sc in next 4 sc, 3 sc in next sc; *sc in next 3 sc, sk next 2 sc, sc in next 3 sc, 3 sc in next sc; rep from * to last 6 sc, sc in next 4 sc, dec over last 2 sc; ch 1, turn.

Rows 3–5: Rep row 2. At end of row 5, do not ch 1. Finish off color A.

Row 6: With right side facing you and color B, working through both lps, sl st loosely in each sc across. Finish off color B.

Row 7: With wrong side facing you and color A, leaving sl sts of prev row unworked and working in back lps only of sc of row 5, rep row 2.

Rep rows 2–7 for patt.

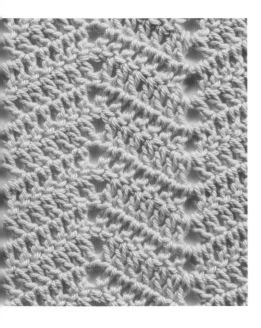

Ripple Stitch

Chain multiple: 16 + 1

Instructions

Row 1 (RS): Dc in 3rd ch from hook and in each of next 5 chs; *in next ch work shell of (dc, ch 2, dc), dc in next 6 chs; sk next 2 chs, dc in next 6 chs; rep from * to last 8 chs; in next ch work shell, dc in next 5 chs, (YO, draw up a lp in next st, YO and draw through 2 lps on hook) twice; YO, draw through all 3 lps on hook: dec made; ch 3, turn.

Row 2: Sk first st, dc in 6 dc; *in next ch-2 sp work shell; dc in 6 dc, sk 2 dc, dc in 6 dc; rep from * to last ch-2 sp; in last sp work shell, dc in 5 dc, dec as before over next 2 dc; ch 3, turn, leaving first 2 skipped chs unworked.

Row 3: Sk first st, dc in 6 dc; *work shell in next ch-2 sp; dc in 6 dc, sk 2 dc, dc in 6 dc; rep from * to last ch-2 sp; in last sp work shell, dc in 5 dc, dec as before over last 2 dc; ch 3, turn, leaving turning ch unworked.

Rep row 3 for patt.

Waves 1

Chain multiple: 17 + 1

Stitch Guide

Cluster (CL): Keeping last lp of each dc on hook, dc in specified sts, chs or sp, YO and draw through all 3 lps on hook: CL made.

Instructions

Row 1 (RS): Dc in 3rd ch from hook, (CL over next 2 chs) twice, ch 1, (dc in next ch, ch 1) 5 times; *(CL over next 2 chs) 6 times; ch 1, (dc in next ch, ch 1) 5 times; rep from * to last 6 chs; (CL over next 2 chs) 3 times; ch 2, turn.

Row 2: Sk first st, dc in next st, (CL over next st and next ch-1 sp) twice; ch 1, dc in next dc, ch 1, (dc in next ch-1 sp, ch 1, dc in next dc, ch 1) twice; *(CL over next ch-1 sp and next st) twice; (CL over next 2 sts) twice; (CL over next st and next ch-1 sp) twice; ch 1, dc in next dc, ch 1, (dc in next ch-1 sp, ch 1, dc in next dc, ch 1) twice; rep from * to last 2 ch-1 sps; (CL over next ch-1 sp and next st) twice; CL over next 2 sts; ch 2, turn, skipping beg 2 skipped chs.

Row 3: Sk first st, dc in next st; (CL over next st and next ch-1 sp) twice; ch 1, dc in next dc, ch 1, (dc in next ch-1 sp, ch 1, dc in next dc, ch 1) twice; *(CL over next ch-1 sp and next st) twice; (CL over next 2 sts) twice; (CL over next st and next ch-1 sp) twice; ch 1, dc in next dc, ch 1, (dc in next ch-1 sp, ch 1, dc in next dc, ch 1) twice; rep from * to last 2 ch-1 sps; (CL over next ch-1 sp and next st) twice; CL over next 2 sts, ch 2, turn, skipping turning ch.

Rep row 3 for patt.

Wings

Chain multiple: 8 + 4

Instructions

Row 1: Sc in 2nd ch from hook and in each rem ch; ch 3 (counts as first dc of following row), turn.

Row 2 (RS): Dc in next sc; *sk next 2 sc, tr in next sc; working behind tr, dc in first skipped sc, dc in next skipped sc; dc in next sc; sk next sc, dc in each of next 2 sc; working in front of last 2 dc, tr in skipped sc; dc in next sc; rep from * across; end dc in last sc; ch 1, turn.

Row 3: Sc in each st across, sc in top of turning ch; ch 3, turn.

Rep rows 2 and 3 for patt.

Filet Ripple

Chain multiple: 20 + 4

Stitch Guide

Cluster (CL): Keeping last lp of each dc on hook, dc in next dc, sk next st, dc in next dc, YO and draw through all 3 lps on hook: CL made.

Instructions

Row 1 (RS): Dc in 6th ch from hook; (ch 1, sk next ch, dc in next ch) 3 times; ch 1, sk next ch, (dc, ch 3, dc) in next ch; *(ch 1, sk next ch, dc in next ch) 3 times, ch 1, sk next ch; keeping last lp of each dc on hook, dc in next ch, sk next 3 chs, dc in next ch, YO and draw through all 3 lps on hook; (ch 1, sk next ch, dc in next ch) 3 times; ch 1, sk next ch, (dc, ch 3, dc) in next ch; rep from * to last 10 chs, (ch 1, sk next ch, dc in next ch) 5 times; ch 3, turn.

Row 2: Sk next ch-1 sp, dc in next dc, (dc in next ch-1 sp and in next dc) 4 times; (2 dc, ch 3, 2 dc) in next ch-3 sp; (dc in next dc and in next ch-1 sp) 3 times; *CL, (dc in next ch-1 sp and in next dc) 3 times; (2 dc, ch 3, 2 dc) in next ch-3 sp; (dc in next dc and in next ch-1 sp) 3 times; rep from * to last 2 dc, dc in next dc, in next ch-1 sp, and in next dc; sk next ch of beg 5 skipped chs, dc in next ch; ch 3, turn.

Row 3: Sk first 2 dc, dc in next dc, ch 1; (sk next dc, dc in next dc, ch 1) 4 times; (dc, ch 3, dc) in next ch-3 sp; *ch 1, sk next dc, (dc in next dc, ch 1, sk next dc) 3 times; CL, ch 1, sk next dc; (dc in next dc, ch 1, sk next dc) 3 times; (dc, ch 3, dc) in next ch-3 sp; rep from * to last 11 dc, (ch 1, sk next dc, dc in next dc) 5 times; sk last dc, dc in top of turning ch; ch 3, turn.

Row 4: Sk first 2 dc and next ch-1 sp; dc in next dc, (dc in next ch-1 sp and in next dc) 4 times; (2 dc, ch 3, 2 dc) in next ch-3 sp; *(dc in next dc and in next ch-1 sp) 3 times; CL, (dc in next ch-1 sp and in next dc) 3 times; in next ch-3 sp work (2 dc, ch 3, 2 dc); rep from * to last 6 dc, (dc in next dc and in next ch-1 sp) 4 times; dc in next dc, sk next ch-1 sp and last dc, dc in top of turning; ch 3, turn.

Rep rows 3 and 4 for patt. End by working a row 3.

Chevron Crowns

Chain multiple: 18 + 2

Stitch Guide

Cluster (CL): YO, draw up a lp to height of a dc in same st as last st worked, YO, draw up lp in next st, YO and draw through all 5 lps on hook: CL made.

Instructions

Row 1 (RS): Sc in 2nd ch from hook; *sk next 2 chs, 5 dc in next ch; sk next 2 chs, sc in next ch; rep from * across; ch 2, turn.

Row 2: 2 dc in first sc; sk next 2 dc, sc in next dc, ch 1; sk next 2 dc and next sc, dc in next dc, ch 2; (CL, ch 2) 4 times, dc in same dc as last CL made; *ch 1, sk next sc and next 2 dc, sc in next dc; sk next 2 dc, 5 dc in next sc; sk next 2 dc, sc in next dc, ch 1, sk next 2 dc and next sc; dc in next dc, ch 2, (CL, ch 2) 4 times, dc in same dc as last CL made; rep from * to last 7 sts; ch 1, sk next sc and next 2 dc, sc in next dc, sk next 2 dc, 3 dc in last sc; ch 1, turn.

Row 3: Sc in first dc, sk next 2 dc and next sc, dc in next dc, ch 2; (CL, ch 2) 5 times, dc in same dc as last CL made; *sk next sc and next 2 dc, sc in next dc, sk next 2 dc and next sc, dc in next dc, ch 2; (CL, ch 2) 5 times; dc in same dc as last CL made; rep from * to last 4 sts, sk next sc and next 2 dc, sc in 2nd ch of turning ch-2; ch 1, turn.

Row 4: Work one sc in each st and 2 sc in each ch-2 sp across; ch 1, turn.

Row 5: Sc in first sc; *sk next 3 sc, 5 dc in next sc; (sk next 2 sc, sc in next sc, sk next 2 sc, 5 dc in next sc) twice; sk next 3 sc, sc in next sc; rep from * across; ch 2, turn.

Rep rows 2–5 for patt.

Clusters

Chain multiple: 5 + 2

Stitch Guide

Cluster (CL): (*YO, insert hook in next ch or sp and draw up a lp, YO and draw through 2 lps) 4 times; YO and draw through all 5 lps on hook: CL made.

Instructions

Row 1: Sc in 2nd ch from hook; *ch 3, CL over next 4 chs; ch 1, sc in next ch; rep from * across, ch 5, turn.

Row 2 (RS): Sc in next CL; *ch 3, CL in next ch-3 sp, ch 1, sc in next CL; rep from * across, end last rep with ch 3, CL in next ch-3 sp, ch 1, dc in last sc; ch 1, turn.

Row 3: Sk next st, sc in next CL; *ch 3, CL in next ch-3 sp, ch 1, sc in next CL; rep from * across, end last rep with sc in turning ch-lp; ch 5, turn.

Rep rows 2 and 3 for patt.

Wheels

Chain multiple: 8 + 2

Stitch Guide

Cluster (CL): Over specified number of sts, in each st work (YO, insert hook in st, YO and draw lp through, YO and draw through 2 lps); YO and draw through all lps on hook: CL made.

Instructions

Row 1 (RS): Sc in 2nd ch from hook; *sk 3 chs, 9 dc in next ch, sk 3 chs, sc in next ch; rep from * across, ch 3, turn.

Row 2: CL over next 4 sts; *loosely ch 3, sc in next st, loosely ch 3, CL over next 9 sts; rep from * across; end last rep with CL over last 5 sts, sk turning ch, ch 3, turn.

Row 3: 4 dc in base of ch; *sk 3 chs, sc in next sc, sk 3 chs, 9 dc in lp which closed next CL; rep from * across; end last rep with 5 dc in top of turning ch; ch 1, turn.

Row 4: Sc in first st; *loosely ch 3, CL over next 9 sts, loosely ch 3, sc in next st; rep from * across; end last rep with sc in top of turning ch; ch 1, turn.

Row 5: Sc in first sc; *sk 3 chs, 9 dc in lp which closed next CL, sk 3 chs, sc in next sc; rep from * across, sk turning ch, ch 3, turn.

Rep rows 2–5 for patt. End by working a row 2.

Shells in a Row

Chain multiple: 8 + 3
Two colors: color A and color B

Stitch Guide

Cluster (CL): Keeping last lp of each dc on hook, dc in each of 5 sts specified, YO and draw through all 6 lps on hook: CL made.

Instructions

Work beg ch with color A.

Row 1 (RS): With color A, work 2 dc in 3rd ch from hook; sk next 3 chs, sc in next ch; *sk next 3 chs, 5 dc in next ch; sk next 3 chs, sc in next ch; rep from * to last 4 chs; sk next 3 chs, 3 dc in last ch; ch 1, turn.

Row 2: Sc in first dc, ch 3, CL over next 5 sts, ch 3; *sc in next dc, ch 3, CL over next 5 sts, ch 3; rep from * to beg 2 skipped chs; sc in 2nd ch of beg 2 skipped chs; change to color B, ch 2, turn. Finish off color A.

Row 3: With color B, 2 dc in first sc, sc in next CL; *5 dc in next sc, sc in next CL; rep from * to last sc, 3 dc in last sc; ch 1, turn.

Row 4: Sc in first dc, ch 3, CL over next 5 sts; *ch 3, sc in next dc, ch 3, CL over next 5 sts; rep from * to turning ch-2, ch 3, sc in 2nd ch of turning ch-2; ch 2, turn.

Row 5: 2 dc in first sc; sc in next CL; *5 dc in next sc, sc in next CL; rep from * to last sc, 3 dc in last sc; ch 1, turn.

Row 6: Sc in first dc, ch 3, CL over next 5 sts; *ch 3, sc in next dc, ch 3, CL over next 5 sts; rep from * to turning ch-2, ch 3, sc in 2nd ch of turning ch; change to color A, ch 2, turn. Finish off color B.

Row 7: With color A, rep row 5.

Row 8: With color A, rep row 6, change to color B, ch 2, turn. Finish off color A.

Rep rows 3–8 for patt, working in color sequence of 2 rows A, 4 rows B.

Cluster Rows

Chain multiple: 7 + 6

Stitch Guide

Cluster (CL): (YO, insert hook in specified st and draw up a ½" lp; YO and draw through 2 lps on hook) 3 times; YO and draw through all 4 lps on hook: CL made.

Instructions

Row 1: Sc in 2nd ch from hook and in each rem ch; ch 1, turn.

Rows 2 and 3: Sc in each sc, ch 1, turn.

Row 4 (WS): Sc in 3 sc; *(CL in next st, sc in next st) 3 times; CL in next st; sc in next 3 sc; rep from * across; ch 1, turn.

Row 5: Sc in each sc and in each CL across; ch 1, turn.

Row 6: Rep row 4.

Row 7: Sc in each sc and in each CL across, ch 1, turn.

Rows 8 and 9: Sc in each sc; ch 1, turn.

Rep rows 4–9 for patt.

Puffy Chevron

Chain multiple: 16 + 2

Stitch Guide

Cluster (CL): Keeping last lp of each dc on hook, dc in 5 sts specified, YO and draw through all 6 lps on hook: CL made.

Instructions

Row 1 (RS): Dec over 3rd and 4th chs from hook (to work dec: YO, draw up lp in 3rd ch from hook, YO; draw through 2 lps on hook; YO, draw up lp in next ch, YO, draw through 2 lps on hook, YO and draw through all 3 lps on hook: dec made); dc in next 5 chs, 4 dc in next ch, dc in next 5 chs; *CL over next 5 chs; dc in next 5 chs, 4 dc in next ch, dc in next 5 chs; rep from * to last 3 chs, dec over last 3 chs [to work dec: (YO, draw up lp in next st, YO, draw through 2 lps on hook) 3 times; YO and draw through all 4 lps on hook: dec made]; ch 2, turn.

Row 2: Sk first st, dec over next 2 sts [to work dec: (YO, draw up lp in next st, YO, draw through 2 lps on hook) twice; YO and draw through all 3 lps on hook: dec made]; sk next 2 dc, 5 dc in next dc; 4 dc in sp between 2nd and 3rd dc of next 4-dc group; 5 dc in first dc of next 5-dc group; *sk next 2 dc, CL over next 5 sts; sk next 2 dc, 5 dc in next dc; 4 dc in sp between 2nd and 3rd dc of next 4-dc group, 5 dc in first dc of next 5-dc group; rep from * to last 5 sts, sk next 2 dc, dec over last 3 sts; ch 2, turn.

Rep row 2 for patt.

Winding Roads

Chain multiple: 9 + 3
Two colors: color A and color B

Stitch Guide

Cluster (CL): Keeping last lp of each dc on hook, dc in specified 2 sts, YO and draw through all 3 lps on hook: CL made.

Instructions

Work beg ch with color A.

Row 1 (RS): With color A, dec over 3rd and 4th chs from hook (to work dec: YO, draw up a lp in 3rd ch from hook, YO, draw through 2 lps on hook, YO, draw up a lp in next ch, YO, draw through 2 lps on hook, YO and draw through all 3 lps on hook: dec made); CL over next 2 chs; *5 dc in next ch, (CL over next 2 chs) 4 times; rep from * to last 6 chs; 5 dc in next ch, (CL over next 2 chs) twice; dc in last ch; ch 2, turn.

Row 2: Sk first dc, working in back lps only, (CL over next 2 sts) twice; *5 dc in next dc; (CL over next 2 sts) 4 times; rep from * to last 6 sts; 5 dc in next dc; (CL over next 2 sts) twice, dc in 2nd ch of beg 2 skipped chs; change to B, ch 2, turn.

Row 3: Sk first dc; working in back lps only, (CL over next 2 sts) twice; *5 dc in next dc, (CL over next 2 sts) 4 times; rep from * to last 6 sts, 5 dc in next dc; (CL over next 2 sts) twice; dc in 2nd ch of turning ch-2; ch 2, turn.

Row 4: Rep row 3.

Rep row 3 for patt, working in color sequence of 2 rows A, 2 rows B.

Elegant Stitch

Chain multiple: any even number

Stitch Guide

Cluster (CL): YO, insert hook in specified ch or st and draw up a lp to height of a dc; (YO, draw up a lp in same ch or st) twice: 7 lps on hook; YO and draw through 6 lps, YO and draw through rem 2 lps: CL made.

Instructions

Row 1 (RS): CL in 5th ch from hook; *ch 1, sk next ch, CL in next ch; rep from * across to last ch, dc in last ch; ch 4, turn.

Row 2: Sk first CL, work CL in next ch-1 sp; *ch 1, CL in next ch-1 sp; rep from * across to turning ch, ch 1, dc in 3rd ch of turning ch; ch 4, turn.

Row 3: CL in first ch-1 sp; *ch 1, CL in next ch-1 sp; rep from * to last sp, ch 1, CL in last sp, dc in 3rd ch of turning ch; ch 4, turn.

Rep rows 2 and 3 for patt.

Crown Clusters

Chain multiple: 3

Stitch Guide

Cluster (CL): Keeping last lp of each dc on hook, dc in each of 3 sts specified; YO and draw through all 4 lps on hook: CL made.

Instructions

Row 1: 3 dc in 5th ch from hook; *sk next 2 chs, 3 dc in next ch; rep from * to last ch, dc in last ch; ch 3, turn.

Row 2 (RS): *CL over next 3 dc, ch 1; rep from * across, end dc in top of turning ch; ch 3, turn.

Row 3: 3 dc in top of each CL across, dc in top of turning ch; ch 3, turn.

Rep rows 2 and 3 for patt.

Hole in the Wall

Chain multiple: 2 + 1

Stitch Guide

Cluster (CL): *YO, insert hook in same sc as last st, YO and draw up a lp to height of a dc; YO and draw through 2 lps; (YO, insert hook in next sc, YO and draw up a lp, YO and draw through 2 lps) twice; YO and draw through all 4 lps: CL made.

Instructions

Row 1: Sc in 2nd ch from hook and in each rem ch; ch 2, turn.

Row 2 (RS): YO, insert hook in first sc, YO and draw up a lp to height of a dc, YO and draw through 2 lps on hook; (YO, insert hook in next sc, YO and draw up a lp, YO and draw through 2 lps on hook) twice; YO and draw through all 4 lps on hook: beg CL made; ch 2; *CL, ch 2; rep from * across, hdc in last sc; ch 1, turn.

Row 3: Sc in first hdc, 2 sc in next ch-2 sp; *sc in next CL, 2 sc in next ch-2 sp; rep from * to last 2 sts, sc in last CL, sc in top of turning ch; ch 2, turn.

Rep rows 2 and 3 for patt.

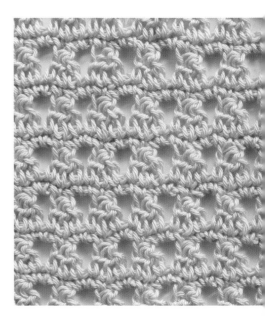

Cute Clusters

Chain multiple: 3 + 2

Stitch Guide

Cluster (CL): (YO, insert hook in specified st, YO and draw up a lp; YO and draw through 2 lps on hook) 5 times; YO and draw through 6 lps on hook: CL made. (Push CL to right side.)

Instructions

Row 1: Sc in 2nd ch from hook and in each rem ch; ch 1, turn.

Row 2 (RS): Sc in first sc; *work CL in next sc, sc in next 2 sc; rep from * across; ch 1, turn.

Rows 3–5: Sc in each st across; ch 1, turn.

Row 6: Sc in first 2 sc, work CL in next sc; *sc in next 2 sc, work CL in next sc; rep from * across, end sc in last sc; ch 1, turn.

Rows 7–9: Sc in each st across; ch 1, turn.

Rep rows 2–9 for patt.

Clusters on a Slant

Chain multiple: 5 + 3

Stitch Guide

Cluster (CL): *YO, insert hook in specified ch or sp, YO and draw up a lp to height of a dc, YO and draw through 2 lps on hook; in same ch or lp rep from * twice, YO and draw through all 4 rem lps: CL made.

Instructions

Row 1 (RS): In 6th ch from hook work CL; *ch 1, sk next 2 chs, dc in next ch; working in front of last dc made, dc in 2nd skipped ch, ch 1, sk next ch, CL in next ch; rep from * to last 2 chs, ch 1, sk next ch, dc in last ch; ch 4, turn.

Row 2: Sk first ch-1 sp, dc in next ch-1 sp; working in front of last dc made, dc in skipped ch-1 sp; *ch 1, CL in sp between next 2 dc, ch 1, sk next ch-1 sp; dc in next ch-1 sp, dc in skipped ch-1 sp; rep from * across, ch 1, dc in 3rd ch of turning ch; ch 4, turn.

Row 3: CL in sp between next 2 dc, ch 1; *sk next ch-1 sp, dc in next ch-1 sp; working in front of last dc made, dc in skipped ch-1 sp, ch 1, CL in sp between next 2 dc, ch 1; rep from * across, dc in 3rd ch of turning ch; ch 4, turn.

Rep rows 2 and 3 for patt.

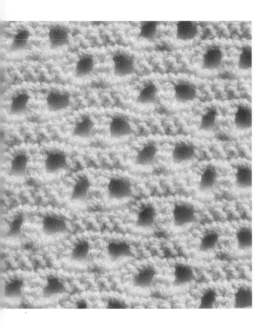

Clusters in Ovals

Chain multiple: 10 + 1

Stitch Guide

Cluster (CL): Keeping last lp of each st on hook, 2 dc in specified st; YO and draw through all 3 lps: CL made.

Instructions

Row 1: Sc in 2nd ch from hook and in each rem ch; ch 1, turn.

Row 2: Sc in each of first 3 sc; *ch 3, sk 2 sc, CL in next sc, ch 3, sc in next 5 sc; rep from * across, ending last rep with sc in each of last 3 (instead of 5) sc; ch 1, turn.

Row 3: Sc in first 3 sc; *2 sc in ch-3 sp, sc in CL, 2 sc in ch-3 sp, sc in each of next 5 sc; rep from * across, end last rep with sc in each of last 3 (instead of 5) sc; ch 6 (counts as a dc and ch-3 sp on following row), turn.

Row 4: Sk first 3 sc, sc in next 5 sc, *ch 3, sk 2 sc, CL in next sc, ch 3, sk 2 sc, sc in next 5 sc; rep from * across; end last rep with ch 3, dc in last sc; ch 1, turn.

Row 5: Sc in first dc, 2 sc in ch-3 sp, sc in next 5 sc; *2 sc in ch-3 sp, sc in CL, 2 sc in ch-3 sp, sc in next 5 sc; rep from * across; end last rep with 3 sc in ch-6 sp; ch 1, turn.

Rep rows 2–5 for patt.

This 'n' That

Chain multiple: 9 + 1

Stitch Guide

Cluster (CL): YO, insert hook in ch or sp indicated, YO and draw up a lp to height of a dc, YO and draw through 2 lps on hook; YO, insert hook in same st or sp, YO and draw through 2 lps on hook; YO and draw through 3 lps on hook: CL made.

Instructions

Row 1 (RS): In 7th ch from hook work (CL, ch 1, CL); *sk next 2 chs, (4 dc, ch 1, dc) in next ch; sk 5 chs, work (CL, ch 1, CL) in next ch; rep from * to last 3 chs, ch 1, sk next 2 chs, dc in last ch; ch 4, turn.

Row 2: Sk first ch-1 sp, work (CL, ch 1, CL) in next ch-1 sp; *(4 dc, ch 1, dc) in next ch-1 sp, (CL, ch 1, CL) in next ch-1 sp; rep from * to last 2 chs, ch 1, sk next ch, dc in last ch; ch 4, turn.

Rep row 2 for patt.

Little Tulips

Chain multiple: 7 + 4

Stitch Guide

Shell: (Dc, ch 2, dc) all in same ch or st: shell made.

Cluster (CL): YO, insert hook in specified sp and draw up a lp, YO and draw through 2 lps on hook; (YO, insert hook in same sp and draw up a lp, YO and draw through 2 lps on hook) twice; YO and draw through all 4 lps on hook: CL made.

Instructions

Row 1: Dc in 4th ch from hook, *sk 2 chs, shell in next ch; sk 2 chs, dc in next 2 chs; rep from * across, ch 3, turn.

Row 2 (RS): Dc in next dc, *ch 2, CL in ch-2 sp of next shell, ch 2, dc in next 2 dc; rep from * across, ch 3, turn.

Row 3: Dc in next dc; *shell in top of next CL, dc in next 2 dc; rep from * across, ch 3, turn.

Row 4: Rep row 2.

Rep rows 3 and 4 for patt.

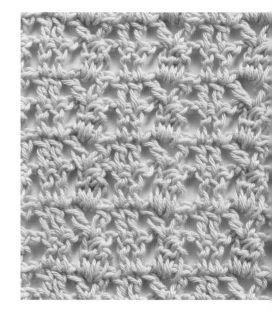

Simply Clusters

Chain multiple: 7 + 4

Stitch Guide

Shell: (Dc, ch 2, dc) all in same ch or st: shell made.

Cluster (CL): YO, insert hook in specified sp and draw up a lp, YO and draw through 2 lps on hook; (YO, insert hook in same sp and draw up a lp, YO and draw through 2 lps on hook) twice; YO and draw through all 4 lps on hook: CL made.

Instructions

Row 1: Dc in 4th ch from hook, *sk 2 chs, shell in next ch; sk 2 chs, dc in next 2 chs; rep from * across, ch 3, turn.

Row 2 (RS): Dc in next dc, *ch 2, CL in ch-2 sp of next shell, ch 2, dc in next 2 dc; rep from * across, ch 3, turn.

Row 3: Dc in next dc; *shell in top of next CL, dc in next 2 dc; rep from * across, ch 3, turn.

Rep rows 2 and 3 for patt.

Pebbles

Chain multiple: 4 + 2

Stitch Guide

Cluster (CL): (YO, insert hook in specified st, and draw up a lp) 3 times, YO and draw through 7 lps on hook: CL made.

Instructions

Row 1 (RS): Sc in 2nd ch from hook and in rem ch; ch 1, turn.

Row 2: Sc in first sc; *CL in next sc, sc in next sc; rep from * across; ch 1, turn.

Row 3: Sc in each st across; ch 1, turn.

Row 4: Sc in first 2 sc, CL in next sc; *sc in next sc, CL in next sc; rep from * across, sc in last 2 sc; ch 1, turn.

Row 5: Rep row 3.

Rep rows 2–5 for patt.

Diamonds in a Row

Chain multiple: 6 + 1

Stitch Guide

Cluster (CL): Keeping last lp of each st on hook, dc in each of next 3 dc; YO and draw through all 4 lps on hook: CL made.

Instructions

Row 1: Sc in 2nd ch from hook and in each rem ch; ch 4 (counts as a dc and ch-1 sp of following row), turn.

Row 2: Sk next 2 sts, 3 dc in next st; *ch 1, sk next 2 sts, dc in next st, ch 1, sk next 2 sts, 3 dc in next st; rep from * to last 3 sts, ch 1, sk 2 sts, dc in last st; ch 5 (counts as a dc and ch-2 sp), turn.

Row 3: *CL over next 3 dc, ch 2, dc in next dc, ch 2; rep from * across; end last rep with CL over next 3 dc, ch 2, dc in 3rd ch of turning ch; ch 1, turn.

Row 4: Sc in first dc; *2 sc in ch-2 sp, sc in CL, 2 sc in ch-2 sp, sc in next dc; rep from * across, end last rep with sc in last CL, 3 sc in ch-5 sp; ch 3, turn.

Row 5: Dc in base of ch, ch 1, sk next 2 sc; dc in next sc; *ch 1, sk next 2 sc, 3 dc in next sc, ch 1, sk 2 sc, dc in next sc; rep from * across, end last rep with ch 1, sk 2 sc, 2 dc in last sc; ch 3 (counts as first dc of following row), turn.

Row 6: Dc in next dc; ch 2, dc in next dc, *ch 2, CL over next 3 dc, ch 2, dc in next dc; rep from * across, end last rep with ch 2; holding back last lp of each dc, dc in last dc and in 3rd ch of turning ch (end CL made); YO and draw through 3 lps; ch 1, turn.

Row 7: Sc in end CL; *2 sc in each ch-2 sp, sc in each dc and sc in each CL; rep from * across, end last rep with sc in last dc (sk turning ch); ch 4, turn.

Rep rows 2–7 for patt.

Tiny Clusters

Chain multiple: 2 + 1

Stitch Guide

Single crochet cluster (scCL): Draw up a lp in each of next 3 sts, YO and draw through all 4 lps on hook: scCL made.

Instructions

Row 1: Sc in 2nd ch from hook and in each rem ch; ch 2, turn.

Row 2: Sk turning ch, *scCL over next 3 sts, ch 1; insert hook in last st of prev scCL; rep from * across, end with sc in last st; ch 2, turn.

Row 3: Starting in base of turning ch, *work scCL over next 3 sts, ch 1; insert hook in last st of prev scCL; rep from * across, end with sc in turning ch; ch 2, turn.

Rep row 3 for patt.

Crazy Clusters

Chain multiple: 4 + 3

Stitch Guide

Cluster (CL): YO, insert hook in specified st and draw up a lp; YO and draw through 2 lps; YO, insert hook in same st and draw up a lp; YO and draw through 2 lps; YO and draw through 3 lps: CL made.

Instructions

Row 1 (RS): Dc in 4th ch from hook and in next 2 chs; *ch 1, sk next ch, dc in next 3 chs; rep from * across to last 5 sts, ch 1, sk next ch, dc in last 4 chs; ch 3 (counts as dc of following row), turn.

Row 2: Sk next dc; *in next dc work (CL, ch 4, CL); sk next dc, next ch-1 sp and next dc; rep from * across to last 3 sts, (CL, ch 4, CL) in next dc, sk next dc, dc in 3rd ch of turning ch; ch 3, turn.

Row 3: *3 dc in next ch-4 sp, ch 1; rep from * across to last ch-4 sp, 3 dc in ch-4 sp, dc in last CL (leave turning ch unworked), ch 3, turn.

Rep rows 2 and 3 for patt.

Cluster Filet

Chain multiple: 6 + 3

Stitch Guide

Cluster (CL): YO, insert hook in specified st and draw up a lp; YO and draw through 2 lps; YO, insert hook in same st and draw up a lp, YO and draw through 2 lps; YO and draw through all 3 lps: CL made.

Instructions

Row 1: Sc in 2nd ch from hook and in each rem ch; ch 4 (counts as a dc and ch-1 sp), turn.

Row 2: Sk next st, dc in next st; *ch 1, sk next st, dc in next st; rep from * across; ch 4, turn.

Row 3: Dc in next dc, ch 1; *CL in next dc, ch 1, (dc in next dc, ch 1) twice; rep from * across, end last rep with dc in 3rd ch of turning ch; ch 4, turn.

Row 4: Dc in next dc; *ch 1, dc in CL, (ch 1, dc in next dc) twice; rep from * across, end last rep with dc in 3rd ch of turning ch; ch 4, turn.

Rep rows 3 and 4 for patt.

Looped Shell

Chain multiple: 8 + 2

Stitch Guide

Cluster (CL): Keeping last lp of each st on hook, 2 dc in specified st; YO and draw through all 3 lps on hook: CL made.

Cluster shell (CL shell): In specified st work (CL, ch 3, CL, ch 3, CL): CL shell made.

Instructions

Row 1: Sc in 2nd ch from hook and in each rem ch; ch 1, turn.

Row 2: Sc in each sc; ch 1, turn.

Row 3: Rep row 2.

Row 4 (RS): Sc in first sc; *sk 3 sc, CL shell in next sc, sk 3 sc, CL in next sc; rep from * across to last 8 sts, sk 3 sc, CL shell in next sc, sk 3 sts, sc in last sc; ch 6 (counts as a dc and ch-3 sp of following row), turn.

Row 5: *Sc in center CL of next CL shell, ch 3, sc in next CL; rep from * across to last CL shell, ch 3, sc in center CL of last CL shell, ch 3, dc in last sc; ch 1, turn.

Row 6: Sc in dc; *3 sc in next ch-3 sp, sc in next sc; rep from * across to turning ch, 4 sc in turning ch-6 lp; ch 1, turn.

Row 7: Sc in each sc; ch 1, turn.

Rep rows 2–7 for patt. End by working a row 3.

Shapely Shells

Chain multiple: 12 + 7

Stitch Guide

Cluster (CL): *YO, insert hook in specified sp and draw up a lp to height of a dc, YO and draw through 2 lps; rep from * once more in same sp, YO and draw through 3 lps: CL made.

Instructions

Row 1: Dc in 4th ch from hook and in each of next 2 chs; *ch 3, sk 2 chs, sc in next ch, ch 3, sk 3 chs, sc in next ch, ch 3, sk 2 chs, dc in each of next 3 chs; rep from * across, ending last rep with dc in each of last 4 (instead of 3) chs; ch 3 (counts as first dc on following row), turn.

Row 2: Dc in next 3 dc; *sk next ch-3 sp, in next ch-3 sp work (CL, ch 3) 4 times, CL in same sp, sk next ch-3 sp, dc in next 3 dc; rep from * across, ending last rep with dc in last 3 dc and in top of turning ch-3; ch 3, turn.

Row 3: *Dc in next 3 dc; *ch 3, sk next ch-3 sp, sc in next ch-3 sp, ch 3, sc in next ch-3 sp; ch 3, sk next ch-3 sp, dc in next 3 dc; rep from * across, ending last rep with dc in last 3 dc and dc in top of turning ch; ch 3, turn.

Rep rows 2 and 3 for patt.

Tall Clusters

Chain multiple: 3 + 2

Stitch Guide

Triple crochet cluster (trCL): *YO 2 times; insert hook in specified st and draw up a lp to height of a tr; (YO and draw through 2 lps on hook) twice; rep from * once, YO and draw through 3 lps: trCL made.

Instructions

Row 1: Sc in 2nd ch from hook and in each rem ch; ch 4 (counts as a tr on following row throughout), turn.

Row 2: *Sk 2 sc, work (trCL, ch 1, trCL) in next sc; rep from * across to last 3 sts, sk 2 sts, tr in last st; ch 4, turn.

Row 3: *Work (trCL, ch 1, trCL) in ch-1 sp of next (trCL, ch 1, trCL) group; rep from * to last st, tr in top of turning ch; ch 4, turn.

Rep row 3 for patt.

My Way, Your Way

Chain multiple: 4 + 2

Stitch Guide

Cluster (CL): (YO, insert hook in specified st and draw up a lp, YO and draw through 2 lps on hook) 2 times; YO and draw through all 3 lps on hook: CL made.

Instructions

Row 1: Sc in 2nd ch from hook; *ch 5, sk next 3 chs, sc in next ch; rep from * across; ch 4, turn.

Row 2: Sc in first ch-5 lp; *ch 3, sc in next ch-5 lp; rep from * across; ch 1, dc in last sc; ch 3 (counts as dc on following row), turn.

Row 3: Work 2 dc in dc; *(sc, ch 2, 2 dc) in next sc; rep from * across to last sc; sc in last sc, ch 2, CL in same sc, sc in 3rd ch of turning ch-4; ch 1, turn.

Row 4: Sc in CL; *ch 2, 2 dc in next ch-2 sp, sk next dc, sc in next dc; rep from * across; end final rep with sc in top of turning ch; ch 5, turn.

Row 5: Sk first dc, sc in next dc; *ch 5, sk next dc, sc in next dc; rep from * across; ch 2, dc in last sc; ch 1, turn. Row 6: Sc in first dc; *ch 5, sc in next ch-5 lp; rep from * across to turning ch-5; ch 5, sc in 3rd ch of turning ch-5; ch 4, turn.

Rep rows 2–6 for patt.

Lacy Mesh

Chain multiple: 4 + 2

Stitch Guide

Cluster (CL): *YO, insert hook in specified st and draw up a lp to height of a dc; YO and draw through 2 lps; rep from * once, YO and draw through 3 lps: CL made.

Instructions

Row 1: Sc in 2nd ch from hook and in each rem ch; ch 1, turn.

Row 2 (RS): Sc in first sc; *ch 2, sk 1 sc, CL in next sc, ch 2, sk 1 sc, sc in next sc; rep from * across; ch 5 (counts as a tr and ch-1 sp), turn.

Row 3: Sc in top of first CL; *ch 5, sc in top of next CL; rep from * across, ending last rep with ch 1, tr in last sc; ch 1, turn.

Row 4: Sc in tr; *ch 2, CL in next sc, ch 2, sc in next ch-5 sp; rep from * across, ending last rep with sc in 3rd ch of turning ch; ch 5, turn.

Rep rows 3 and 4 for patt.

Mesh Diamonds

Chain multiple: 20 + 18

Stitch Guide

Cluster (CL): (YO, insert hook in specified st and draw up a lp, YO and draw through 2 lps on hook) 2 times; YO and draw through all 3 lps on hook: CL made.

Instructions

Row 1: Sc in 2nd ch from hook; *ch 5, sk next 3 chs, sc in next ch; rep from * across; ch 6, turn.

Row 2: Sc in first ch-5 lp, ch 5, sc in next ch-5 lp; *(CL, ch 3, CL) in next sc, sc in next ch-5 lp**; (ch 5, sc in next ch-5 lp) 4 times; rep from * across, ending final rep at **; ch 5, sc in last ch-5 lp, ch 2, tr in last sc; ch 1, turn.

Row 3: Sc in tr, ch 5, sc in next ch-5 lp; *(CL, ch 3, CL) in next sc, sc in next ch-3 sp, (CL, ch 3, CL) in next sc, sc in next ch-5 lp**; (ch 5, sc in next ch-5 lp) 3 times; rep from * across, ending final rep at **; ch 5, sc in 4th ch of turning ch-6; ch 6, turn.

Row 4: Sc in first ch-5 lp; *ch 5, sc in next ch-3 sp, (CL, ch 3, CL) in next sc, sc in next ch-3 sp**; (ch 5, sc in next ch-5 lp) 3 times; rep from * across, ending final rep at **; ch 5, sc in last ch-5 lp, ch 2, tr in last sc; ch 1, turn.

Row 5: Sc in tr; *ch 5, sc in next ch-5 lp, ch 5, sc in next ch-3 sp**; (ch 5, sc in next ch-5 lp) 2 times, (CL, ch 3, CL) in next sc, sc in next ch-5 lp; rep from * across, ending final rep at **; ch 5, sc in next ch-5 lp, ch 5, sc in 4th ch of turning ch-6; ch 6, turn.

Row 6: Sc in first ch-5 lp; *(ch 5, sc in next ch-5 lp) 3 times**; (CL, ch 3, CL) in next sc, sc in next ch-3 sp, (CL, ch 3, CL) in next sc, sc in next ch-5 lp; rep from * across, ending final rep at **; ch 2, tr in last sc; ch 1, turn.

Row 7: Sc in tr; *(ch 5, sc in next ch-5 lp) 3 times, ch 5**; sc in next ch-3 sp, (CL, ch 3, CL) in next sc, sc in next ch-3 sp; rep from * across, ending final rep at **; sc in 4th ch of turning ch-6; ch 6, turn.

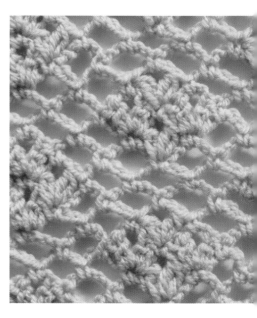

Row 8: Sc in first ch-5 lp, ch 5, sc in next ch-5 lp; *(CL, ch 3, CL) in next sc**; (sc in next ch-5 lp, ch 5) 2 times, sc in next ch-3 sp, (ch 5, sc in next ch-5 lp, ch 5) 2 times; rep from * across, ending final rep at **; sc in next ch-5 lp, ch 5, sc in last ch-5 lp, ch 2, tr in last sc; ch 1, turn.

Rep rows 3–8 for patt.

Cluster Ladders

Chain multiple: 24 + 17

Stitch Guide

Cluster (CL): (YO, insert hook in specified sp and draw up a lp) 4 times; YO and draw through all 9 lps on hook: CL made.

Instructions

Row 1: Sl st in 8th ch from hook; *ch 4, sk next 2 chs, sl st in next ch; rep from * across; ch 5, turn.

Row 2: Sl st in first ch-4 lp; *ch 4, sl st in next ch-4 lp; rep from * across to last ch-lp; ch 4, sl st in last ch-lp, ch 2, dc in 5th skipped ch at beg of row 1; turn.

Row 3 (RS): Sl st in dc, ch 4, sl st in first ch-4 lp; *in next ch-4 lp work [(CL, ch 1) 2 times, CL], sl st in next ch-4 lp**; (ch 4, sl st in next ch-4 lp) 6 times; rep from * across, ending final rep at **; ch 4, sl st in 3rd ch of turning ch-5; ch 5, turn.

Row 4: Sl st in first ch-4 lp; *(ch 4, sl st in next ch-1 sp) 2 times**; (ch 4, sl st in next ch-4 lp) 6 times; rep from * across, ending final rep at **; ch 4, sl st in next ch-4 lp, ch 2, dc in last sl st; turn.

Row 5: Sl st in dc; *(ch 4, sl st in next ch-4 lp) 5 times; in next ch-4 lp work [(CL, ch 1) 2 times, CL], sl st in next ch-4 lp, ch 4, sl st in next ch-4 lp; rep from * across to last 3 ch-4 lps; (ch 4, sl st in next ch-4 lp) 3 times; ch 4, sl st in 3rd ch of turning ch-5; ch 5, turn.

Row 6: Sl st in first ch-4 lp; (ch 4, sl st in next ch-4 lp) 4 times; *(ch 4, sl st in next ch-1 lp) 2 times**; (ch 4, sl st in next ch-4 lp) 6 times; rep from * across, ending final rep at **; (ch 4, sl st in next ch-4 lp) 5 times; ch 2, dc in last sl st; turn.

Rep rows 3–6 for patt.

Soft Clusters

Chain multiple: 7 + 2

Stitch Guide

Cluster (CL): *YO, insert hook in specified st or sp and draw up a lp, YO and draw through 2 lps on hook; rep from * once more in same st or sp; YO and draw through all 3 lps on hook: CL made.

Instructions

Row 1 (RS): (CL, ch 3, CL) in 6th ch from hook; *sk next 2 chs, dc in next 2 chs, sk next 2 chs, (CL, ch 3, CL) in next ch; rep from * across to last 3 chs; sk next 2 chs, dc in last ch; ch 6, turn.

Row 2: Sc in first ch-3 sp; *ch 3, dc in next 2 dc, ch 3, sc in next ch-3 sp; rep from * across; ch 3, dc in first skipped ch of foundation ch; ch 5, turn.

Row 3: CL in first sc; *ch 2, dc in next 2 dc; ch 2, CL in next sc; rep from * across; ch 2, dc in 3rd ch of turning ch-6; ch 3, turn.

Row 4: (CL, ch 3, CL) in first CL; *dc in next 2 dc, (CL, ch 3, CL) in next CL; rep from * across; dc in 3rd ch of turning ch-5; ch 6, turn.

Row 5: Sc in first ch-3 sp; *ch 3, dc in next 2 dc, ch 3, sc in next ch-3 sp; rep from * across; ch 3, dc in 3rd ch of turning ch-3; ch 5, turn.

Rep rows 3–5 for patt.

Wacky Wicker

Chain multiple: 4 + 2

Stitch Guide

Cluster (CL): YO, insert hook in specified st and draw up a lp, YO and draw through 2 lps on hook; YO, insert hook in same st and draw up a lp, YO and draw through 2 lps; YO and draw through all 3 lps on hook: CL made.

Instructions

Row 1 (RS): Sc in 2nd ch from hook; *ch 2, sk next ch, CL in next ch, ch 2, sk next ch, sc in next ch; rep from * across; ch 5, turn.

Row 2: Sc in first CL; *ch 5, sc in next CL; rep from * across; ch 2, dc in last sc; ch 1, turn.

Row 3: Sc in first dc; *ch 2, CL in next sc, ch 2, sc in next ch-5 lp; rep from * across, ending with sc in 3rd ch of turning ch-5; ch 5, turn.

Rep rows 2 and 3 for patt.

Breath of Spring

Chain multiple: 16 + 15

Stitch Guide

Cluster (CL): (YO, insert hook in specified st or sp and draw up a lp, YO and draw through 2 lps on hook) 3 times; YO and draw through all 4 lps on hook: CL made.

Beginning cluster (beg CL): Ch 3, (YO, insert hook in top of last st made and draw up a lp, YO and draw through 2 lps on hook) 2 times; YO and draw through all 3 lps on hook: beg CL made.

Instructions

Row 1: Work (CL, ch 3, CL) in 11th ch from hook; *ch 3, sk next 3 chs, dc in next ch, ch 3, sk next 3 chs, sc in next ch, ch 3, sk next 3 chs, dc in next ch, ch 3, sk next 3 chs, (CL, ch 3, CL) in next ch; rep from * across to last 4 chs; ch 3, sk next 3 chs, dc in last ch; ch 6, turn.

Row 2: Sk first ch-3 sp, sc in next ch-3 sp; *ch 3, dc in next dc, work beg CL; CL in each of next 2 ch-3 sps, work beg CL, dc in next dc, ch 3, sk next ch-3 sp, sc in next ch-3 sp; rep from * across; end final rep with ch 3, dc in 3rd ch of turning ch; ch 6, turn.

Row 3: Sc in first sc; *ch 3, dc in next dc, ch 3, (CL, ch 3, CL) in same st as next beg CL, ch 3, dc in next dc, ch 3, sc in next sc; rep from * across; end final rep with ch 3, dc in 3rd ch of turning ch; ch 6, turn.

Row 4: *Work beg CL; CL in each of next 2 ch-3 sps, work beg CL; dc in next dc, ch 3, sk next ch-3 sp, sc in next ch-3 sp, ch 3, dc in next dc; rep from * across; end final rep with: work beg CL; CL in next ch-3 sp, CL in turning ch-6 sp; work beg CL, dc in 3rd ch of turning ch; ch 6, turn.

Row 5: *Work (CL, ch 3, CL) in same st as next beg CL, ch 3**; dc in next dc, ch 3, sc in next sc, ch 3, dc in next dc, ch 3; rep from * across, ending final rep at **; dc in 3rd ch of turning ch-3; ch 6, turn.

Rep rows 2–5 for patt.

Deep Clusters

Chain multiple: 12 + 2

Stitch Guide

Cluster (CL): (YO, insert hook in specified st or sp and draw up a lp, YO and draw through 2 lps on hook) 5 times; YO and draw through all 6 lps on hook, ch 1: CL made.

Instructions

Row 1: Work (sc, ch 5, sc) in 2nd ch from hook; *ch 5, sk next 5 chs, CL in next ch, ch 5, sk next 5 chs**; (sc, ch 5, sc, ch 5, sc) in next ch; rep from * across, ending final rep at **; (sc, ch 5, sc) in last ch; ch 8, turn.

Row 2: *Work (sc, ch 5, sc, ch 5, sc) in next CL, ch 5, sk next sc**; CL in next sc, ch 5; rep from * across, ending final rep at **; dc in last sc; ch 1, turn.

Row 3: Work (sc, ch 5, sc) in dc; *ch 5, sk next sc, CL in next sc, ch 5**; (sc, ch 5, sc, ch 5, sc) in next CL; rep from * across, ending final rep at **; (sc, ch 5, sc) in 3rd ch of turning ch-8; ch 8, turn.

Rep rows 2 and 3 for patt.

Bunny Ears

Chain multiple: 5 + 3

Stitch Guide

Cluster (CL): *YO, insert hook in specified st and draw up a lp to height of a dc; YO and draw through 2 lps on hook; rep from * once more in same st, YO and draw through 3 lps on hook: CL made.

Picot: Ch 3, sl st in base of ch: picot made.

Shell: (Picot, CL, ch 3, CL) all in same st: shell made.

Instructions

Row 1: Work shell in 6th ch from hook; *sk 4 chs, shell in next ch; rep from * to last 3 chs, work picot, sk 2 chs, dc in last ch; ch 4, turn.

Row 2: CL in first picot; *shell in next picot; rep from * across, ending last rep with CL in last picot, ch 1, dc in top of turning ch; ch 3, turn.

Row 3: *Shell in next picot; rep from * across, ending last rep with work picot, dc in 3rd ch of turning ch; ch 4, turn.

Rep rows 2 and 3 for patt.

Looped Clusters

Chain multiple: 6 + 2

Stitch Guide

Cluster (CL): *YO, insert hook in specified st and draw up a lp to height of a dc, YO and draw through 2 lps on hook; rep from * 2 times more in same st, YO and draw through 4 lps: CL made.

Instructions

Row 1: Sc in 2nd ch from hook and in each rem ch; ch 1, turn.

Row 2: Sc in first sc; *ch 3, sk 2 sc, CL in next sc, ch 3, sk 2 sc, sc in next sc; rep from * across; ch 6 (counts as a dc and ch-3 sp of following row), turn.

Row 3: Sc in top of first CL; *ch 3, dc in next sc, ch 3, sc in top of next CL; rep from * across, ending last rep with ch 3, dc in last sc; ch 1, turn.

Row 4: Sc in first dc; *ch 3, CL in next sc, ch 3, sc in next dc; rep from * across, ending last rep with ch 3, CL in last sc, ch 3, sc in 3rd ch of turning ch-6; ch 6, turn.

Rep rows 3 and 4 for patt.

Doing Wheelies

Chain multiple: 10 + 4

Stitch Guide

Cluster (CL): YO, insert hook in first specified st and draw up a lp to height of a dc, YO and draw through 2 lps; (YO, insert hook in next st and draw up a lp, YO and draw through 2 lps) 2 times; YO and draw through all 4 lps on hook: CL made.

Half cluster (hCL): YO, insert hook in first specified st and draw up a lp to height of a dc, YO and draw through 2 lps; YO, insert hook in next specified st and draw up a lp, YO and draw through 2 lps; YO and draw through all 3 lps on hook: hCL made.

Double triple crochet (dtr): YO 3 times; insert hook in specified st and draw up a lp; (YO and draw through 2 lps) 4 times: dtr made.

Instructions

Row 1: Dc in 5th ch from hook; *ch 3, sk 3 chs, 3 dc in next ch, ch 3, sk 3 chs, CL over next 3 chs; rep from * across, ending last rep with ch 3, sk 3 chs, 3 dc in next ch, ch 3, sk 3 chs, hCL over last 2 chs; ch 8, turn.

Row 2: *Dc in each of next 3 dc, ch 7, sk CL; rep from * across, ending last rep with ch 3 (instead of 7), dtr in top of turning ch; ch 3, turn.

Row 3: Dc in dtr; *ch 3, CL over next 3 dc, ch 3, 3 dc in 4th ch of ch-7 lp; rep from * across, ending last rep with ch 3, 2 dc in 5th ch of turning ch; ch 3, turn.

Row 4: Dc in next dc; *ch 7, sk CL, dc in each of next 3 dc; rep from * across, ending last rep with ch 7, dc in last dc and in top of turning ch; ch 3, turn.

Row 5: Dc in next dc; *ch 3, 3 dc in 4th ch of ch-7 lp, ch 3, CL over next 3 dc; rep from * across, ending last rep with ch 3, hCL over last dc and top of turning ch; ch 8, turn.

Rep rows 2–5 for patt.

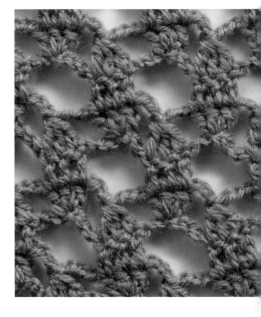

Crossed Over

Chain multiple: 6 + 1

Stitch Guide

Cluster (CL): *YO, insert hook in specified st and draw up a lp to height of a dc; YO and draw through 2 lps; rep from * in same st 2 more times; YO and draw through 4 lps: CL made.

Double triple crochet (dtr): YO 3 times; insert hook in specified st and draw up a lp; (YO and draw through 2 lps) 4 times: dtr made.

Instructions

Row 1: Dc in 4th ch from hook; *ch 1, sk next ch, dc in next ch; rep from * to last ch, dc in last ch; ch 4, turn.

Row 2: *Sk next dc and next ch-1 sp, dtr in next dc, ch 1, dtr in skipped dc (crossed dtr made), ch 1; rep from * across, ending last rep with dtr in top of turning ch; ch 4, turn.

Row 3 (RS): *CL in ch-1 sp of next crossed dtr, ch 1, dc in next ch-1 sp, ch 1; rep from * across to last crossed dtr, CL in ch-1 sp of last crossed dtr, ch 1, dc in top of turning ch; ch 4, turn.

Row 4: *Sk next ch-1 sp, sk next CL, dtr in next ch-1 sp, ch 1, dtr in skipped ch-1 sp; ch 1**, sk next dc; rep from * across, ending last rep at **, dtr in turning ch-4 sp, ch 4, turn.

Row 5: *Dc in next dtr, ch 1; rep from * across, ending last rep with dc in 3rd ch of turning ch; ch 4, turn.

Rep rows 2–5 for patt.

City Clusters

Chain multiple: 16 + 13

Stitch Guide

Cluster (CL): *YO, insert hook in specified st or sp and draw up a lp, YO and draw through 2 lps on hook; rep from * once more in same st or sp; YO and draw through all 3 lps on hook: CL made.

Instructions

Row 1: Dc in 7th ch from hook, (ch 1, sk next ch, dc in next ch) 3 times; *sk next 3 chs, (CL, ch 3, dc, ch 3, CL) in next ch, ch 1, sk next 3 chs, dc in next ch, (ch 1, sk next ch, dc in next ch) 4 times; rep from * across; ch 3, turn.

Row 2 (RS): Sk first 2 dc; *(CL, ch 3, dc, ch 3, CL) in next dc, ch 1, sk next dc**; dc in next dc, (ch 2, sc in next ch-3 sp) 2 times, ch 2, dc in next dc, sk next dc; rep from * across, ending final rep at **; sk next ch, dc in next ch; ch 5, turn.

Row 3: *(Sc in next ch-3 sp, ch 2) 2 times**; dc in next dc, (ch 1, dc in next ch-2 sp) 3 times, ch 1, dc in next dc, ch 2; rep from * across, ending final rep at **; dc in 3rd ch of turning ch-3; ch 4, turn.

Row 4: *(Dc in next ch-2 sp, ch 1) 3 times; dc in next dc, sk next dc (CL, ch 3, dc, ch 3, CL) in next dc, ch 1, sk next dc, dc in next dc, ch 1; rep from * across; (dc in next ch-2 sp, ch 1) 2 times; dc in turning ch-5 lp, ch 1, dc in 3rd ch of turning ch-5; ch 3, turn.

Rep rows 2–4 for patt.

Simple Clusters

Chain multiple: any uneven number

Stitch Guide

Cluster (CL): YO, insert hook in specified st and draw up a lp, YO and draw through 2 lps; YO, insert hook in next st and draw up a lp, YO and draw through 2 lps; YO and draw through 3 lps: CL made.

Instructions

Row 1: Sc in 2nd ch from hook and in each rem ch; ch 3 (counts as a dc of following row), turn.

Row 2: *Sk next sc, 2 dc in next sc; rep from * across, ending last rep by skipping next sc, dc in last sc; ch 4 (counts as a dc and ch-1 sp), turn.

Row 3: *CL over next 2 dc, ch 1; rep from * across to last 3 sts, CL over next 2 dc, dc in top of turning ch; ch 1, turn.

Row 4: Sc in first dc, sc in each CL and in each ch-1 sp across, ending last rep with sc in ch-4 sp, sc in 3rd ch of turning ch, ch 3, turn.

Row 5: Dc in each sc across, ch 3, turn.

Row 6: Sk first dc, *2 dc in next dc, sk next dc; rep from * across, ending last rep with dc in top of turning ch; ch 4, turn.

Rep rows 3–6 for patt. End by working a row 3.

Cluster Play

Chain multiple: 8 + 3

Stitch Guide

Cluster (CL): *YO, insert hook around specified st and draw up a lp, YO and draw through 2 lps; rep from * twice around same st, YO and draw through 4 lps: CL made.

Instructions

Row 1: Dc in 4th ch from hook and each of next 6 chs; *ch 1, sk next ch, dc in each of next 7 chs; rep from * across to last 9 chs, ch 1, sk next ch, dc in each of last 8 chs; ch 3 (counts as a dc of following row throughout), turn.

Row 2 (RS): *Dc in each of next 2 dc, ch 1, sk 1 dc, dc in next dc, work CL around dc just made; sk next dc, dc in next 2 dc, ch 1; rep from * across, ending last rep with dc in each of last 2 dc, dc in top of turning ch; ch 3, turn.

Row 3: *Dc in next 2 dc, dc in top of CL, dc in next dc (around which CL was made), dc in ch-1 sp, dc in next 2 dc**, ch 1; rep from * across, ending last rep at **; dc in top of turning ch; ch 3, turn.

Row 4: Dc in next dc; *(ch 1, sk next dc, dc in next dc) 3 times**, ch 1, dc in next dc; rep from * across, ending last rep at **; dc in top of turning ch, ch 3, turn.

Row 5: *Dc in next dc; (dc in ch-1 sp, dc in dc) 3 times, ch 1; (dc in dc, dc in ch-1 sp) 3 times, dc in next dc**, ch 1; rep from * across, ending last rep at **; dc in top of turning ch; ch 3, turn.

Rep rows 2–5 for patt.

Clusters Galore

Chain multiple: 10 + 2

Stitch Guide

Cluster (CL): *YO, insert hook in first specified st and draw up a lp, YO and draw through 2 lps on hook; rep from * in next specified st; YO and draw through all 3 lps on hook: CL made.

Instructions

Row 1: Sc in 2nd ch from hook; *ch 3, sk 2 chs, sc in next ch; ch 5, sk 3 chs, sc in next ch, ch 3, sk 2 chs, sc in next ch; rep from * across; ch 1, turn.

Row 2: Sc in first sc; *ch 2, (dc, ch 3, sc in top of last dc) 4 times in next ch-5 lp; dc in same ch-5 lp; ch 2, sk next ch-3 sp, sc in next sc; rep from * across; ch 8, turn.

Row 3: Sk first ch-3 sp; *sc in next ch-3 sp, ch 5, sc in next ch-3 sp, ch 3**; CL in next 2 ch-3 sps, ch 3; rep from * across, ending final rep at **; dtr in last sc; ch 1, turn.

Row 4: Sc in dtr; *ch 2, (dc, ch 3, sc in top of last dc) 4 times in next ch-5 lp; dc in same ch-5 lp; ch 2**; sk next ch-3 sp, sc in sp between CLs; rep from * across, ending final rep at **; sc in 5th ch of turning ch-8; ch 8, turn.

Rep rows 3 and 4 for patt. End by working a row 3.

Clusters and Shells

Chain multiple: 6 + 2

Stitch Guide

Cluster (CL): YO, insert hook in specified st and draw up a lp, YO and draw through 2 lps on hook; YO, insert hook in same st and draw up a lp, YO and draw through 2 lps on hook; YO and draw through 3 lps: CL made.

Shell: In specified st work (dc, ch 1) twice, dc in same st: shell made.

Instructions

Row 1: Sc in 2nd ch from hook and in each rem ch; ch 4 (counts as a dc and ch-1 sp), turn.

Row 2: Dc in base of ch; *ch 2, sk 2 sc, sc in next sc, ch 2, sk 2 sc, shell in next sc; rep from * across to last 3 sts, ch 2, sk 2 sc, in last sc work (dc, ch 1, dc); ch 1, turn.

Row 3: Sc in first dc, sc in next ch-1 sp; *ch 2, CL in next sc, ch 2, sc in first ch-1 sp of shell, ch 2, sc in next ch-1 sp of shell; rep from * across, ending last rep with ch 2, CL in last sc, ch 2, sc in 4th and in 3rd chs of turning ch; ch 4, turn.

Row 4: Dc in base of prev row turning ch; ch 2, sc in next CL; *ch 2, sk next ch-2 sp, shell in next ch-2 sp, ch 2, sk next ch-2 sp, sc in next CL; rep from * across, ending last rep with ch 2, (dc, ch 1, dc) in last sc; ch 1, turn.

Rep rows 3 and 4 for patt.

Cluster Waves

Chain multiple: 8 + 6

Stitch Guide

Cluster (CL): *YO, insert hook in specified st and draw up a lp, YO and draw through 2 lps on hook; rep from * 2 more times in same st; YO and draw through all 4 lps on hook: CL made.

Instructions

Row 1 (RS): Sc in 2nd ch from hook; *ch 3, sk next 3 chs, CL in next ch, ch 3, sk next 3 chs, sc in next ch; rep from * across to last 4 chs; ch 3, sk next 3 chs, dc in last ch; ch 1, turn.

Row 2: Sc in first dc; *ch 3; sc in next sc, ch 3, sc in next CL; rep from * across to last sc; ch 3, sc in last sc; ch 6, turn.

Row 3: Sk first sc, sc in next sc; *ch 3, CL in next sc, ch 3, sc in next sc; rep from * across; ch 1, turn.

Row 4: Sc in first sc; *ch 3, sc in next CL, ch 3, sc in next sc; rep from * across to turning ch; sk next 3 chs, sc in next ch of turning ch; ch 1, turn.

Row 5: Sc in first sc; *ch 3, CL in next sc, ch 3, sc in next sc; rep from * across to last sc; ch 3, dc in last sc; ch 1, turn.

Rep rows 2–5 for patt.

Rondelay

Chain multiple: 5

Stitch Guide

Cluster (CL): *YO, insert hook in specified st or sp and draw up a lp, YO and draw through 2 lps on hook; rep from * once more in same st or sp; YO and draw through all 3 lps on hook: CL made.

Instructions

Row 1 (RS): Work CL in 5th ch from hook; *sk next 4 chs, (CL, ch 1, dc, ch 1, CL) in next ch; rep from * across to last 5 chs; sk next 4 chs, (CL, ch 1, dc) in last ch; ch 3, turn.

Row 2: Dc in first ch-1 sp; *ch 3, sc in sp between next 2 CL, ch 3**; dc in next ch-1 sp, ch 1, dc in next ch-1 sp; rep from * across, ending final rep at **; sk next CL, 2 dc in next ch-sp; ch 4, turn.

Row 3: Work CL in first dc; *(CL, ch 1, dc, ch 1, CL) in next ch-1 sp; rep from * across; (CL, ch 1, dc) in 3rd ch of turning ch-3; ch 3, turn.

Rep rows 2 and 3 for patt.

Post Clusters

Chain multiple: 5 + 1

Stitch Guide

Cluster (CL): (YO, insert hook from front to back to front around post of next dc, YO and draw up a lp; YO and draw through first 2 lps on hook) 3 times; YO and draw through all 4 lps on hook: CL made.

Instructions

Row 1: Sc in 2nd ch from hook and in each rem ch; ch 3 (counts as a dc of following row throughout), turn.

Row 2: Dc in next sc and in each rem sc; ch 3, turn.

Row 3 (RS): Dc in base of ch; *CL over next 3 dc, 2 dc in each of next 2 dc; rep from * across to last 4 sts, CL over next 3 dc, 2 dc in last dc; ch 3, turn.

Row 4: Dc in each dc and CL across, ch 3, turn.

Rep rows 3 and 4 for patt.

Clustered Shells

Chain multiple: 6 + 2

Stitch Guide

Cluster (CL): YO, insert hook in specified st and draw up a lp to height of a dc; YO and draw through 2 lps on hook; YO, insert hook in same st and draw up a lp to height of a dc; YO and draw through 2 lps on hook; YO and draw through all 3 lps: CL made.

Cluster shell (CL shell): In specified st work [(CL, ch 1) twice, CL]: CL shell made.

Instructions

Row 1: Sc in 2nd ch from hook and in each rem ch; ch 3 (counts as a dc of following row throughout), turn.

Row 2: *Sk 2 sts, CL shell in next st, sk 2 sts, dc in next st; rep from * across; ch 3, turn.

Row 3: *CL shell in center CL of next CL shell, dc in next dc; rep from * across, ending last rep with dc in top of turning ch; ch 3, turn.

Rep row 3 for patt.

Shells and Clusters

Chain multiple: 8 + 2

Stitch Guide

Cluster (CL): *YO, insert hook in specified st or sp and draw up a lp to height of a dc; YO and draw through 2 lps; rep from * once in same st, YO and draw through 3 lps: CL made.

Cluster shell (CL shell): In specified st work (CL, ch 2) twice, CL in same st: CL shell made.

V-stitch (V-st): Work (dc, ch 1, dc) in specified st or sp: V-st made.

Instructions

Row 1: Work CL in 6th ch from hook; *sk next 3 chs, V-st in next ch, sk next 3 chs, CL shell in next ch; rep from * across to last 4 chs; sk next 3 chs, 2 dc in last ch; ch 5, turn.

Row 2 (RS): Work CL in first cl; *V-st in center CL of next CL shell; CL shell in ch-1 sp of next V-st; rep from * across, ending with 2 dc in 2nd skipped ch of foundation ch; ch 5, turn.

Row 3: CL in first dc; *V-st in center CL of next CL shell; CL shell in ch-1 sp of next V-st; rep from * across, ending with 2 dc in 3rd ch of turning ch-5; ch 5, turn.

Rep rows 2 and 3 for patt.

Crossed Clusters

Chain multiple: 3 + 2

Stitch Guide

Cluster (CL): YO, insert hook in specified st and draw up a lp to height of a dc, YO and draw through 2 lps on hook; YO, insert hook in same st and draw up a lp to height of a dc, YO and draw through 2 lps on hook; YO and draw through 3 lps on hook: CL made.

Instructions

Row 1: Sc in 2nd ch from hook and in each rem ch; ch 3 (counts as a dc throughout), turn.

Row 2 (RS): *Sk next sc, CL in next sc; working in front of CL just made, CL in skipped sc; dc in next sc; rep from * across; ch 1, turn.

Row 3: Sc in each dc and in each CL across; ch 3, turn.

Rep rows 2 and 3 for patt. End by working a row 3.

Shells and Loops

Chain multiple: 11 + 5

Stitch Guide

Cluster (CL): (YO, insert hook in specified st or sp and draw up a lp, YO and draw through 2 lps on hook) 2 times; YO and draw through all 3 lps on hook: CL made.

Instructions

Row 1: Sc in 2nd ch from hook and in each rem ch; ch 5 (counts as a dc and ch-2 sp on throughout), turn.

Row 2: Sk next 2 sc, sc in next sc; *sk next 3 sc, in next sc work [(CL, ch 1) 4 times, CL]; sk next 3 sc, sc in next sc**; ch 5, sk next 2 sc, sc in next sc; rep from * across, ending final rep at **; ch 2, sk 2 sc, dc in last sc; ch 5, turn.

Row 3: Sc in ch-2 sp; *ch 1, (sc in next ch-1 sp, ch 3) 3 times, sc in next ch-1 sp, ch 1**; (sc, ch 5, sc) in next ch-5 lp; rep from * across, ending final rep at **; sc in turning ch-sp, ch 2, dc in 3rd ch of turning ch; ch 5, turn.

Row 4: Sc in ch-2 sp; *sk next ch-3 sp, [(CL, ch 1) 4 times, CL] in next ch-3 sp**; (sc, ch 5, sc) in next ch-5 lp; rep from * across, ending final rep at **; sc in turning ch-sp, ch 2, dc in 3rd ch of turning ch; ch 5, turn.

Rep rows 3 and 4 for patt.

Climbing Clusters

Chain multiple: 8 + 7

Stitch Guide

Cluster (CL): (YO, insert hook in specified st and draw up a lp) 3 times; YO and draw through all 7 lps on hook: CL made.

Instructions

Row 1: CL in 7th ch from hook; *ch 3, sk next 3 chs, sc in next ch, ch 3, sk next 3 chs**; (CL, ch 5, CL) in next ch; rep from * across, ending final rep at **; (CL, ch 2, tr) in last ch; ch 1, turn.

Row 2: Sc in tr; *ch 2, 3 dc in next sc, ch 2**; sc in next ch-5 lp; rep from * across, ending final rep at **; sk next CL and next 2 chs, sc in next ch; ch 1, turn.

Row 3: Sc in first sc; *ch 3, sk next dc, (CL, ch 5, CL) in next dc, ch 3, sc in next sc; rep from * across; ch 3, turn.

Row 4: Dc in first sc; *ch 2, sc in next ch-5 lp, ch 2**; 3 dc in next sc; rep from * across, ending final rep at **; 2 dc in last sc; ch 6, turn.

Row 5: CL in first dc; *ch 3, sc in next sc, ch 3, sk next dc**; (CL, ch 5, CL) in next dc; rep from * across, ending final rep at **; (CL, ch 2, tr) in 3rd ch of turning ch-3; ch 1, turn.

Rep rows 2–5 for patt.

Four Candles

Chain multiple: 14 + 5

Stitch Guide

V-stitch (V-st): In same st work (dc, ch 2, dc): V-st made.

Shell: Work 7 dc all in same st: shell made.

Cluster (CL): *YO, insert hook in specified st and draw up a lp to height of a dc, YO and draw through 2 lps; rep from * once more in same st, YO and draw through 3 lps: CL made.

Picot: Ch 3, sl st in first ch made: picot made.

Instructions

Row 1: Dc in 13th ch from hook; *ch 5, sk 5 chs, dc in each of next 3 chs, ch 5, sk 5 chs, dc in next ch; rep from * across, ending last rep with ch 5, sk 5 chs, dc in last ch; ch 6 (counts as a dc and ch-3 sp on following row), turn.

Row 2: *V-st in next dc, ch 3, dc in each of next 3 dc, ch 3; rep from * across, ending last rep with V-st in last dc, ch 3, sk next 5 chs, dc in next ch of turning ch; ch 5, turn.

Row 3: *Shell in ch-2 sp of next V-st, ch 2, dc in each of next 3 dc, ch 2; rep from * across, ending last rep with shell in last V-st, ch 2, dc in 3rd ch of turning ch; ch 4, turn.

Row 4: *CL in first dc of shell, work picot, ch 2; (sk next dc, CL in next dc, work picot, ch 2) 2 times; sk next dc, CL in next dc, picot, ch 1**; dc in each of next 3 dc, ch 1; rep from * across, ending last rep at **; dc in 3rd ch of turning ch; ch 8, turn.

Row 5: *Dc in center ch-2 sp of next CL group, ch 5, dc in each of

next 3 dc, ch 5; rep from * across, ending last rep with ch 5, dc in 3rd ch of turning ch; ch 6, turn.

Rep rows 2–5 for patt.

Winging

Chain multiple: 12 + 4

Stitch Guide

Cluster (CL): *YO, insert hook in specified st and draw up a lp to height of a dc; YO and draw through 2 lps; rep from * once in same st, YO and draw through 3 lps: CL made.

Instructions

Row 1: Dc in 6th ch from hook; *(ch 3, sk 3 chs, dc in next ch) 2 times; (ch 1, sk 1 ch, dc in next ch) 2 times; rep from * across, ending last rep with ch 1, sk next ch, dc in last ch; ch 4 (counts as a dc and ch-1 sp on following row), turn.

Row 2: Dc in next dc; *in next st work (CL, ch 3, sc, ch 3, CL); (dc in next dc, ch 1) twice, dc in next dc; rep from * across, ending last rep with dc in last dc, ch 1, dc in 3rd ch of turning ch; ch 4, turn.

Row 3: Dc in next dc; *ch 3, tr in next sc, ch 3**, (dc in next dc, ch 1) 2 times, dc in next dc; rep from * across, ending last rep at **; dc in next dc, ch 1, dc in 3rd ch of turning ch; ch 4, turn.

Rep rows 2 and 3 for patt.

Dancing Clusters

Chain multiple: 6 + 2

Stitch Guide

Cluster (CL): (YO, insert hook in specified st and draw up a lp, YO and draw through 2 lps on hook) 4 times; YO and draw through all 5 lps on hook: CL made.

Instructions

Row 1: Sc in 2nd ch from hook and in each rem ch across; ch 1, turn.

Row 2 (RS): Sc in first sc; *ch 3, sk next 2 sc, CL in next sc, ch 3, sk next 2 sc, sc in next sc; rep from * across; ch 5, turn.

Row 3: Sc in top of first CL; *ch 2, dc in next sc, ch 2, sc in top of next CL; rep from * across; ch 2, dc in last sc; ch 1, turn.

Row 4: Sc in dc; *2 sc in next ch-2 sp, sc in next sc**; 2 sc in next ch-2 sp, sc in next dc; rep from * across, ending final rep at **; 3 sc in turning ch-sp; ch 1, turn.

Row 5: Sc in first sc and in each sc across; ch 1, turn.

Rep rows 2–5 for patt.

Oval Windows

Chain multiple: 14 + 2

Stitch Guide

Cluster (CL): *YO twice; insert hook in next tr and draw up a lp to height of a tr; (YO and draw through 2 lps) 2 times; rep from * twice, YO and draw through 4 lps: CL made.

Instructions

Row 1: Sc in 2nd ch from hook and in each rem ch across; ch 6 (counts as a tr and ch-2 sp of following row), turn.

Row 2: *Sk 6 sc, in next sc work (3 tr, ch 2, tr, ch 2, 3 tr); ch 2, sk 6 sc**; dc in next sc, ch 2; rep from * across, ending last rep at **; dc in last sc; ch 4 (counts as first tr on following row), turn.

Row 3: *CL over next 3 tr, ch 5, dc in next tr, ch 5, CL over next 3 tr**; tr in next dc; rep from * across, ending last rep at **; tr in 3rd ch of turning ch-6; ch 6, turn.

Row 4: *3 tr in top of next CL, ch 2, dc in next dc, ch 2, 3 tr in top of CL, ch 2**; tr in next tr, ch 2; rep from * across, ending last rep at **; tr in 4th ch of turning ch-4; ch 8, turn.

Row 5: *CL over next 3 tr, tr in next dc; CL over next 3 tr**; ch 5, dc in next tr; ch 5; rep from * across, ending last rep at **; dc in 4th ch of turning ch-6; ch 5, turn.

Row 6: *Work 3 tr in top of next CL, ch 2, tr in next tr; ch 2, 3 tr in top of next CL**; ch 2, dc in next dc, ch 2; rep from * across, ending last rep at **; dc in 3rd ch of turning ch-8; ch 4, turn.

Row 7: *CL over next 3 dc, ch 5, dc in next tr, ch 5, CL over next 3 tr**; tr in next dc; rep from * across, ending last rep at **; tr in 3rd ch of turning ch-5; ch 6, turn.

Rep rows 4–7 for patt.

Joined Shells

Chain multiple: 8 + 2

Stitch Guide

Shell: In specified st work (dc, ch 1) twice, dc in same st: shell made.

Cluster (CL): YO, insert hook in specified st and draw up a lp; YO and draw through 2 lps; YO, insert hook in same st and draw up a lp, YO and draw through 2 lps; YO and draw through 3 lps: CL made.

Instructions

Row 1: Sc in 2nd ch from hook and in each rem ch; ch 4 (counts as a dc and ch-1 sp), turn.

Row 2 (RS): Dc in base of turning ch, ch 2, sk 3 sc, sc in next sc; *ch 2, sk 3 sc, shell in next sc, ch 2, sk 3 sc, sc in next sc; rep from * across, ending last rep with ch 2, sk 3 sc, work (dc, ch 1, dc) in last sc; ch 1, turn.

Row 3: Sc in first dc and in first ch-1 sp; *ch 3, CL in next sc, ch 3, sc in first ch-1 sp of next shell, ch 1, sc in 2nd ch-1 sp of same shell; rep from * across, ending last rep with ch 2, 2 dc in turning ch-sp; ch 4, turn.

Row 4: Dc in base of turning ch, ch 2, sc in top of CL; *ch 2, shell in next ch-1 sp, ch 2, sc in top of next CL; rep from * across, ending last rep with ch 2, (dc, ch 1, dc) in last sc; ch 1, turn.

Rep rows 3 and 4 for patt.

Little Spiders

Chain multiple: 14 + 11

Stitch Guide

Cluster (CL): *YO, insert hook in specified st and draw up a lp to height of a dc, YO and draw through 2 lps; rep from * twice more in same st, YO and draw through 4 lps: CL made.

Instructions

Row 1 (RS): Dc in 7th ch from hook; *ch 1, sk next ch, dc in next ch; rep from * across, ch 4, turn.

Row 2: Dc in next dc, ch 1, dc in next dc; *ch 5, sk 2 dc, CL in next dc; ch 5, sk 2 dc, dc in next dc, ch 1, dc in next dc; rep from * across, ending last rep with ch 1, dc in 3rd ch of turning ch; ch 4, turn.

Row 3: Dc in next dc, ch 1, dc in next dc; *ch 4, sc in next ch-5 sp, ch 1, sk CL, sc in next ch-5 sp; ch 4, dc in next dc, ch 1, dc in next dc; rep from * across, ending last rep with ch 1, dc in 3rd ch of turning ch; ch 4, turn.

Row 4: Dc in next dc, ch 1, dc in next dc; *ch 4, sc in next sc, sc in next ch-1 sp, sc in next sc; ch 4, dc in next dc, ch 1, dc in next dc; rep from * across, ending last rep with ch 1, dc in 3rd ch of turning ch; ch 4, turn.

Row 5: Dc in next dc, ch 1, dc in next dc; *ch 5, sk next sc, CL in next sc, ch 5, dc in next dc, ch 1, dc in next dc; rep from * across, ending last rep with ch 1, dc in 3rd ch of turning ch; ch 4, turn.

Row 6: Dc in next dc, ch 1, dc in next dc; *(ch 1, dc) twice in next ch-5 sp; ch 1, dc in CL; (ch 1, dc) twice in next ch-5 sp; (ch 1, dc in

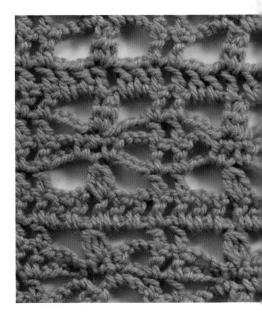

next dc) twice; rep from * across, ending last rep with ch 1, dc in 3rd ch of turning ch; ch 4, turn.

Rep rows 2–6 for patt.

Offset Clusters

Chain multiple: 3 + 2

Stitch Guide

Cluster (CL): *YO, insert hook in specified st and draw up a lp to height of a dc; YO and draw through 2 lps; rep from * two more times in same st, YO and draw through 4 lps: CL made.

Shell: In specified st work (dc, ch 1, CL): shell made.

Instructions

Row 1: CL in 5th ch from hook; *sk 2 chs, work shell in next ch; rep from * across, ending last rep with dc (instead of shell) in last ch; ch 4, turn.

Row 2: CL in base of ch; *work shell in top of dc of next shell; rep from * across, ending last rep with dc (instead of shell) in 3rd ch of turning ch; ch 4, turn.

Rep row 2 for patt.

Classy Clusters

Chain multiple: 4

Stitch Guide

Cluster (CL): YO, insert hook in first specified st and draw up a lp to height of a dc, YO and draw through 2 lps; (YO, insert hook in next specified st and draw up a lp to height of a dc, YO and draw through 2 lps) twice; YO and draw through 4 lps: CL made.

Half cluster (hCL): *YO, insert hook in first specified st and draw up a lp to height of a dc, YO and draw through 2 lps; YO, insert hook in next specified st and draw up a lp to height of a dc; YO and draw through 3 lps: hCL made.

Small cluster (sCL): YO, insert hook in specified st and draw up a lp to height of a dc, YO and draw through 2 lps; YO, insert hook in same st and draw up a lp to height of a dc, YO and draw through 3 lps; YO and draw through 2 lps: sCL made.

Instructions

Row 1: Dc in 5th ch from hook, ch 3, work sCL in top of dc just made; *sk next ch, CL over next 3 chs, ch 3, sCL in top of CL just made; rep from * across to last 3 chs, sk next ch, hCL over next 2 chs; ch 3 (counts as first dc of following row), turn.

Row 2: Dc in top of hCL; *ch 1, 3 dc in top of next CL; rep from * across, ending last rep with ch 1, 2 dc in last dc; ch 3, turn.

Row 3: Dc in next dc, ch 3, work sCL in top of dc just made; *CL over next 3 dc, ch 3, work sCL in top of CL just made; rep from * across, ending last rep with hCL over last dc and top of turning ch; ch 3, turn.

Rep rows 2 and 3 for patt.

Clever Cluster

Chain multiple: any even number

Stitch Guide

Cluster (CL): YO, insert hook in specified st and draw up a lp to height of a dc; YO and draw through 2 lps; (YO, insert hook in same st and draw up a lp to same height, YO and draw through 2 lps) twice; YO and draw through 4 lps; ch 1: CL made.

Instructions

Row 1: Sc in 2nd ch from hook and in next ch; *ch 1, sk next ch, sc in next ch; rep from * across to last 3 chs, ch 1, sk next ch, sc in last 2 chs; ch 4 (counts as a dc and ch-1 sp of following row), turn.

Row 2 (RS): *Sk next sc, CL in next ch-1 sp, ch 1; rep from * across to last ch-1 sp, CL in last ch-1 sp, ch 1, sk next sc, dc in last sc; ch 1, turn.

Row 3: Sc in first dc, sc in first ch-1 sp; *ch 1, sk next CL, sc in next ch-1 sp; rep from * across, ending last rep with sc in turning ch-sp, sc in 3rd ch of turning ch; ch 4, turn.

Rep rows 2 and 3 for patt.

Parasols

Chain multiple: 8 + 2

Stitch Guide

Cluster (CL): *YO, insert hook in first specified st and draw up a lp to height of a dc; YO and draw through 2 lps; YO, insert hook in next st and draw up a lp to height of a dc, YO and draw through 2 lps**; sk next st, rep from * to ** once in next 2 sts; YO and draw through all 5 lps on hook: CL made.

Half cluster (half CL): (YO, insert hook in specified sp and draw up a lp; YO and draw through 2 lps on hook) 2 times; YO and draw through all 3 lps on hook: half CL made.

Instructions

Row 1 (RS): Sc in 2nd ch from hook; *ch 4, sk next ch, CL over next 5 chs, ch 4, sk next ch, sc in next ch; rep from * across; ch 6 (counts as a dc and ch-3 sp), turn.

Row 2: *Sc in top of next CL, ch 3, dc in next sc, ch 3; rep from * across, ending last rep with dc in last sc; ch 3, turn.

Row 3: Work half CL in next ch-3 sp, ch 4, sc in next sc; *ch 4, CL in next 2 ch-3 sps, working half of CL in each ch-3 sp, ch 4, sc in next sc; rep from * across, ending last rep with ch 4, work half CL in turning ch-sp, dc in 3rd ch of turning ch, ch 1, turn.

Row 4: Sc in first dc; *ch 3, dc in next sc, ch 3, sc in top of next CL; rep from * across, ending last rep with sc in top of turning ch; ch 1, turn.

Row 5: Sc in first sc; *ch 4, CL in next 2 ch-3 sps, ch 4, sc in next sc; rep from * across, ending last rep with sc in last sc, ch 6, turn.

Rep rows 2–5 for patt.

Cluster Shells

Chain multiple: 5 + 2

Stitch Guide

Cluster (CL): *YO, insert hook in specified st and draw up a lp to height of a dc; YO and draw through 2 lps; rep from * once more in same st, YO and draw through 3 lps: CL made.

Cluster shell (CL shell): In specified st work (CL, ch 1, dc, ch 1, CL): CL shell made.

Instructions

Row 1: Sc in 2nd ch from hook and in each rem ch; ch 4, turn.

Row 2: CL in base of turning ch; *sk 4 sc, CL shell in next sc; rep from * across to last 5 sts, sk 4 sc, (CL, ch 1, dc) in last sc; ch 3, turn.

Row 3: Dc in ch-1 sp, ch 3, sc between next CL and next CL shell; *ch 3, dc in next ch-1 sp, ch 1, dc in next ch-1 sp, ch 3, sc between CLs; rep from * across, ending last rep with ch 3, dc in 4th and in 3rd chs of turning ch; ch 4, turn.

Row 4: CL in base of turning ch; *work CL shell in ch-1 sp between dc sts; rep from * across, ending last rep with (CL, ch 1, dc) in the ch-4 turning ch-sp; ch 4, turn.

Rep rows 3 and 4 for patt.

Cluster Crowns

Chain multiple: 12 + 1

Stitch Guide

Cluster (CL): *YO, insert hook in specified st and draw up a lp to height of a dc, YO and draw through 2 lps; rep from * 2 more times in same st, YO and draw through 4 lps: CL made.

Instructions

Row 1: Sc in 2nd ch from hook; *ch 4, sk 3 chs, sc in next ch; ch 4, sk 2 chs, sc in next ch; ch 4, sk 3 chs**, sc in next 2 chs; rep from * across, ending last rep at **; sc in last ch, ch 3, turn.

Row 2: *CL in next ch-4 sp, ch 3, work (CL, ch 5, CL) in next ch-4 sp, ch 3, CL in next ch-4 sp**, ch 1; rep from * across, ending last rep at **; dc in last sc; ch 1, turn.

Row 3: Sc in first dc; *3 sc in ch-3 sp, 5 sc in ch-5 sp, 3 sc in ch-3 sp, sc in ch-1 sp; rep from * across, ending last rep with sc in top of turning ch (instead of in ch-1 sp); ch 3, turn.

Row 4: Sk first 4 sc; *(CL in next sc, ch 3) 4 times, CL in next sc; sk next 3 sc, dc in next sc**; sk next 3 sc; rep from * across, ending last rep at **; ch 1, turn.

Row 5: Sc in first dc; *(sc in next ch-3 sp, ch 4) 3 times, sc in next ch-3 sp, sc in dc; rep from * across, ending last rep with sc in top of turning ch (instead of in dc); ch 3, turn.

Rep rows 2–5 for patt. End by working a row 2.

Slanted Clusters

Chain multiple: 6 + 5

Stitch Guide

Cluster (CL): *YO, insert hook in specified sp and draw up a lp to height of a dc; YO and draw through 2 lps; rep from * twice in same sp, YO and draw through 4 lps: CL made.

Shell: In specified sp work (tr, ch 4, CL): shell made.

Instructions

Row 1: Dc in 5th ch from hook; *ch 2, sk 2 chs, dc in next ch; rep from * across; ch 3, turn.

Row 2: Sk first ch-2 sp; *shell in next ch-2 sp, sk next ch-2 sp; rep from * across to last ch-2 sp, shell in last sp, dc in 3rd ch of turning ch; ch 3, turn.

Row 3: *Dc in top of first CL; ch 2, dc in 3rd ch of next ch-4 sp; rep from * across, ending last rep with ch 2, dc in top of turning ch; ch 3, turn.

Rep rows 2 and 3 for patt.

Fans and Clusters

Stitch multiple: 10 + 4

Stitch Guide

Cluster (CL): Keeping last lp of each dc on hook, work 3 dc in indicated st; YO and draw through all 4 lps on hook: CL made.

Double cluster (dCL): Keeping last lp of each dc on hook, dc in next dc, sk next CL, dc in next dc; YO and draw through all 3 lps on hook: dCL made.

Instructions

Row 1: Work 2 dc in 4th ch from hook, ch 3, sk next 4 chs, sc in next ch, ch 3, sk next 4 chs; *work 5 dc in next ch, ch 3, sk next 4 chs, sc in next ch; ch 3, sk next 4 chs; rep from * to last ch, work 3 dc in last ch; ch 4 (counts as a dc and ch-1 sp of following row), turn.

Row 2 (RS): (Dc in next dc, ch 1) twice; CL in next sc, ch 1; *(dc in next dc, ch 1) 5 times; CL in next sc, ch 1; rep from * to last 3 sts, (dc in next dc, ch 1) twice, dc in top of turning ch; ch 5 (counts as first dc and ch-2 sp of following row), turn.

Row 3: Dc in next dc, ch 2; work dCL, ch 2; *(dc in next dc, ch 2) 3 times, work dCL, ch 2; rep from * to last dc, dc in last dc, ch 2, dc in 3rd ch of turning ch; ch 1, turn.

Row 4: Sc in first dc, ch 1; *sc in next ch-2 sp, ch 3; rep from * across to turning ch, sc in 3rd ch of turning ch; ch 3, turn.

Row 5: Work 2 dc in first sc, ch 3, sk next ch-3 sp, sc in next ch-3 sp, ch 3, sk next ch-3 sp; *5 dc in next ch-3 sp, ch 3, sk next ch-3 sp, sc in next ch-3 sp, ch 3, sk next ch-3 sp; rep from * to last 2 sc, sk next sc, 3 dc in last sc; ch 4, turn.

Rep rows 2–5 for patt.

Clusters and Picots

Chain multiple: 5

Stitch Guide

Cluster (CL): *YO, insert hook in specified st and draw up a lp to height of a dc; YO and draw through 2 lps; rep from * two more times in same st, YO and draw through 4 lps: CL made.

Shell: Work (CL, ch 3, CL) all in same st: shell made.

Picot: Ch 3, sl st in first ch made: picot made.

Instructions

Row 1: Work CL in 5th ch from hook; *sk 4 chs, shell in next ch; rep from * across to last 5 chs, sk 4 chs, (CL, ch 1, dc) in last ch; ch 1, turn.

Row 2: Sc in first dc; *ch 5, work (sc, picot) in next ch-3 sp; rep from * across, ending last rep with ch 5, sc in turning ch-sp; ch 5, turn.

Row 3: *Sc in next ch-5 sp, ch 5; rep from * across, ending last rep with sc in last ch-5 sp, ch 2, dc in last sc; ch 4, turn.

Row 4: CL in dc; *shell in 3rd ch of next ch-5 sp; rep from * across, ending last rep with (CL, ch 1, dc) in turning ch-sp; ch 1, turn.

Rep rows 2–4 for patt.

Chained Melody

Chain multiple: 8 + 2

Stitch Guide

Cluster (CL): (YO, insert hook in specified st and draw up a lp to height of a dc, YO and draw through 2 lps) 2 times; YO, draw through 3 lps: CL made.

Shell: In specified st work (sc, ch 3, CL, ch 3, sl st): shell made.

Instructions

Row 1 (RS): Sc in 2nd ch from hook; *ch 5, sk 3 chs, sc in next ch, ch 5, sk 3 chs**, in next ch work shell; rep from * across, ending last rep at **; sc in last ch, ch 4, turn.

Row 2: *Sc in next ch-5 sp, ch 5; rep from * across, ending last rep with sc in last ch-5 sp, ch 2, tr in last sc; ch 1, turn.

Row 3: Sc in first tr; *ch 5, shell in 3rd ch of next ch-5 sp, ch 5**, sc in next ch-5 sp; rep from * across, ending last rep at **; sc in turning ch-sp, ch 5, turn.

Row 4: *Sc in next ch-5 lp, ch 5; rep from * across, ending last rep with sc in last ch-5 lp, ch 2, tr in last sc; ch 1, turn.

Row 5: Sc in first tr; *ch 5, sc in 3rd ch of next ch-5 sp; ch 5**, shell in next ch-5 sp; rep from * across, ending last rep at **; sc in last ch-5 sp, ch 2, tr in sc at base of prev row turning ch; ch 5, turn.

Rep rows 2–5 for patt.

Posies

Chain multiple: 16 + 2

Stitch Guide

Shell: In specified sp work (3 dc, ch 3, 3 dc): shell made.

Cluster (CL): *YO, insert hook in specified sp and draw up a lp, YO and draw through 2 lps; rep from * twice in same sp, YO and draw through 4 lps: CL made.

Instructions

Row 1: Sc in 2nd ch from hook; * ch 5, sk 3 chs, sc in next ch; rep from * across, turn.

Row 2: *Ch 5, sc in next ch-5 sp; rep from * across to last sp, ch 5, sc in last sp, ch 2, dc in sc; ch 1, turn.

Row 3: Sc in dc, ch 5, sc in next ch-5 sp; *shell in next ch-5 sp, sc in next ch-5 sp; (ch 5, sc in next ch-5 sp) 2 times; rep from * across, ending last rep with ch 5, sc in last ch-5 sp, ch 2, dc in sc; ch 1, turn.

Row 4 (RS): Sc in dc; *ch 5, sc in next ch-5 sp; (CL, ch 3, sc, ch 3, CL, ch 3, sc, ch 3, CL) in center ch-3 sp of shell; sc in next ch-5 sp; rep from * across, ending last rep with ch 2, dc in sc; ch 1, turn.

Row 5: Sc in dc; *ch 5, sc in top of next ch-3, ch 5, sc in top of next CL, ch 5, sc in top of ch-3 before last CL, ch 5, sc in next ch-5 sp; rep from * across, ending last rep with sc in last ch-5 sp, ch 2, dc in sc; ch 1, turn.

Row 6: Sc in dc; *ch 5, sc in next ch-5 sp; rep from * across, ending last rep with ch 2, dc in sc; ch 1, turn.

Rep rows 3–6 for patt.

Clusters in Rows

Chain multiple: 8 + 3

Stitch Guide

Cluster (CL): (YO, insert hook in specified st or sp and draw up a lp, YO and draw through 2 lps) twice; YO and draw through 3 lps: CL made.

Cluster shell (CL shell): In specified st work (CL, ch 3, CL): CL shell made.

Instructions

Row 1: Dc in 4th ch from hook and in each rem ch; ch 5 (counts as first dc and ch-2 sp of following row), turn.

Row 2: Sk next dc, sc in next dc; *ch 5, sk 3 dc, sc in next dc; rep from * across, ending last rep with ch 2, dc in top of turning ch; ch 4, turn.

Row 3: CL in base of turning ch; *ch 3, sc in next ch-5 lp, ch 3, work CL shell in next ch-5 lp; rep from * across, ending last rep with sc in next ch-5 lp, ch 3, work (CL, ch 1, dc) in last ch-5 lp; ch 1, turn.

Row 4: Sc in dc; *ch 3, (YO insert hook in next ch-3 sp and draw up a lp to height of a dc, YO and draw through 2 lps) twice; YO and draw through 3 lps: joined dc made; ch 3**, sc in ch-3 sp of next CL shell; rep from * across, ending last rep at **; sc in 3rd ch of turning ch; ch 3, turn.

Row 5: *Work 3 dc in next ch-3 sp, dc in top of next joined dc; 3 dc in next ch-3 sp, dc in next sc; rep from * across, ending last rep with dc in last sc; ch 5, turn.

Row 6: *Sc in center dc of next 3-dc group, ch 5; rep from * across,

ending last rep with ch 2 (instead of ch 5), dc in top of turning ch; ch 4, turn.

Rep rows 3–6 for patt. End by working a row 5.

Tundra

Chain multiple: 20 + 6

Stitch guide

Double crochet cluster (dcCL):
*YO, insert hook in specified st and draw up a lp, YO and draw through 2 lps on hook; rep from * once more; YO and draw through all 3 lps on hook: dcCL made.

Instructions

Row 1: Sc in 8th ch from hook, ch 4, sk next 3 chs, sc in next ch, ch 4, sk next 3 chs, dc in next ch; *(ch 4, sk next 3 chs, sc in next ch) 4 times; ch 4, sk next 3 chs, dc in next ch; rep from * across to last 10 chs; (ch 4, sk next 3 chs, sc in next ch) 2 times, ch 2, sk next ch, dc in last ch; ch 1, turn.

Row 2: Sc in first dc, ch 4, sc in next ch-4 sp; *ch 3, sk next ch-4 sp, 5 dc in next dc, ch 3, sk next ch-4 sp, sc in next ch-4 sp**; (ch 4, sc in next ch-4 sp) 2 times; rep from * across, ending final rep at **; ch 4, sk next sc and next 2 chs, sc in next ch; ch 6, turn.

Row 3: Sc in first ch-4 sp; *ch 3, sk next ch-3 sp, (dcCL in next dc, ch 3) 5 times, sk next ch-3 sp, sc in next ch-4 sp**; ch 4, sc in next ch-4 sp; rep from * across, ending final rep at **; ch 2, tr in last sc; ch 1, turn.

Row 4: Sc in first tr; *(ch 4, sc in next ch-3 sp, ch 4, sk next ch-3 sp, sc in next ch-3 sp) 2 times, ch 4**; dc in next ch-4 sp; rep from * across, ending final rep at **; sc in 4th ch of turning ch-6; ch 5, turn.

Row 5: Sc in first ch-4 sp, (ch 4, sc in next ch-4 sp) 3 times; *ch 3, sk next ch-4 sp, 5 dc in next dc, ch 3, sk next ch-4 sp, sc in next ch-4 sp, (ch 4, sc in next ch-4 sp) 2 times; rep from * across; ch 4, sc in next ch-4 sp, ch 2, dc in last sc; ch 1, turn.

Row 6: Sc in first dc, (ch 4, sc in next ch-4 sp) 3 times; *ch 3, sk next ch-3 sp, (dcCL in next dc, ch 3) 5 times, sk next ch-3 sp, sc in next ch-4 sp, ch 4, sc in next ch-4 sp; rep from * across; ch 4, sc in next ch-4 sp, ch 4, sc in 3rd ch of turning ch-5; ch 5, turn.

Row 7: Sc in first ch-4 sp, ch 4, sc in next ch-4 sp; *ch 4, dc in next ch-4 sp**; (ch 4, sc in next ch-3 sp, ch 4, sk next ch-3 sp, sc in next ch-3 sp) 2 times; rep from * across, ending final rep at **; (ch 4, sc in next ch-4 sp) 2 times, ch 2, dc in last sc; ch 1, turn.

Row 8: Sc in first dc, ch 4, sc in next ch-4 sp; *ch 3, sk next ch-4 sp, 5 dc in next dc, ch 3, sk next ch-4 sp, sc in next ch-4 sp**; (ch 4, sc in next ch-4 sp) 2 times; rep from * across, ending final rep at **; ch 4, sc in 3rd ch of turning ch-5; ch 6, turn.

Rep rows 3–8 for patt.

Cross Stitch

Chain multiple: 4 + 3

Instructions

Row 1 (WS): Hdc in 3rd ch from hook and in each rem ch; ch 5, turn.

Row 2: Sk first hdc; †YO twice, insert hook in back lp of next hdc, YO and draw up a lp: 4 lps on hook; YO and draw through 2 lps on hook: 3 lps rem on hook; YO, sk next 2 hdc, insert hook in back lp of next hdc, YO and draw up a lp: 5 lps on hook; *YO and draw through 2 lps on hook*; rep between * and * once more; mark last 2 lps worked off for center of cross st; rep between * and * twice more: one lp on hook; ch 2, YO, insert hook through 2 marked lps, YO and draw up a lp: 3 lps on hook; rep between * and * twice: cross st made; rep from † across, tr in top of turning ch; ch 2, turn.

Row 3: Sk first tr, hdc in next st, 2 hdc in next ch-2 sp; *hdc in each of next 2 sts, 2 hdc in next ch-2 sp; rep from * across to last 2 sts, hdc in top 2 sts of turning ch; ch 5, turn.

Rep rows 2 and 3 for patt.

Spiked Columns

Chain multiple: 4 + 3

Instructions

Row 1: Sc in 2nd ch from hook and in each rem ch; ch 3 (counts as first dc of following row throughout), turn.

Row 2 (RS): *Dc in each of next 3 sts, dc in same st as first dc of group was worked, sk next st; rep from * across to last st, dc in last st; ch 3, turn.

Row 3: *Dc in each of next 3 dc, dc in same st as first dc of group was worked; rep from * across, end last rep with dc in last st; ch 3, turn.

Rep row 3 for patt.

Bird Wings

Chain multiple: 8 + 2

Instructions

Row 1: Sc in 2nd ch from hook and in each rem ch; ch 3 (counts as a dc on following row throughout), turn.

Row 2 (RS): *Sk next 2 sc, tr in next sc; working behind last tr made, dc in each of 2 skipped sts; dc in next sc; sk next sc, dc in each of next 2 sc; working in front of last 2 dc made, tr into the skipped sc, dc in next dc; rep from * across, ch 1, turn.

Rows 3 and 4: Sc in each st across to turning ch, sc in top of turning ch; ch 1, turn.

Row 5: Sc in each sc across, ch 3, turn.

Rep rows 2–5 for patt.

Crossing Over

Chain multiple: 2 + 1

Instructions

Row 1: Sc in 2nd ch from hook and in each rem ch; ch 3 (counts as a dc of following rows), turn.

Row 2 (RS): *Sk next sc, tr in next sc, ch 1; working in front of tr just made, tr in first skipped sc; rep from * to last sc, dc in last sc; ch 1, turn.

Row 3: Sc in first dc; *sc in next tr, sc in next ch-1 sp; sk next tr; rep from * to last 2 sts, sk last tr, sc in top of turning ch; ch 3, turn.

Rep rows 2 and 3 for patt.

Simple Stitch

Chain multiple: any number

Instructions

Row 1 (RS): Sc in 2nd ch from hook and in each rem ch; ch 1, turn.

Row 2: Sc in each sc across, ch 3 (counts as first dc of following row), turn.

Row 3: Dc in each sc across; ch 1, turn.

Row 4: Sc in each dc across, ch 1, turn.

Row 5: Sc in each sc across, ch 3, turn.

Rep rows 3–5 for patt.

Sideways

Chain multiple: 4

Instructions

Row 1 (RS): Dc in 4th ch from hook; *sk next 3 chs, work (sc, ch 3, 3 dc) all in next ch; rep from * to last 4 chs, sk 3 chs, sc in last ch; ch 3, turn.

Row 2: Dc in first sc; *sk next 3 dc, work (sc, ch 3, 3 dc) all in next ch-3 sp; rep from * across, sc in top of turning ch; ch 3, turn.

Rep row 2 for patt, then work final row.

Final row: Dc in first sc, ch 1, sc in next ch-3 sp; *ch 3, sc in next ch-3 sp; rep from * to last 2 sts, dc in next sc, dc in top of turning ch.

Corn Rows

Chain multiple: 2 + 1

Instructions

Row 1 (RS): Sc in 2nd ch from hook, 2 sc in next ch; *sk next ch, 2 sc in next ch; rep from * to last 2 chs, sk next ch, ch 1, sc in last ch; ch 1, turn.

Row 2: Sc in first sc, 2 sc in next sc; *sk 1 sc, 2 sc in next sc; rep from * to last 2 sts, sk next sc, sc in last sc; ch 1, turn.

Rep row 2 for patt.

Topsy Turvy

Chain multiple: 4 + 1

Instructions

Row 1: Sc in 2nd ch from hook and in each rem ch; ch 4 (counts as a dc and ch-1 sp), turn.

Row 2 (RS): *Sk next 2 sc, 4 dc in next sc; rep from * to last 3 sts, ch 1, sk 2 sc, dc in last sc; ch 1, turn.

Row 3: Sc in first dc, sc in ch-1 sp; sc in each dc across, sc in ch-sp and in 3rd ch of ch-4; ch 6, turn.

Row 4: Sk first 2 sc; *(YO, insert hook in next sc, YO and draw up a lp to height of a dc, YO and draw through 2 lps on hook) 4 times; YO and draw through all 5 lps on hook, ch 1 for eye, ch 3; rep from * to last 2 sc, sk next sc, dc in last sc; ch 1, turn.

Row 5: Sc in first dc; *2 sc in next ch-3 sp, sc in ch-1 eye; rep from * across, to ch-6 sp, 3 sc in ch-6 sp; ch 4, turn.

Rep rows 2–5 for patt.

Arches

Chain multiple: 4

Instructions

Row 1 (RS): Dc in 4th ch from hook and in each rem ch; ch 3 (counts as first dc of following row), turn.

Row 2: Dc in next dc; *ch 2, sk next 2 dc, dc in next 2 dc; rep from * across; ch 3, turn.

Row 3: Dc in next dc; *2 dc in next ch-2 sp, dc in each of next 2 dc; rep from * across; ch 3, turn.

Rep rows 2 and 3 for patt.

Cross Over

Chain multiple: 2 + 1

Instructions

Row 1 (RS): Sc in 2nd ch from hook; *insert hook in last ch used, YO and draw up a lp, sk next ch, insert hook in next ch, YO and draw up a lp, YO and draw through all 3 lps on hook, ch 1; rep from * to last ch, sc in last ch; ch 1, turn.

Row 2: Sc in first sc; *draw up a lp in last st used, sk next st, draw up a lp in next st, YO and draw through all 3 lps on hook, ch 1; rep from * to last st, sc in last st; ch 1, turn.

Rep row 2 for patt.

All in a Row

Chain multiple: any number

Instructions

Row 1 (RS): Dc in 4th ch from hook and in each rem ch; ch 1, turn.

Row 2: Sc in both lps of first dc; sc in front lp only of each dc across, sc in 3rd ch of turning chain; ch 3 (counts as first dc of following row), turn.

Row 3: Dc in back lp only of each sc to last sc, dc in both lps of last sc; ch 1, turn.

Rep rows 2 and 3 for patt.

Chinese Lanterns

Chain multiple: 8 + 2

Instructions

Row 1 (RS): Dc in 4th ch from hook and in next 4 chs; *ch 4, sk next 4 chs, dc in next 4 chs; rep from * to last 2 chs, dc in last 2 chs; ch 3 (counts as first dc of next row), turn.

Row 2: Dc in next 5 dc; *ch 4, sk next ch-4 lp, dc in next 4 dc; rep from * to last 2 sts, dc in last 2 sts; ch 3, turn.

Row 3: Dc in next 5 dc; *ch 2, insert hook under both ch-4 lps and work one sc, ch 2; dc in next 4 dc; rep from * to last 2 sts, dc in last 2 sts, ch 3, turn.

Row 4: Dc in next 5 dc; *ch 4, dc in next 4 dc; rep from * to last 2 sts, dc in last 2 sts; ch 3, turn.

Row 5: Dc in next dc; *ch 4, sk next 4 dc; dc in each of next 4 chs; rep from * across to last 6 dc, ch 4, sk next 4 dc, dc in last 2 dc; ch 3, turn.

Row 6: Dc in next dc; *ch 4, dc in next 4 dc; rep from * to last 2 dc, ch 4, dc in last 2 dc; ch 3, turn.

Row 7: Dc in next dc; *ch 2, sc under both ch-4 lps as before, ch 2; dc in each of next 4 dc; rep from * across, ending last rep dc in last 2 dc; ch 3, turn.

Row 8: Rep row 6.

Row 9: Dc in next dc, dc in each of next 4 chs; *ch 4, sk 4 dc, dc in each of next 4 chs; rep from * to last 2 sts, dc in last 2 sts; ch 3, turn.

Rep rows 2–9 for patt. End last rep after working row 8.

Parallels

Chain multiple: 4 + 2

Instructions

Row 1: Sc in 2nd ch from hook and in each rem ch; ch 1, turn.

Row 2: Sc in first sc; *ch 4, sk next 3 sc, sc in next sc; rep from * across; ch 1, turn.

Row 3: Sc in first sc; *ch 4, sk next ch-4 lp, sc in next sc; rep from * across; ch 1, turn.

Rep row 3 for patt, then work final row.

Final row: Sc in first sc; *3 sc in next ch-4 sp, sc in next sc; rep from * across.

Garden Trellis

Chain multiple: 9 + 8

Instructions

Row 1 (RS): Sc in 2nd ch from hook and in each rem ch; ch 1, turn.

Row 2: Sc in first sc, sk 2 sc, (sc, ch 3, sc) in next sc; *(sk 2 sc, sc in next sc, ch 3) twice; sk 2 sc, (sc, ch 3, sc) in next sc; rep from * to last 3 sc; sk 2 sc, sc in last sc; ch 1, turn.

Row 3: Sc in first sc, (sc, ch 3, sc) in next ch-3 sp; *(sc in next ch-3 sp, ch 3) twice; (sc, ch 3, sc) in next ch-3 sp; rep from * to last 2 sc; sk next sc, sc in last sc; ch 1, turn.

Rep row 3 for patt.

Final row: Sc in first sc; *sc in next sc, sc in ch-3 sp, sc in next sc; (2 sc in ch-3 sp, sc in next sc) twice; rep from * across; end with sc in last 2 sc.

Optical

Chain multiple: 8 + 6

Instructions

Row 1: Sc in 2nd ch from hook; *ch 3, sk next 3 chs, sc in next ch; rep from * across; ch 3, turn.

Row 2 (RS): In first ch-3 sp, work 4 dc; *ch 1, dc in next ch-3 sp, ch 1, 4 dc in next ch-3 sp; rep from * across to last sc, dc in last sc; ch 1, turn.

Row 3: Sc in first dc, ch 3; *sc in next ch-1 sp, ch 3; rep from * across, sc in turning ch; ch 4, turn.

Row 4: Dc in first ch-3 sp, ch 1; *4 dc in next ch-3 sp, ch 1, dc in next ch-3 sp, ch 1; rep from * across, dc in last sc; ch 1, turn.

Row 5: Sc in first dc, ch 3, sk first ch-1 sp, sc in next ch-1 sp; *ch 3, sc in next ch-1 sp; rep from * across to last sp, ch 3, sk next dc and next ch, sc in next ch; ch 3, turn.

Rep rows 2–5 for patt.

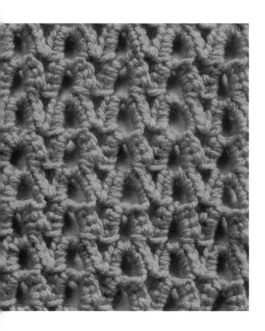

Hooked Up

Chain multiple: 4 + 2

Instructions

Row 1: Sc in 2nd ch from hook; *ch 5, sk next 2 chs, sc in each of next 2 chs; rep from * across to last 3 chs, sk next 2 chs, sc in last ch; ch 1, turn.

Row 2: *Work (4 sc, ch 5, 4 sc) in next ch-5 lp; rep from * across, ch 3, turn.

Rep row 2 for patt, then work final row.

Final row: *Work 9 sc in next ch-5 sp; rep from * across.

Open and Shut

Chain multiple: 2

Instructions

Row 1 (RS): Sc in 2nd ch from hook; *ch 1, sk next ch, sc in next ch; rep from * across; ch 2 (counts as first hdc of following row), turn.

Row 2: Hdc in next ch-1 sp; *ch 1, hdc in next ch-1 sp; rep from * across, hdc in last sc; ch 4 (counts as a dc and ch-1 sp), turn.

Row 3: *Dc in next ch-1 sp, ch 1; rep from * to last 2 hdc, sk next hdc, dc in last hdc; ch 2, turn.

Row 4: Hdc in next ch-1 sp; *ch 1, hdc in next ch-1 sp; rep from * to last dc, hdc in last dc; ch 1, turn.

Row 5: Sc in first hdc, ch 1; *sc in next ch-1 sp, ch 1; rep from * to last 2 hdc, sk next hdc, sc in last hdc; ch 1, turn.

Row 6: Sc in each sc and in each ch-1 sp; ch 1, turn.

Row 7: Sc in first sc; *ch 1, sk next sc, sc in next sc; rep from * across; ch 2, turn.

Rep rows 2–7 for patt.

Chain Link

Chain multiple: 7

Instructions

Row 1: 3 dc in 4th ch from hook, sk 2 chs, sc in next ch; *ch 3, sk 3 chs, 3 dc in next ch, sk 2 chs, sc in next ch; rep from * across; ch 2, turn.

Row 2 (RS): 3 dc in first sc; *sk 2 dc, sc in next dc, ch 3, 3 dc in next sc; rep from * to last 4 sts, sk 3 dc, sc in top of turning ch; ch 2, turn.

Rep row 2 for patt.

Kernels

Chain multiple: 2 + 1

Instructions

Row 1: Sc in 2nd ch from hook and in each rem ch; ch 1, turn.

Row 2 (RS): Sk first sc, (sc, dc) in next sc; *sk next sc, (sc, dc) in next sc; rep from * across; ch 1, turn.

Row 3: (Sc, dc) in each dc across; end sc in last sc; ch 1, turn.

Rep row 3 for patt.

Lattice

Chain multiple: 3 + 1

Instructions

Row 1 (RS): Dc in 4th ch from hook, sc in same ch; *ch 2, sk next 2 chs, work (dc, sc) in next ch; rep from * across; ch 3, turn.

Row 2: Sk first sc, work (dc, sc) in first dc; *ch 2, sk next ch-2 and sc, work (dc, sc) in next dc; rep from * across; ch 3, turn.

Rep row 2 for patt.

Clovers

Chain multiple: 4 + 5

Instructions

Row 1 (RS): Dc in 4th ch from hook (3 skipped chs count as first dc) and in next ch; *ch 1, sk next ch, dc in next 3 chs; rep from * across, ch 4 (counts as first dc and ch-1 sp of following row), turn.

Row 2: Dc in next dc; *dc in next ch-1 sp and in next dc, ch 1, sk next dc, dc in next dc; rep from * across, ch 3, turn.

Row 3: Dc in next ch-1 sp and in next dc; *ch 1, sk next dc, dc in next dc, dc in next ch-1 sp and in next dc; rep from * across; ch 4, turn.

Rep rows 2 and 3 for patt.

Shells in Line

Chain multiple: 9 + 2

Instructions

Row 1 (RS): Dc in 4th ch from hook; *sk next 2 chs, work (2 dc, ch 2, 2 dc) in next ch for shell; sk 2 chs, dc in next 4 chs; rep from * across to last 7 chs, sk next 2 chs, shell in next ch, sk next 2 chs, dc in each of last 2 chs; ch 3 (counts as first dc of following row), turn.

Row 2: Dc in next dc; *ch 2, sk first 2 dc of shell, work (sc, ch 3, sc) in ch-2 sp of shell, sk last 2 dc of shell, ch 2, dc in next 4 dc; rep from * across to last shell, sk first 2 dc of shell, ch 2, (sc, ch 3, sc) in ch-2 sp of shell, sk last 2 dc of shell, ch 2, dc in last 2 sts; ch 3, turn.

Row 3: Dc in next dc; *shell in next ch-3 sp, dc in next 4 dc; rep from * to last ch-3 sp, shell in ch-3 sp, dc in last 2 sts; ch 3, turn.

Rep rows 2 and 3 for patt.

Basic Background

Chain multiple: 2 + 1

Instructions

Row 1: Sc in 2nd ch from hook and in each rem ch; ch 1, turn.

Row 2 (RS): Sk first sc, 2 sc in next sc; *sk next sc, 2 sc in next sc; rep from * across; ch 1, turn.

Rep row 2 for patt.

Joined Arches

Chain multiple: 8 + 5

Instructions

Row 1: Dc in 4th and 5th chs from hook; *ch 5, sk next 5 chs, dc in next 3 chs; rep from * across; ch 3 (counts as first dc of following row), turn.

Row 2: Dc in next 2 dc; *ch 2, sc in 3rd ch of ch-5 lp, ch 2, dc in next 3 dc; rep from * across, working final dc in top of turning ch; ch 3, turn.

Row 3: Dc in next 2 dc; *ch 2, sc in next sc, ch 2, dc in next 3 dc; rep from * across, working final dc in top of turning ch; ch 3, turn.

Row 4: Dc in next 2 dc; *ch 5, dc in next 3 dc; rep from * across, working final dc in top of turning ch; ch 3, turn.

Rep rows 2–4 for patt.

Reflections

Chain multiple: 2 + 1

Instructions

Row 1 (RS): Hdc in 5th ch from hook; *ch 1, sk next ch, hdc in next ch; rep from * across; ch 2 (counts as first hdc of following row here and throughout patt), turn.

Row 2: Hdc in first ch-1 sp; *ch 1, hdc in next ch-1 sp; rep from * across, end hdc in last ch; ch 3 (counts as a hdc and ch-1 sp), turn.

Row 3: Hdc in first ch-1 sp, ch 1; *hdc in next ch-1 sp, ch 1; rep from * across to last 2 sts, sk next st, hdc in last st; ch 2, turn.

Row 4: Hdc in first ch-1 sp; *ch 1, hdc in next ch-1 sp; rep from * across, end hdc in last st; ch 3, turn.

Rep rows 3 and 4 for patt.

Little Mesh

Chain multiple: 3 + 2

Instructions

Row 1 (RS): Sc in 2nd ch from hook; *ch 3, dc in prev sc, sk 2 chs, sc in next ch; rep from * across; ch 3 (counts as a dc of following row), turn.

Row 2: Dc in first st, sc in next ch-3 sp, *ch 3, dc in same ch-3 sp, sc in next ch-3 sp; rep from * across, end last rep with sc in last ch-3 sp, ch 2, dc in last sc; ch 1, turn.

Row 3: Sc in first st, ch 3, dc in next ch-2 sp, *work (sc, ch 3, dc) in next ch-3 sp; rep from * across; ending last rep with sc in top of turning ch; ch 3, turn.

Rep rows 2 and 3 for patt.

Open Mesh

Chain multiple: any even number

Instructions

Row 1: Sc in 2nd ch from hook and in each rem ch; ch 4 (counts as a dc and ch-1 sp of following row), turn.

Row 2: Sk first st, dc in next st; *ch 1, sk next st, dc in next st; rep from * across; ch 4, turn.

Row 3: Dc in next dc; *ch 1, dc in next dc; rep from * across; ch 4, turn.

Rep row 3 for patt.

Lacy Diamonds

Chain multiple: 12 + 10

Instructions

Turning ch-3 does not count as a st in this patt. *Do not* work into the turning ch.

Row 1: Dc in 4th ch from hook; *ch 5, sk next 5 chs, dc in next 7 chs; rep from * across to last 6 chs, ch 5, sk next 5 chs, dc in last ch; ch 3, turn.

Row 2: Dc in first dc, ch 2; *dc in next ch-sp, ch 3, sk next dc, dc in next 5 dc, ch 3; rep from * across to last ch-sp; dc in last ch-sp, ch 2, dc in last dc; ch 3, turn.

Row 3: Dc in first dc, ch 1; *dc in next ch-sp, dc in next dc, dc in next ch-sp**; ch 3, sk next dc, dc in next 3 dc, ch 3; rep from * across, ending final rep at **; ch 1, dc in last dc; ch 3, turn.

Row 4: Dc in first dc; *dc in next ch-sp, dc in next 3 dc, dc in next ch-sp**; ch 3, sk next dc, dc in next dc, ch 3; rep from * across, ending final rep at **; dc in last dc; ch 3, turn.

Row 5: Dc in first dc; *dc in next 5 dc, dc in next ch-sp, ch 5, dc in next ch-sp; rep from * across to last 6 dc; dc in last 6 dc; ch 3, turn.

Row 6: Dc in first dc; *dc in next 5 dc, ch 3, dc in next ch-sp, ch 3, sk next dc; rep from * across to last 6 dc; dc in last 6 dc; ch 3, turn.

Row 7: Dc in first dc, ch 1; *sk next dc, dc in next 3 dc**; ch 3, dc in next ch-sp, dc in next dc, dc in next ch-sp, ch 3; rep from * across, ending final rep at **; ch 1, sk next dc, dc in last dc; ch 3, turn.

Row 8: Dc in first dc, ch 2; *sk next dc, dc in next dc**; ch 3, dc in next ch-sp, dc in next 3 dc, dc in next ch-sp, ch 3; rep from * across, ending final rep at **; ch 2, sk next dc, dc in last dc; ch 3, turn.

Row 9: Dc in first dc, ch 5, sk first ch-sp; *dc in next ch-sp, dc in next 5 dc, dc in next ch-sp, ch 5; rep from * across to last ch-sp; sk last ch-sp, dc in last dc; ch 3, turn.

Rep rows 2–9 for patt.

Matchsticks

Chain multiple: 2 + 1

Instructions

Row 1: Sc in 2nd ch from hook and in each rem ch; ch 1, turn.

Row 2: Sc in each sc across, ch 1, turn.

Row 3: Sc in each sc across; ch 4 (counts as a dc and ch-1 sp of following row), turn.

Row 4: *Sk next sc, dc in next sc, ch 1; rep from * across, end with skipping next sc, dc in last st; ch 1, turn.

Row 5: Sc in each dc and in each ch-1 sp to turning ch-sp, sc in 3rd ch of turning ch; ch 1, turn.

Rep rows 2–5 for patt.

Quads

Chain multiple: 6 + 2

Instructions

Row 1: Sc in 2nd ch from hook and in each rem ch; ch 5 (counts as a dc and ch 2 sp on following rows), turn.

Row 2: Sk next 2 sts, dc in each of next 4 sts; *ch 2, sk 2 sts, dc in each of next 4 sts; rep from * across; ch 5, turn.

Row 3: Sk next 2 dc, dc in next dc; *2 dc in ch-2 sp, dc in next dc, ch 2; sk next 2 dc, dc in next dc; rep from * across to turning ch; 2 dc in ch-5 sp, dc in 3rd ch of turning ch; ch 5, turn.

Rep row 3 for patt.

Tidy Little Stitch

Chain multiple: 5 + 2

Instructions

Row 1: Sc in 2nd ch from hook and in each rem ch; ch 4 (counts as a dc and ch-1 sp of following row), turn.

Row 2 (RS): Sk first sc, dc in next sc; *ch 1, sk next sc, dc in next sc; rep from * across, ch 1, turn.

Row 3: Draw up a lp in first dc, draw up a lp in next ch-1 sp, draw up a lp in next dc; YO and draw through all 4 lps on hook, ch 1; *draw up a lp in dc just worked, draw up a lp in next ch-1 sp, draw up a lp in next dc; YO and draw through all 4 lps on hook, ch 1; rep from * across; to end last rep draw up a lp in dc just worked, draw up a lp in ch-4 sp, draw up a lp in 3rd ch of turning ch, YO and draw through all 4 lps on hook; ch 4, turn.

Row 4: *Dc in 2 strands of st above next dc, ch 1; rep from * to last dc, dc in last dc, ch 1, turn.

Rep rows 3 and 4 for patt.

Two on Two

Chain multiple: 4 + 1

Instructions

Row 1: Sc in 2nd ch from hook and in each rem ch; ch 1, turn.

Row 2: Sc in first 2 sts; *ch 2, sk next 2 sts, sc in next 2 sts; rep from * across; end last rep with ch 2, sk 2 sts, sc in last st; ch 3 (counts as first dc of following row), turn.

Row 3: Dc in next st; *ch 2, dc in next 2 sc; rep from * across; ch 1, turn.

Row 4: Sc in first 2 dc; *ch 2, sc in next 2 dc; rep from * across, end last rep with sc in 3rd ch of turning ch; ch 3, turn.

Rep rows 3 and 4 for patt.

Between the Lines

Chain multiple: any uneven number

Instructions

Count sts carefully at end of each row.

Row 1: Sc in 2nd ch from hook and in each rem ch; ch 3 (counts as first dc of following row throughout), turn.

Row 2: Dc in each sc across, ch 3, turn.

Row 3: Dc between turning ch and next dc; *sk next dc, dc between skipped dc and next dc; rep from * to turning ch, dc in 3rd ch of turning ch; ch 3, turn.

Rep row 3 for patt.

Hill and Dale

Chain multiple: 8 + 5

Instructions

Row 1 (RS): Dc in 4th ch from hook (3 skipped chs count as a dc) and in next ch; *sk 2 chs, dc in next ch, ch 3, 3 dc around post (vertical bar) of last dc made, sk next 2 chs, dc in next 3 chs; rep from * across; ch 3 (counts as a dc on following row), turn.

Row 2: Dc in next 2 dc; *ch 2, sc in next ch-3 sp, ch 2, dc in next 3 dc; rep from * across, end dc in last 2 dc, dc in turning ch; ch 3, turn.

Row 3: Dc in next 2 dc; *dc in next sc, ch 3, 3 dc around post of last dc made, dc in next 3 dc; rep from * across; end with dc in last 2 dc, dc in top of turning ch; ch 3, turn.

Rep rows 2 and 3 for patt. End by working a row 2.

Very Basic

Chain multiple: 2

Instructions

Row 1: Sc in 2nd ch from hook and in each rem ch; ch 1, turn.

Row 2 (RS): Sc in first sc; *sk next sc, sc in next sc, working in front of sc just made, sc in skipped sc; rep from * across; ch 1, turn.

Rep row 2 for patt.

Take It Easy

Chain multiple: any even number

Instructions

Row 1 (RS): Sc in 2nd ch from hook; *ch 1, sk next ch, sc in next ch; rep from * across; ch 1, turn.

Row 2: Sc in first sc; *ch 1, sk next ch-1 sp, sc in next sc; rep from * across.

Rep row 2 for patt.

Ups and Downs

Chain multiple: any even number

Instructions

Row 1 (RS): Sc in 2nd ch from hook and in each rem ch; ch 1, turn.

Row 2: *Sc in first st, dc in next st; rep from * across to last st, sc in last st; ch 1, turn.

Row 3: *Sc in sc, dc in dc; rep from * across; ch 1, turn.

Rep row 3 for patt.

Staggered Blocks

Chain multiple: 18 + 1

Instructions

Row 1: Sc in 2nd ch from hook and in each rem ch; ch 3 (counts as first dc of following row), turn.

Row 2: Dc in next 3 sts; *(ch 2, sk 2 sts, dc in next st) 4 times, ch 2, sk 2 sts, dc in each of next 4 sts; rep from * to last 15 sts, (ch 2, sk 2 sts, dc in next st) 5 times; ch 5 (counts as a dc and ch-2 sp of following row), turn.

Row 3: (Dc in next dc, ch 2) 3 times; *dc in next dc, 2 dc in ch-2 sp, dc in next dc**; ch 2, sk 2 dc, dc in next dc; (ch 2, dc in next dc) 3 times, ch 2; rep from * across, end last rep at **, ch 2, sk 2 dc, dc in top of turning ch; ch 5, turn.

Row 4: Dc in next dc, ch 2, sk 2 dc, dc in next dc; 2 dc in ch-2 sp, dc in next dc; *(ch 2, dc in next dc) 4 times, ch 2, sk 2 dc, dc in next dc, 2 dc in ch-2 sp, dc in next dc; rep from * across; end last rep with (ch 2, dc in next dc) twice, ch 2, dc in 3rd ch of turning ch; ch 5, turn.

Row 5: (Dc in next dc, ch 2) twice, dc in next dc, sk 2 dc, dc in next dc; 2 dc in ch-2 sp, dc in next dc; *(ch 2, dc in next dc) 4 times, ch 2, sk 2 dc, dc in next dc; 2 dc in ch-2 sp, dc in next dc; rep from * across; end last rep with ch 2, dc in 3rd ch of turning ch; ch 3, turn.

Row 6: *2 dc in ch-2 sp, dc in next dc, ch 2, sk 2 dc, dc in next dc, (ch 2, dc in next dc) 4 times**; 2 dc in next ch-2 sp, dc in next dc, ch 2, sk 2 dc, (dc in next dc, ch 2) 4 times, dc in next dc; rep from * across; end last rep at **, ch 2, dc in 3rd ch of turning ch; ch 5, turn.

Rep rows 2–6 for patt.

Filet Blocks

Chain multiple: 8 + 5

Instructions

Row 1: Sc in 2nd ch from hook and in each rem ch; ch 4 (counts as a dc and ch-1 sp of following row), turn.

Row 2: Sk next st, dc in next st; *ch 1, sk next st, dc in next st; rep from * across, ch 4, turn.

Row 3: Dc in next dc, ch 1; *(dc in next dc, dc in ch-1 sp) twice, dc in next dc; ch 1, dc in next dc, ch 1; rep from * across; end last rep with dc in 3rd ch of turning ch; ch 4, turn.

Row 4: Rep row 3.

Rep rows 2–4 for patt.

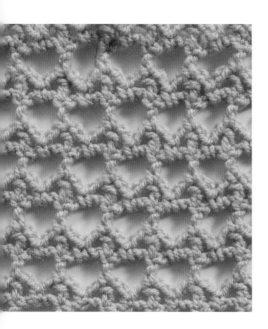

Ironwork

Chain multiple: 4 + 2

Instructions

Row 1: Sc in 2nd ch from hook and in each rem ch; ch 6 (counts as a dc and ch-3 lp on following row), turn.

Row 2: Sk first 4 sc, dc in next sc, *ch 3, sk next 3 sc, dc in next sc; rep from * across; ch 5, turn.

Row 3: *Sc in next ch-3 lp, ch 2, dc in next dc, ch 2; rep from * across to turning ch-5 sp, sc in ch-5 sp, ch 2, dc in 3rd ch of ch-5 sp; ch 5, turn.

Row 4: *Dc in next dc, ch 3; rep from * to turning ch-5 lp, dc in third ch of ch-5 lp; ch 5, turn.

Rep rows 3 and 4 for patt.

Crosses and Arches

Chain multiple: 4 + 3

Instructions

Row 1: Sc in 2nd ch from hook and in each rem ch; ch 3 (counts as first dc of following row), turn.

Row 2: Dc in next st; *sk next st, dc in next st, dc in skipped st; dc in next 2 sts; rep from * across; ch 1, turn.

Row 3: Sc in each st, ch 3, turn.

Row 4: Dc in next st; *ch 2, sk 2 sts, dc in next 2 sts; rep from * across; ch 1, turn.

Row 5: Sc in first 2 sts; *2 sc in ch-2 sp, sc in next 2 dc; rep from * across; ch 3, turn.

Rep rows 2–5 for patt.

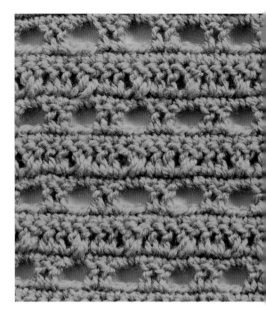

Triangles

Chain multiple: 4 + 2

Instructions

Row 1: Sc in 2nd ch from hook and in each rem ch; ch 1, turn.

Row 2: Sc in first st; *ch 3, sk 3 sts, sc in next st; rep from * across; ch 1, turn.

Row 3: *Sc in next ch-3 sp, ch 3, in same sp work (tr, dc, hdc, sc); rep from * across, end last rep with sc in last sc; ch 6, turn.

Row 4: Sc in 3rd ch of next ch-3; *ch 3, sc in 3rd ch of next ch-3; rep from * across; ch 1, turn.

Rep rows 3 and 4 for patt.

Third Time's a Charm

Chain multiple: 4 + 2

Instructions

Row 1: Dc in 5th ch from hook (counts as first 2 dc of row), dc in next ch; *ch 1, sk next ch, dc in next 3 chs; rep from * across; ch 4, turn.

Row 2: Sk next dc, dc in next dc, dc in next ch-sp, dc in next dc; *ch 1, sk next dc, dc in next dc, dc in next ch-sp, dc in next dc; rep from * across to last dc; ch 1, sk last dc, dc in top of turning ch; ch 3, turn.

Row 3: Dc in first ch-sp, dc in next dc; *ch 1, sk next dc, dc in next dc, dc in next ch-sp, dc in next dc; rep from * across to last 2 dc; ch 1, sk next dc, dc in last dc, dc in next 2 chs of turning ch-4; ch 4, turn.

Rep rows 2 and 3 for patt.

Linked Crowns

Chain multiple: 12

Instructions

Row 1: Sc in 2nd ch from hook; *ch 5, sk next 3 chs, sc in next ch; rep from * across to last 2 chs; ch 2, sk next ch, dc in last ch; ch 1, turn.

Row 2: Sc in first st; *7 dc in next ch-5 lp, sc in next ch-5 lp**; ch 5, sc in next ch-5 lp; rep from * across, ending final rep at **; ch 2, tr in last sc; ch 1, turn.

Row 3: Sc in first st; *ch 5, sk next dc, sc in next dc, ch 5, sk next 3 dc, sc in next dc**; ch 5, sc in next ch-5 lp; rep from * across, ending final rep at **; ch 2, tr in last sc; ch 1, turn.

Rep rows 2 and 3 for patt.

Winging It

Chain multiple: 6 + 2

Instructions

Row 1: Sc in 2nd ch from hook; *ch 5, sk next 5 chs, sc in next ch; rep from * across; ch 1, turn.

Row 2: Sc in first sc; *ch 5, sc in next sc; rep from * across; ch 1, turn.

Row 3: Sc in first sc; *ch 7, sc in next sc; rep from * across; ch 1, turn.

Row 4: Sc in first sc; *ch 7, sc in next sc; rep from * across; ch 5, turn.

Row 5: Sk first sc; *sc around next ch-7 lps on last 2 rows at same time**; ch 5; rep from * across, ending final rep at **; ch 2, dc in last sc; ch 1, turn.

Row 6: Sc in first dc, ch 2, sc in next sc; *ch 5, sc in next sc; rep from * across; ch 2, sc in 3rd ch of turning ch-5; ch 6, turn.

Row 7: Sk first sc, sc in next sc; *ch 7, sc in next sc; rep from * across to last sc; ch 3, dc in last sc; ch 1, turn.

Row 8: Sc in first dc, ch 3, sc in next sc; *ch 7, sc in next sc; rep from * across; ch 3, sc in 3rd ch of turning ch-6; ch 1, turn.

Row 9: Sc in first sc; *ch 5, sk next sc, sc around next ch-7 lps on last 2 rows at same time; rep from * across; ch 5, sc in last sc; ch 1, turn.

Rep rows 2–9 for patt.

Doublets

Chain multiple: 2 + 1

Instructions

Row 1: Sc in 2nd ch from hook and in each rem ch; ch 3 (counts as a dc throughout), turn.

Row 2: 2 dc in next sc; *ch 1, sk next sc, 2 dc in next sc; rep from * across to last 2 sc, sk next sc, dc in last sc; ch 3, turn.

Row 3: 2 dc in next dc; *sk next dc, 2 dc in next dc; rep from * across, sk last dc, dc in top of turning ch; ch 3, turn.

Rep row 3 for patt.

Tiny Crosses

Chain multiple: 3 + 2

Instructions

Row 1: Sc in 2nd ch from hook and in each rem ch; ch 1, turn.

Row 2: Sc in first sc; *ch 2, sk 2 sc, sc in next sc; rep from * across; ch 3, turn.

Row 3 (RS): Dc in ch-2 sp, ch 1, dc in next ch-2 sp, dc again in preceding ch-2 sp, ch 1; *dc in next ch-2 sp, dc in preceding ch-2 sp, ch 1; rep from * across; end last rep with dc in last sc; ch 1, turn.

Row 4: Sc in first dc; sc in each ch-1 sp and in each dc across; ch 1, turn.

Rep rows 2–4 for patt.

Dainty Doubles

Chain multiple: 6 + 3

Instructions

Row 1: Sc in 2nd ch from hook and in next ch; *ch 4, sk next 4 chs, sc in next 2 chs; rep from * across; ch 3, turn.

Row 2 (RS): *Work (2 dc, ch 2, 2 dc) in in next ch-4 lp; rep from * across; sk next sc, dc in last sc; ch 5, turn.

Row 3: 2 sc in first ch-2 sp; *ch 4, 2 sc in next ch-2 sp; rep from * across; ch 2, dc in 3rd ch of turning ch-3; ch 4, turn.

Row 4: 2 dc in first ch-2 sp; *(2 dc, ch 2, 2 dc) in next ch-4 lp; rep from * across; 2 dc in turning ch-5 lp, ch 1, dc in 3rd ch of turning ch-5; ch 1, turn.

Row 5: Sc in first dc, sc in next ch-1 sp; *ch 4, 2 sc in next ch-2 sp; rep from * across, working final 2 sc in turning ch-4 lp; ch 3, turn.

Rep rows 2–5 for patt.

Cross Patch

Chain multiple: 4

Instructions

Row 1: Sc in 2nd ch from hook; *ch 1, sk next ch, sc in next ch; rep from * across; ch 1, turn.

Row 2: Sc in first sc; *ch 1, sc in next sc; rep from * across; ch 4 (counts as a dc and ch-1 sp), turn.

Row 3: *Sk next ch-1 sp, sk next sc, sk next ch-1 sp, dc in next sc; ch 1, dc in skipped sc, ch 1; rep from * across, ending last rep by skipping last ch-1 sp, dc in last st; ch 1, turn.

Row 4: Sc in first dc; *ch 1, sc in next dc; rep from * across, ending last rep with ch 1, sc in 3rd ch of turning ch; ch 3, turn.

Row 5: Sk next ch-1 sp, dc in next sc, ch 1, dc in base of turning ch; *ch 1, sk next ch-1 sp, sk next sc, sk next ch-1 sp; dc in next sc, ch 1, dc in skipped dc; rep from * across, ending with dc in same st as final crossed dc; ch 2, turn.

Row 6: Sk next dc, sk next ch-1 sp, sc in next dc; *ch 1, sc in next dc; rep from * across, ending with ch-1, sk last ch-1 sp, sk last dc, sc in top of turning ch, ch 4, turn.

Rep rows 3–6 for patt.

On the Diagonal

Chain multiple: 7 + 5

Instructions

Row 1: Sc in 2nd ch from hook and in each rem ch; ch 3 (counts as a dc of following row), turn.

Row 2: Dc in next 2 sc; *in next sc work (dc, ch 2, dc), sk 3 sc, dc in next 3 sc; rep from * across, ending last rep with dc in last 4 (instead of 3) sc; ch 3 (counts as a dc of following row), turn.

Row 3: Dc in next 2 dc; *(dc, ch 2, dc) in next dc; sk next dc and ch-2 sp, dc in next 3 dc; rep from * across, ending last rep with dc in last 3 dc and in top of turning ch; ch 3, turn.

Rep row 3 for patt.

Fans

Fans

Chain multiple: 12 + 6

Instructions

Row 1 (RS): Dc in 6th ch from hook, sk 3 chs, sc in 5 chs; *sk 3 chs, dc in next ch; (ch 2, dc in same ch) twice, sk 3 chs, sc in 5 chs; rep from * to last 4 chs, sk next 3 chs, (dc, ch 2, dc) in last ch; ch 3, turn.

Row 2: 4 dc in next ch-2 sp, sk 2 sts, sc in 3 sc, 4 dc in next ch-2 sp; *dc in next dc, 4 dc in next ch-2 sp, sk 2 sts, sc in 3 sc, 4 dc in next sp; rep from * across, end dc in top of turning ch; ch 1, turn.

Row 3: Sc in first 3 dc, sk next 3 sts, dc in next sc; (ch 2, dc in same st) twice; *sk 3 sts, sc in 5 dc, sk 3 sts, dc in next sc, (ch 2, dc in same st) twice; rep from * to last 6 sts, sk next 3 sts, sc in next 2 dc and in top of turning ch; ch 1, turn.

Row 4: Sc in first 2 sc, 4 dc in ch-2 sp, dc in next dc, 4 dc in next ch-2 sp; *sk 2 sts, sc in 3 sc, 4 dc in next ch-2 sp, dc in next dc, 4 dc in next ch-2 sp; rep from * to last 4 sts, sk 2 sts, sc in last 2 sc; ch 5, turn.

Row 5: Dc in first sc, sk 3 sts, sc in 5 dc; *sk 3 sts, dc in next sc; (ch 2, dc in same st) twice, sk 3 sts, sc in 5 dc; rep from * across to last 4 sts, sk 3 sts, (dc, ch 2, dc) in last sc; ch 3, turn.

Rep rows 2–5 for patt.

Irish Fans

Chain multiple: 7

Instructions

Row 1 (RS): 2 dc in 4th ch from hook; *sk 2 chs, 5 dc in next ch (5-dc group made); sk next 2 chs, dc in next 2 chs (2-dc group made); rep from * to last 3 chs, sk next 2 chs, 3 dc in last ch; ch 3, turn.

Row 2: Dc between first 2 dc, *5 dc between dc of next 2-dc group, dc between 2nd and 3rd dc of next 5-dc group and between 3rd and 4th dc of same group); rep from * to last 4 sts, 3 dc between last dc and turning ch; ch 3, turn.

Rep row 2 for patt.

Fantastic Fans

Chain multiple: 12 + 2

Stitch Guide

Fan: In specified st or ch work (6 tr, ch 1, 6 tr): fan made.

Instructions

Row 1: Sc in 2nd ch from hook and in each rem ch; ch 1, turn.

Row 2 (RS): Sc in first sc; *sk 5 sts, work fan in next st, sk 5 sts, sc in next st; rep from * across; ch 5 (counts as a tr and ch-1 sp), turn.

Row 3: Tr in base of ch; *ch 6, sc in ch-1 sp of next fan, ch 6, (tr, ch 1, tr) in next sc; rep from * across, ch 1, turn.

Row 4: *Sc in ch-1 sp of next (tr, ch 1, tr) group; work fan in sc in ch-1 sp of next fan; rep from * across; end last rep with sc in ch-1 sp of last (tr, ch 1, tr) group; ch 5, turn.

Rep rows 3 and 4 for patt.

Crowned Fans

Chain multiple: 12 + 2

Stitch Guide

Shell: Work 8 dc in same lp: shell made.

Picot: Ch 4, sl st in first ch made: picot made.

Instructions

Row 1: Sc in 2nd ch from hook; *ch 5, sk 3 chs, sc in next ch; rep from * across; ch 6, turn.

Row 2: Sc in first ch-5 lp; *shell in next lp, sc in next lp; ch 5, sc in next lp; rep from * across, ending last rep with ch 3, tr in next sc; ch 1, turn.

Row 3: Sc in tr; *(dc in next dc, work picot) 7 times; dc in next dc, sc in next ch-5 lp; rep from * across, ending last rep with sc in 3rd ch of turning ch; ch 9, turn.

Row 4: Sc in 3rd picot, *ch 5, sk next picot, sc in next picot, ch 5, dc in next sc, ch 5, sc in 3rd picot; rep from * across, ending last rep with ch 5, tr in last sc; ch 6, turn.

Row 5: *Sc in next ch-5 lp, ch 5; rep from * across, ending last rep with sc in ch-9 lp, ch 2, tr in 5th ch of ch-9 lp; ch 3, turn.

Row 6: Work 4 dc in ch-2 sp, sc in next ch-5 lp, ch 5, *sc in next ch-5 lp, shell in next ch-5 lp, sc in next ch-5 lp, ch 5; rep from * across, ending last rep with 5 dc in ch-6 lp; ch 4, turn.

Row 7: (Work picot, dc in next dc) 4 times, sc in next ch-5 lp; *(dc in next dc, work picot) 7 times, dc in next dc, sc in next ch-5 sp; rep from * across, ending last rep with (dc in next dc, work picot) 4 times, dc in top of turning ch; ch 8, turn.

Row 8: Sc in 2nd picot, ch 5, dc in next sc; *ch 5, sc in 3rd picot, ch 5, sk next picot, sc in next picot, ch 5, dc in next sc; rep from * across, ending last rep with ch 5, sc in 3rd picot, ch 2, dc in top of turning ch; ch 6, turn.

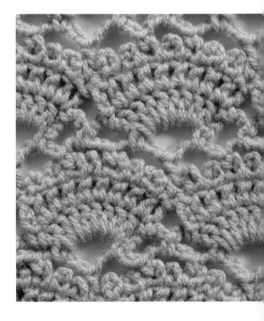

Row 9: *Sc in next ch 5 lp, ch 5; rep from * across, ending last rep with ch 2, tr in 3rd ch of turning ch; ch 6, turn.

Rep rows 2–9 for patt.

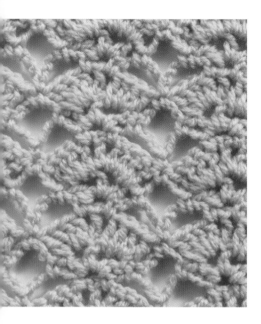

Fabulous Fans

Chain multiple: 12 + 2

Stitch Guide

Shell: In specified sp work (dc, ch 2) twice, dc in same sp: shell made.

Instructions

Row 1: Sc in 2nd ch from hook and in each rem ch; ch 1, turn.

Row 2 (RS): Sc in first sc; *ch 5, sk 3 sc, sc in next sc, ch 3, sk 3 sc, sc in next sc; ch 5, sk 3 sc, sc in next sc; rep from * across; ch 7 (counts as a tr and ch-2 sp), turn.

Row 3: Sc in next ch-5 sp; *shell in next ch-3 sp, sc in next ch-5 sp, ch 5, sc in next ch-5 sp; rep from * across, ending last rep with shell in last ch-3 sp, sc in last ch-5 sp, ch 2, tr in last sc; ch 1, turn.

Row 4: Sc in tr; *4 dc in first ch-2 sp of next shell, ch 1, dc in next dc of same shell, ch 1, 4 dc in next ch-2 sp of same shell, sc in next ch-5 sp; rep from * across, ending last rep with sc in 5th ch of turning ch-7; ch 1, turn.

Row 5: Sc in first sc; *ch 5, sc in next ch-1 sp, ch 3, sc in next ch-1 sp, ch 5, sc in next sc; rep from * across, ending last rep with sc in tr; ch 7, turn.

Rep rows 3–5 for patt. End by working a row 4.

Frisky Fans

Chain multiple: 8 + 2

Stitch Guide

V-stitch (V-st): In specified st work (dc, ch 3, dc): V-st made.

Picot: Ch 3, sl st in base of ch: picot made.

Fan shell: In specified sp work (3 dc, work picot, 3 dc, work picot, 3 dc): fan shell made.

Instructions

Row 1: Sc in 2nd ch from hook; *ch 2, sk next ch, dc in next 5 chs, ch 2, sk next ch, sc in next ch; rep from * across; ch 4, turn.

Row 2: Dc in base of ch; *ch 1, sc in center dc of next 5-dc group**, ch 1, V-st in next sc; rep from * across, ending last rep at **; ch 1, (dc, ch 1, dc) in last sc; ch 3, turn.

Row 3: In next ch-1 sp work (2 dc, picot, 2 dc); *dc in next sc, fan shell in next ch-3 sp; rep from * across to last sc, dc in last sc, in turning ch-lp work (2 dc, picot, 2 dc; dc in top of turning ch, ch 3 (counts as first dc of following row), turn.

Row 4: Dc in next dc, *ch 2, dc in dc between next 2 fan shells, ch 2, dc in each of center 3 dc in next fan shell; rep from * across, ending last rep with ch 2, dc in last dc and dc in top of turning ch; ch 1, turn.

Row 5: Sc in first dc; ch 2, 2 dc in next ch-2 sp; *dc in next dc, 2 dc in next ch-2 sp, ch 2, sk next dc, sc in next dc, ch 2, sk next dc, 2 dc in next ch-2 sp; rep from * across, ending last rep with ch 2, sk last dc, dc in top of turning ch; ch 4, turn.

Rep rows 2–5 for patt.

Flirty Fans

Chain multiple: 8 + 2

Stitch Guide

Fan: In specified st work (dc, ch 1) 4 times, dc in same st: fan made.

Back-post double crochet (BPdc): YO, insert hook from back to front to back around post (vertical bar) of specified st; YO and draw up a lp to height of a dc; (YO and draw through 2 lps) twice: BPdc made.

Instructions

Row 1 (RS): Sc in 2nd ch from hook; *sk 3 chs, work fan in next ch**, sk 3 chs, sc in next ch; rep from * across, ending last rep at **; sk 3 chs, sc in last ch; ch 3 (counts as a dc of following row), turn.

Row 2: *BPdc around 2nd dc of next fan, ch 2, sc in next dc, ch 2, BPdc around next dc, dc in next sc; rep from * across; ch 4 (counts as a dc and ch-1 sp), turn.

Row 3: (Dc, ch 1, dc) in base of ch; *sc in next sc, sk next st, work fan in next dc; rep from * across to last sc, sc in last sc, in top of turning ch work (dc, ch 1) twice, dc in same place; ch 1, turn.

Row 4: Sc in first dc, ch 2, BPdc around next dc; dc in next sc; *BPdc around 2nd dc of next fan, ch 2, sc in next dc, ch 2, BPdc around next dc, dc in next sc; rep from * across, ending last rep with BPdc around last dc, ch 2, sc in top of turning ch; ch 1, turn.

Row 5: Sc in first sc; *sk next st, work fan in next dc, sc in next sc; rep from * across; ch 3, turn.

Rep rows 2–5 for patt.

Crowns

Chain multiple: 14 + 5

Stitch Guide

V-stitch (V-st): Work (dc, ch 2, dc) in same ch or sp: V-st made.

Shell: Work 7 dc in same sp: shell made.

Cluster (CL): *YO, insert hook in specified st and draw up a lp to height of a dc, YO and draw through 2 lps; rep from * once in same st, YO and draw through 3 lps: CL made.

Instructions

Row 1: Dc in 4th ch from hook and in next ch; *ch 3, sk 5 chs, V-st in next ch, ch 3, sk 5 chs, dc in each of next 3 chs; rep from * across; ch 3 (counts as first dc of following row), turn.

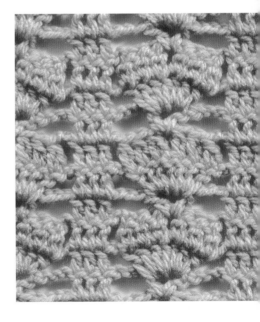

Row 2: Dc in each of next 2 dc; *ch 2, shell in ch-2 sp of next V-st, ch 2, dc in each of next 3 dc; rep from * across, ending last rep with dc in last 2 dc, dc in top of turning ch; ch 3, turn.

Row 3: Dc in each of next 2 dc; *ch 2, CL in each of next 3 dc, ch 1, sk next dc, CL in each of next 3 dc, ch 2, dc in each of next 3 dc; rep from * across, ending last rep with dc in last 2 dc, dc in top of turning ch; ch 3, turn.

Row 4: Dc in each of next 2 dc; *ch 3, V-st in next ch-1 sp, ch 3, dc in each of next 3 dc; rep from * across, ending last rep with dc in last 2 dc, dc in top of turning ch; ch 3, turn.

Rep rows 2–4 for patt.

Glorious Crowns

Chain multiple: 12 + 2

Stitch Guide

Picot: Ch 3, sl st in first ch made: picot made.

Instructions

Row 1: Sc in 2nd ch from hook; *ch 5, sk 3 chs, sc in next ch; rep from * across; ch 5, turn.

Row 2: *Sc in next ch-5 sp, work 8 dc in next ch-5 sp, sc in next ch-5 sp, ch 4; rep from * across, ending last rep with ch 2 (instead of ch 4), dc in last sc; ch 1, turn.

Row 3: Sc in first dc; *(dc, work picot) in each of next 8 dc, ch 1**, sc in ch-4 sp, ch 1; rep from * across, ending last rep at **; sc in 3rd ch of turning ch; ch 4, turn.

Row 4: *(Tr in next dc, ch 1) 8 times, tr in next ch-1 sp, ch 1, tr in next ch-1 sp, ch 1; rep from * across, ending last rep with tr in last sc; ch 1, turn.

Row 5: Sc in first tr; *(ch 4, sk 2 ch-1 sps, sc in next ch-1 sp) 3 times; rep from * across, ending last rep with sc in top of turning ch; ch 5, turn.

Row 6: Sc in next ch-4 sp; *work 8 dc in next ch-4 sp, sc in next ch-4 sp**, ch 4, sc in next ch-4 sp; rep from * across, ending last rep at **; ch 2, dc in last sc; ch 1, turn.

Rep rows 3–6 for patt.

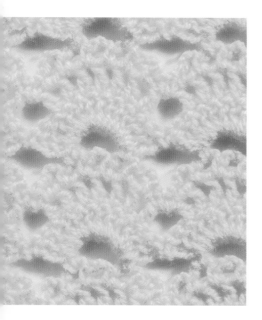

Delicate Fans

Chain multiple: 10 + 5

Instructions

Row 1: Sc in 8th ch from hook; *ch 5, sk next 3 chs, sc in next ch**; ch 6, sk next 5 chs, sc in next ch; rep from * across, ending final rep at **; ch 2, sk next 2 chs, dc in last ch; ch 1, turn.

Row 2: Sc in first st; *11 dc in next ch-5 lp**; sc in next ch-6 lp; rep from * across, ending final rep at **; sk next 2 chs, sc in next ch; ch 4, turn.

Row 3: Sk first 2 dc, *dc in next dc, (ch 1, dc in next dc) 6 times**; sk next 4 dc; rep from * across, ending final rep at **; tr in last sc; ch 1, turn.

Row 4: Sc in tr; *ch 1, sc in next ch-1 sp, (ch 3, sc in next ch-1 sp) 5 times, ch 1**; sc in sp between next 2 dc; rep from * across, ending final rep at **; sc in 4th ch of turning ch-4; ch 6, turn.

Row 5: Sk first ch-3 sp; *sc in next ch-3 sp, ch 5, sk next ch-3 sp, sc in next ch-3 sp**; ch 6, sk next 2 ch-3 sps; rep from * across, ending final rep at **; ch 2, tr in last sc; ch 1, turn.

Rep rows 2–5 for patt.

Elongated Fans

Chain multiple: 14 + 3

Stitch Guide

Triple triple crochet (trtr): YO 4 times; insert hook in specified st and draw up a long lp; (YO and draw through 2 lps) 5 times: trtr made.

Shell: In specified st work (trtr, ch 1) 6 times, trtr in same st: shell made.

Instructions

Row 1: Work shell in 10th ch from hook; *sk 6 chs, dc in next ch, sk 6 chs, work shell in next ch; rep from * across, ending last rep by skipping 6 chs, dc in last ch; ch 1, turn.

Row 2: Sc in dc; *(sc in next trtr, sc in next ch-1 sp) 6 times, sc in next trtr, sc in next dc; rep from * across, ending last rep with sc in top of turning ch; ch 7, turn.

Row 3: Work (trtr, ch 1) twice in base of turning ch, trtr in same place; sc in sc above center trtr of next shell; *shell in sc above next dc, sc in sc above center trtr of next shell; rep from * across, ending last rep with (trtr, ch 1) 3 times in sc above last dc, trtr in same st; ch 1, turn.

Row 4: (Sc in next trtr, sc in ch-1 sp) 3 times, sc in next trtr, sc in next sc; *(sc in next trtr, sc in ch-1 sp) 6 times, sc in next trtr, sc in next sc; rep from * across, ending last rep with (sc in next trtr, sc in ch-1 sp) twice, sc in last trtr; sc in 6th ch of of turning ch, ch 1, turn.

Row 5: Sc in first sc; *shell in next sc above center trtr of prev shell, sc in sc at top of center trtr of next shell; rep from * across, ending last rep with sc in last sc, ch 1, turn.

Row 6: Sc in sc; *(sc in next trtr, sc in next ch-1 sp) 6 times, sc in next trtr, sc in next dc; rep from * across, ending last rep with sc in top of turning ch; ch 7, turn.

Row 7: Work (trtr, ch 1) twice in base of turning ch, trtr in same place; sc in sc above center trtr of next shell; *shell in sc, sc in sc above center trtr of shell; rep from * across, ending last rep with (trtr, ch 1) 3 times in last sc; trtr in same st, ch 1, turn.

Rep rows 4–7 for patt.

Lovely Lace

Chain multiple: 5 + 1

Instructions

Row 1 (RS): Dc in 4th ch from hook; *sc in next ch, draw up lp on hook to ¾", sk next 3 chs, work (dc, ch 1, dc) in next ch; rep from * to last 2 chs, sk next ch, sc in last ch; ch 3 (counts as first dc of following row throughout), turn.

Row 2: Dc in next dc; *sc in next ch-1 sp, draw up lp on hook to ¾" (dc, ch 1, dc) in next sc; rep from * to last 2 sts, sk next dc, sc in turning ch; ch 3, turn.

Rep row 2 for patt.

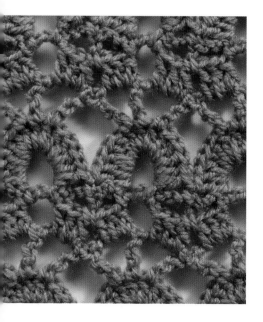

Lucky Horseshoes

Chain multiple: 9 + 1

Instructions

Row 1: Sc in 2nd ch from hook and in each rem ch; ch 1, turn.

Row 2: Sc in first sc; *ch 3, sk 3 sc, sc in next sc, ch 7, sc in next sc, ch 3, sk 3 sc, sc in next sc; rep from * across; ch 1, turn.

Row 3 (RS): Sc in first sc; *sk 3 chs and next sc, 13 dc in ch-7 lp, sk next sc and 3 chs, sc in next sc; rep from * across; loosely ch 6, turn.

Note: On following row, work chs loosely.

Row 4: Sk 5 dc, (tr in next dc, ch 4) twice, tr in next dc, *sk next 5 dc, next sc, and next 5 dc; (tr in next dc, ch 4) twice, tr in next dc; rep from * across; end last rep with sk last 5 dc; YO 4 times, insert hook in last sc, (YO and draw through 2 lps) 5 times; ch 3, turn.

Row 5: *3 dc in next ch-4 sp, ch 4, 3 dc in next ch-4 sp; rep from * across; end last rep with dc in 6th ch of turning ch-6; ch 6 (counts as a dc and ch-3 sp on following row), turn.

Row 6: *Sk 3 dc, in next ch-4 sp work (sc, ch 7, sc); ch 3, dc between next two 3-dc groups, ch 3; rep from * across; end last rep with ch 3, dc in top of turning ch; ch 1, turn.

Row 7: Sc in first dc; *sk 3 chs and next sc, 13 dc in ch-7 lp, sk next sc and 3 chs, sc in next dc; rep from * across; end last rep with sc in 3rd ch of turning ch; loosely ch 6, turn.

Rep rows 4–7 for patt.

Loop-the-Loop

Chain multiple: 6 + 2

Instructions

Row 1: Sc in 10th ch from hook; *ch 3, sk 2 chs, dc in next ch, ch 3, sk 2 chs, sc in next ch; rep from * to last 3 chs, ch 3, sk 2 chs, dc in last ch; ch 3, turn.

Row 2: Dc in next ch-3 sp; *ch 3, dc in next sp, dc in next dc, dc in next sp; rep from * across to last sp, end last rep with ch 3, 2 dc in last sp; ch 6, turn.

Row 3: *Sc in next sp, ch 3, dc in center dc of next 3-dc group, ch 3; rep from * across, end last rep with dc in top of turning ch; ch 3, turn.

Rep rows 2 and 3 for patt.

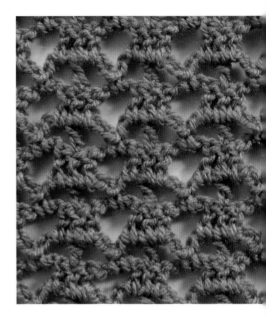

Quads in a Loop

Chain multiple: 5 + 1

Instructions

Row 1 (RS): Dc in 4th ch from hook and in next 2 chs; *ch 1, sk next ch, dc in next 4 chs; rep from * across; ch 1, turn.

Row 2: Sc in first dc; *ch 5, sc in next ch-1 sp; rep from * across, end ch 5, sc in top of turning ch; ch 3, turn.

Row 3: 3 dc in first ch-5 sp; *ch 1, 4 dc in next ch-5 sp; rep from * across, end ch 1, 3 dc in last sp, dc in last sc; ch 1, turn.

Rep rows 2 and 3 for patt.

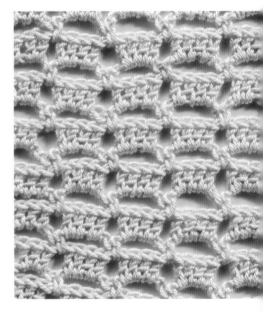

Tied Lace

Chain multiple: 12 + 1

Instructions

Row 1: Sc in 10th ch from hook; *ch 3, sk next 2 chs, dc in next ch**; ch 5, sk next 5 chs, dc in next ch, ch 3, sk next 2 chs, sc in next ch; rep from * across, ending final rep at **; ch 8 (counts as dc and ch-5 sp of next row throughout), turn.

Row 2: Sk first 2 ch-3 sps, dc in next dc; *ch 3, sc in next ch-5 sp, ch 3, dc in next dc, ch 5, sk next 2 ch-3 sps, dc in next dc; rep from * across, working last dc of final rep in 4th skipped ch at beg of row 1; ch 6 (counts as dc and ch-3 sp of next row throughout), turn.

Row 3: Sc in first ch-5 sp; *ch 3, dc in next dc; ch 5, sk next 2 ch-3 sps, dc in next dc, ch 3, sc in next ch-5 sp; rep from * across; ch 3, dc in 3rd ch of turning ch-8; ch 8, turn.

Row 4: Sk first 2 ch-3 sps, dc in next dc; *ch 3, sc in next ch-5 sp, ch 3, dc in next dc, ch 5, sk next 2 ch-3 sps, dc in next dc; rep from * across, working last dc of final rep in 3rd ch of turning ch-6; ch 6, turn.

Rep rows 3 and 4 for patt.

Ropes and Ladders

Chain multiple: 4 + 2

Stitch Guide

Loop (lp): Work (sc, ch 3, sc) in specified st: lp made.

Double loop (Dlp): Work (sc, ch 3, sc) twice in specified st: Dlp made.

Instructions

Row 1: Sc in 2nd ch from hook and in each rem ch; ch 1, turn.

Row 2: Sc in first sc; *ch 3, sk 3 sc, in next sc work lp; rep from * across, ending last rep with ch 3, sk 3 sc, sc in last sc; ch 1, turn.

Row 3 (RS): Sc in first sc; *ch 3, work Dlp in ch 3-sp of next lp; rep from * across, ending last rep with ch 3, sc in last sc; ch 6, turn.

Row 4: *Sc in next lp, ch 3, sc in next lp, ch 3; rep from * across, ending last rep with dc in last sc; ch 1, turn.

Row 5: Sc in first dc; *ch 3, Dlp in ch-3 sp between lps; rep from * across, ending last rep with ch 3, sc in 3rd ch of ch-6 sp; ch 6, turn.

Rep rows 4 and 5 for patt, ending with row 4 on last rep.

Lazy Loops

Chain multiple: 3 + 2

Instructions

Row 1: Sc in 2nd ch from hook and in each rem ch; ch 1, turn.

Row 2: Sc in first sc; *ch 5, sk 2 sc, sc in next sc; rep from * across to last 3 sc, ch 2, sk 2 sc, dc in last sc; ch 1, turn.

Row 3: Sc in dc; *ch 5, sc in next ch-5 lp; rep from * across, ending last rep with ch 2, tr in last sc, ch 5 (counts as a tr and ch-1 sp), turn.

Row 4 (RS): *2 dc in next ch-5 lp, ch 1; rep from * across to last ch-5 lp, 2 dc in last lp, tr in last sc; ch 1, turn.

Row 5: Sc in tr; *ch 5, sc in next ch-1 sp; rep from * across, ending last rep with ch 5, sc in turning ch-sp; ch 6, turn.

Row 6: *Sc in next ch-5 lp, ch 5; rep from * across, ending last rep with sc in last ch-5 lp, ch 2, tr in sc; ch 3, turn.

Row 7: Dc in tr; *ch 1, 2 dc in next ch-5 lp; rep from * across, ending last rep with ch 1, 2 dc in turning ch-sp; ch 5, turn.

Row 8: *Sc in ch-1 sp, ch 5; rep from * across, ending last rep with tr, ch 2, tr in top of turning ch; ch 1, turn.

Row 9: Sc in first tr; *ch 5, sc in next ch-5 lp; rep from * across, ending last rep with sc in last ch-5 lp, ch 5, turn.

Rep rows 4–9 for patt. End after working row 4 or row 7 on last rep.

Faux Fur

Chain multiple: any number

Stitch Guide

Front loop only (FLO): Work in front lp only (lp facing you) of each st.

Instructions

Row 1: Sc in 2nd ch from hook and in each rem ch; ch 1, turn.

Row 2: Sc in each sc across, ch 1, turn.

Row 3 (RS): Working in FLO of each st across row, sc in first sc; *ch 6, sc in next sc; rep from * across; ch 1, turn.

Row 4: Working in unused lps of row 3, sc in each lp across, ch 1, turn.

Rows 5 and 6: Sc in each sc, ch 1, turn.

Rep rows 3–6 for patt. End after working row 4 on last rep.

Lively Loops

Chain multiple: 6 + 1

Stitch Guide

Beginning loop single crochet (beg lp sc): Sc in specified st or sp, pull up lp on hook to height of dc, remove hook from lp and leave lp standing alone: beg lp sc made.

Loop single crochet (lp sc): Wrap free end of yarn around hook, insert hook in specified st or sp and draw up a lp, YO and draw through both lps on hook, pull up lp on hook to height of dc, remove hook from lp and leave lp standing alone: lp sc made.

Beginning single crochet (beg sc): Wrap free end of yarn around hook, insert hook in specified st or sp and draw up a lp, YO and draw through both lps on hook: beg sc made.

Instructions

Row 1: Sc in 2nd and 3rd chs from hook; *ch 4, sk next 2 chs, sc in next 4 chs; rep from * across to last 4 chs, ch 4, sk next 2 chs, sc in last 2 chs; ch 1, turn.

Row 2: Work beg lp sc in first sc; work 6 lp sc in next ch-4 lp, sk next sc; *work beg sc in next sc, sc in next sc, work (beg lp sc, 5 lp sc) in next ch-4 lp, sk next sc; rep from * across; work beg lp sc in last sc, but do not remove hook from lp; turn.

Row 3: Sl st in next 2 lp sc tog, sl st in next lp sc; *ch 4, sl st in next lp sc**; sl st in next 4 lp sc tog, sl st in next lp sc; rep from * across, ending final rep at **; sl st in last 3 lp sc; ch 4, turn.

Row 4: *Work 4 sc in next ch-4 lp**; ch 4; rep from * across, ending final rep at **; ch 1, sk next sl st, dc in last sl st; turn.

Row 5: Pull up lp to height of dc, remove hook from lp and leave lp standing alone, work 3 lp sc in ch-1 sp; *sk next sc, work beg sc in next sc, sc in next sc**; work (beg lp sc, 5 lp sc) in next ch-4 lp; rep from * across, ending final rep at **; work (beg lp sc, 3 lp sc) in turning ch-4 lp, but do not remove hook from lp on last lp sc; turn.

Row 6: Sl st in lp sc on hook, ch 2; *sl st in next lp sc, sl st in next 4 lp sc tog, sl st in next lp sc**; ch 4; rep from * across, ending final rep at **; ch 2, sl st in next lp; ch 1, turn.

Row 7: Work 2 sc in ch-2 sp; *ch 4, 4 sc in next ch-4 lp; rep from * across to last ch-2 sp, sc in last ch-2 sp, sc in last sl st; ch 1, turn.

Rep rows 2–7 for patt.

Vertical Shells

Chain multiple: 10 + 7
Two colors: color A and color B

Instructions

Work beg ch with color A.

Row 1 (RS): With color A, dc in 4th ch from hook (3 skipped chs count as a dc) and in next 3 chs; *sk 2 chs, (2 dc, ch 2, 2 dc) in next ch; sk 2 chs, dc in 5 chs; rep from * across, ch 3, turn.

Row 2: Dc in next 4 dc; *(2 dc, ch 2, 2 dc) in next ch-2 sp, sk 2 dc, dc in 5 dc; rep from * across; ch 3, turn.

Repeat row 2 for patt, changing to alternate color on every other row in last dc. Work in color sequence of 2 rows A, 2 rows B.

Rapid Ripple

Chain multiple: 11 + 2
Two colors: color A and color B

Instructions

Work beg ch with color A.

Row 1 (RS): With color A, 2 sc in 2nd ch from hook, sc in next 4 chs, sk 2 chs, sc in 4 chs; *3 sc in next ch, sc in 4 chs, sk 2 chs, sc in 4 chs; rep from * across, 2 sc in last ch; ch 1, turn.

Row 2: 2 sc in first sc; sc in 4 sc, sk 2 sc, sc in 4 sc; *3 sc in next sc, sc in 4 sc, sk 2 sc, sc in 4 sc; rep from * across, 2 sc in last sc; ch 1, turn.

Rows 3 and 4: Rep row 2.

Rep row 2 for patt in this color sequence: 2 rows color B, 4 rows color A.

Blackberry

Chain multiple: 2
Two colors: color A and color B

Instructions

Work beg chain with color A.

Row 1 (RS): With color A, sc in 2nd ch from hook and in each rem ch across; ch 1, turn.

Row 2: Sc in first sc; *tr in next sc, sc in next sc; rep from * across; change to color B, ch 1, turn.

Row 3: Sc in each st across; ch 1, turn.

Row 4: Sc in first sc; *tr in next sc, sc in next sc; rep from * across, change to color A, ch 1, turn.

Rep rows 3 and 4 for patt, working in color sequence of 2 rows A, 2 rows B.

Peppermint Twist

Chain multiple: 4
Two colors: color A and color B

Stitch Guide

Front-post double crochet (FPdc): YO, insert hook from front to back to front around post (vertical bar) of specified st and draw up a lp; (YO and draw through 2 lps) twice: FPdc made.

Front-post triple crochet (FPtr): YO twice, insert hook from front to back to front around post (vertical bar) of specified st and draw up a lp; (YO and draw through 2 lps) 3 times: FPtr made.

Instructions

Work beg ch with color A.

Row 1 (RS): With color A, sc in 2nd ch from hook and in next 2 chs; *ch 1, sk next ch, sc in next 3 chs; rep from * across; ch 1, turn.

Row 2: Sc in each sc and in each ch-1 sp across; change to color B, ch 1, turn.

Row 3: With color B, sc in first 3 sc; *dc in ch-1 sp of row 1, sc in next 3 sc; rep from * across, ch 1, turn.

Row 4: Sc in each st; change to color A, ch 1, turn.

Rows 5 and 6: Sc in each st, ch 1, turn.

Row 7: Sc in first 3 sc; *FPtr around dc 4 rows below, sc in next 3 sts; rep from * across, ch 1, turn.

Row 8: Sc in each st, change to color B, ch 1, turn.

Row 9: Sc in first 3 sc, *FPdc around tr 3 rows below, sc in next 3 sc; rep from * across, ch 1, turn.

Row 10: Sc in each st; change to color A, ch 1, turn.

Rep rows 5–10 for patt.

Alternating Single Crochet

Chain multiple: any even number
Two colors: color A and color B

Instructions

Work beg ch with color A.

Row 1: With color A, sc in 2nd ch from hook; *ch 1, sk next ch, sc in next ch; rep from * across, ch 1, turn.

Row 2: With color A, sc in first sc, sc in next ch-1 sp; *ch 1, sk next sc, sc in next ch-1 sp; rep from * to last sc, sc in last st; change to color B, ch 1, turn.

Row 3: With color B, sc in first sc; *ch 1, sk next sc, sc in next ch-1 sp; rep from * to last 2 sts, ch 1, sk next sc, sc in last sc; ch 1, turn.

Row 4: With color B, rep row 2, change to color A, ch 1, turn.

Row 5: With color A, rep row 3.

Rep rows 2–5 for patt.

Ripple Lace

Chain multiple: 12 + 2
Two colors: color A and color B

Stitch Guide

Double triple crochet (dtr): YO 3 times, draw up a lp in specified st, (YO and draw through 2 lps on hook) 4 times: dtr made.

Double triple crochet cluster (dtrCL): Keeping last lp of each dtr on hook, dtr in next dc, sk next sc, dtr in next dc; YO and draw through all 3 lps on hook: dtrCL made.

Instructions

Work beg ch with color A.

Row 1 (WS): With A, sc in 2nd ch from hook and in next ch; *ch 1, sk next ch, sc in next ch; rep from * across, sc in last ch; ch 1, turn.

Row 2 (RS): Sc in first sc, ch 1, sk next sc, sc in next ch-1 sp; ch 1, sk next ch-1 sp, in next ch-1 sp work (tr, ch 1) 4 times; *sk next ch-1 sp, (sc in next ch-1 sp, ch 1) 3 times; sk next ch-1 sp, in next ch-1 sp work (tr, ch 1) 4 times; rep from * to last 2 ch-1 sps, sk next ch-1 sp, sc in last ch-1 sp, ch 1, sk next sc, sc in last sc; ch 1, turn.

Row 3: Sc in first sc; *dc in next sc, ch 1, dc in next tr, ch 1; in each of next 2 tr work (dc, ch 1) twice; dc in next tr, ch 1, dc in next sc, sc in next sc; rep from * across; at end of row change to color B, finish off color A; with color B, ch 4, turn.

Row 4: Sk first sc, dtr in next dc, tr in next dc; ch 1, dc in next dc, ch 1, (sc in next dc, ch 1) twice; dc in next dc, ch 1, tr in next dc; sk next ch-1 sp; *dtrCL over next 3 sts; tr in next dc, ch 1, dc in next dc, ch 1; (sc in next dc, ch 1) twice, dc in next dc, ch 1, tr in next dc; rep from * to last 2 sts; keeping last lp of each dtr on hook, dtr in next dc and in last sc, YO and draw through all 3 lps on hook; ch 1, turn.

Row 5: Sc in first st and in next tr; (ch 1, sk next ch-1 sp, sc in next st) 5 times; *ch 1, sk next dtrCL, sc in

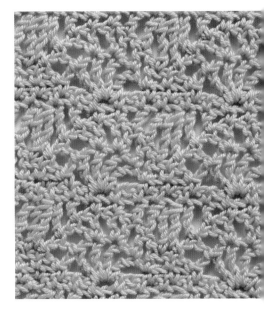

next st; (ch 1, sk next ch-1 sp, sc in next st) 5 times; rep from * to last 2 sts, sk last dtr, sc in top ch of turning ch-4; change to color A, finish off color B; with color A, ch 1, turn.

Rep rows 2–5 for patt.

Tulips in a Row

Chain multiple: 3
Three colors: color A, color B, and color C

Stitch Guide

Shell: (Dc, ch 1, dc) in specified st or sp: shell made.

Cluster (CL): (YO, insert hook in specified st and draw up a lp to height of a dc) 4 times; YO and draw through all 9 lps on hook: CL made.

Instructions

Work beg ch with color A.

Row 1 (RS): With color A, sc in 2nd ch from hook and in each rem ch; ch 1, turn.

Row 2: Sc in each sc; at end of row, finish off color A.

Row 3 (RS): With right side facing you, join color B with sl st in first sc at right; ch 4 (counts as a dc and ch-1 sp), sk next sc, shell in next sc; *sk next 2 sc, shell in next sc; rep from * to last 2 sc, sk next sc, dc in last sc. Finish off color B; do not turn.

Row 4 (RS): With right side facing you, join color C with sl st in 3rd ch of ch-4 at right; ch 4 (counts as a dc and ch-1 sp); *CL in ch-1 sp of next shell, ch 2; rep from * across to last shell, CL in last shell, ch 1, dc in dc. Finish off color C; do not turn.

Row 5 (RS): With right side facing you, join color A in 3rd ch of ch-4 at right; ch 1, sc in same st; sc in next ch-1 sp; *sc in CL, 2 sc in ch-2 sp; rep from * across to last CL, sc in CL, sc in ch-1 sp, sc in dc; ch 1, turn.

Row 6: Rep row 2.

Rep rows 3–6 for patt.

Popcorn Stripes

Chain multiple: 8 + 2
Two colors: color A and color B

Stitch Guide

Popcorn stitch (PC): Work 5 dc in specified st; drop lp from hook, insert hook from front to back in top of first dc worked, insert hook in dropped lp and draw through, ch 1: PC made.

Instructions

Work beg ch with color A.

Row 1: With color A, sc in 2nd ch from hook and in each rem ch; ch 1, turn.

Row 2 (RS): Sc in first 2 sc; *ch 2, sk next sc, PC in next sc, ch 2, sk next sc, sc in next sc; rep from * across; end last rep with ch 2, sk next sc, PC in next sc, dc in last sc; finish off color A; do not turn.

Row 3 (RS): With right side facing you, join color B in first sc at right; ch 2, PC in next st; *ch 2, sc in top of next PC, ch 2, PC in next sc; rep from * across; end last rep with ch 2, sc in last PC, sc in top of dc; finish off color B; do not turn.

Row 4 (RS): With right side facing you, join color A in first sc at right, sc in ch-2 sp, sc in first PC; *ch 2, PC in next sc, ch 2, sc in next PC; rep from * across; end last rep with ch 2, PC in next sc, dc in last st; finish off color A; do not turn.

Rep rows 3 and 4 for patt.

Color Rows

Chain multiple: any even number
Three colors: color A, color B, and color C

Instructions

Work beg ch with color A.

Row 1: With color A, sc in 2nd ch from hook and in each rem ch; ch 1, turn.

Row 2: Sc in first sc; *ch 1, sk next sc, sc in next sc; rep from * across; change to color B, ch 1, turn.

Row 3: With color B, *sk next sc, sc in ch-1 sp, ch 1; rep from * across, end with sc in turning ch; ch 1, turn.

Row 4: With color B, sc in first sc; *ch 1, sc in next sc; rep from * across, change to color C, ch 1, turn.

Rep rows 3 and 4 for patt, alternating 2 rows of each color.

Rail Fence

Chain multiple: 6
Two colors: color A and color B

Instructions

Work beg ch with color A.

Row 1 (RS): With color A, sc in 2nd ch from hook and in next 3 chs; *ch 3, sk 3 chs, sc in next 3 chs; rep from * across, end last rep with sc in last 4 (rather than 3) chs; ch 1, turn.

Row 2: Sc in first 4 sc; *ch 3, sk ch-3 sp, sc in next 3 sc; rep from * across, end last rep with sc in last 4 (rather than 3) sc; change to color B, ch 1, turn.

Row 3: With color B, sc in first sc; *ch 3, sk next 3 sc, 3 sc in next ch-3 sp; rep from * across to last 4 sc, ch 3, sk 3 sc, sc in last sc; ch 1, turn.

Row 4: Sc in first sc; *ch 3, sk ch-3 sp, sc in next 3 sc; rep from * across to last 4 sts, ch 3, sk ch-3 sp, sc in last sc.

Rows 5 and 6: Rep row 4 two times more; at end of last row, change to color A, ch 1, turn.

Row 7: With color A, sc in first sc; 3 sc in ch-3 sp, *ch 3, sk next 3 sc, 3 sc in ch-3 sp; rep from * across, end sc in last sc; ch 1, turn.

Row 8: Sc in first sc; *sc in next 3 sc, ch 3, sk ch-3 sp; rep from * across; end sc in last 4 sc; change to color B, ch 1, turn.

Rep rows 3–8 for patt.

Seafoam

Chain multiple: 6 + 3
Two colors: color A and color B

Stitch Guide

Picot: Ch 3, sl st in 3rd ch from hook: picot made.

Shell: In specified st work (3 dc, work picot, 3 dc): shell made.

Instructions

Work beg ch with color A.

Base Rows

Row 1: With color A, sc in 2nd ch from hook and in each rem sc; ch 1, turn.

Row 2 (RS): Hdc in each st, ch 1, turn.

Rows 3 and 4: Hdc in each st, ch 1, turn.

Row 5 (RS): Working in back lps only of each st, hdc in each st across; ch 1, turn.

Rep rows 2–5 for desired length. End by working a row 5. Finish off color A.

Shell Rows

With right side facing you, turn piece upside down. Starting at bottom, working in unused lps of each row 5 of base, work shell row (above right).

Shell Row: Join color B with sc in first unused lp at right, sc in next lp; *sk 2 lps, shell in next lp, sk 2 lps, sc in next lp; rep from * across to last lp, sc in last lp. Finish off.

Lightly steam each shell row if needed to keep shells flat.

Three Cheers

Chain multiple: any uneven number
Three colors: color A, color B, and color C

Instructions

Alternate two rows of each color for patt. Work beg ch with first color.

Row 1: With first color, sc in 2nd ch from hook and in each rem ch; ch 3 (counts as first dc of following row throughout), turn.

Row 2 (RS): *Sk next sc, dc in next sc, dc in skipped sc; rep from * across to last st, dc in last st, changing to next color; with new color, ch 1, turn.

Row 3: Sc in each dc across, ch 3, turn.

Rep rows 2 and 3 for patt, working 2 rows of each color. End by working a row 2.

Ribbons

Chain multiple: 6 + 4
Two colors: color A and color B

Instructions

Work beg ch with color A.

Row 1 (RS): With color A, sc in 2nd ch from hook and in next 2 chs; *ch 3, sk 3 chs, sc in next 3 chs; rep from * across; ch 1, turn.

Row 2: Sc in first 3 sc; *ch 3, sk next ch-3 sp, sc in next 3 sc; rep from * across; finish off color A.

Row 3: With right side facing you, join color B with sl st in first st at right; ch 1, sc in same st and in next 2 sc; *ch 3, sk next ch-3 sp, sc in next 3 sc; rep from * across; ch 1, turn.

Row 4: Sc in first 3 sc; *ch 3, sk next ch-3 sp, sc in next 3 sc; rep from * across; finish off color B.

Rep rows 3 and 4 for patt, alternating 2 rows of color A with 2 rows of color B.

Alternations

Chain multiple: 5 + 4
Two colors: color A and color B

Stitch Guide

Shell: Work 3 dc in specified st: shell made.

Front-post single crochet (FPsc): Insert hook from front to back to front around post (vertical bar) of specified st and draw up a lp; YO and draw through 2 lps: FPsc made.

Instructions

Work beg ch with color A.

Row 1 (RS): With color A, dc in 4th ch from hook, dc in next ch; *sk 2 chs, dc in next ch, shell in next ch, dc in next ch; rep from * across to last 2 chs, dc in next ch, 2 dc in last ch; finish off color A; do not ch or turn.

Row 2 (RS): With right side facing you, join color B with sc in top of turning ch at right of prev row, sc in next dc; *ch 3, sk next 2 dc, sc in first dc of next shell, FPsc around next dc, sc in next dc; rep from * across, ending last rep with ch 3, sk 2 dc, sc in last 2 dc; finish off color B; join color A and ch 3, turn.

Row 3 (WS): *With color A, work 5 dc in next ch-3 sp; rep from * across, ending last rep with dc in last sc; finish off color A, join color B; ch 1, turn.

Row 4 (RS): Sc in top of first dc of prev row, ch 1, sk first dc of next shell; *sc in next dc, FPsc around next dc, sc in next dc**, ch 3, sk next 2 dc; rep from * across, ending last rep at **; ch 1, sc in top of turning ch; finish off color B, join color A; ch 3, turn.

Row 5 (WS): Work 2 dc in base of ch; *5 dc in ch-3 sp; rep from * across ending last rep with dc in last sc; finish off color A, join color B, ch 1, turn.

Row 6 (RS): Sc in top of turning ch, sc in next dc; *ch 3, sk next 2 dc, sc in first dc of next shell; FPsc

around next dc, sc in next dc; rep from * across, ending last rep with ch 3, sk 2 dc, sc in last 2 dc; finish off color B, join color A; ch 1, turn.

Rep rows 3–6 for patt.

Interlacements

Chain multiple: 4 + 2
Three colors: color A, color B, and color C

Instructions

Work beg ch with color A.

Row 1: With color A, work 3 dc in 6th ch from hook; *ch 1, sk 3 chs, 3 dc in next ch; rep from * across, ending last rep with 2 dc (instead of 3) in last ch, changing to color B in last st; with color B, ch 2, turn.

Row 2: *With color B, dc in next ch-1 sp, tr in skipped ch in row 1, dc in same ch-1 sp, ch 1; rep from * across, ending last rep with 2 dc in top of beg skipped chs, changing to color C in last st; with color C, ch 2, turn.

Row 3: *With color C, dc in next ch-1 sp, tr in skipped st in row below, dc in same ch-1 sp, ch 1; rep from * across, ending last rep with 2 dc in top of turning ch; changing to color A in last st; with color A, ch 2, turn.

Rep row 3 for patt, working in alternating rows of color A, color B, and color C.

Tri-Color Shells

Chain multiple: 6 + 2
Three colors: color A, color B, and color C

Stitch Guide

Shell: Work 5 dc in specified ch or sp: shell made.

Instructions

Work beg ch with color A.

Row 1: With color A, sc in 2nd ch from hook; *sk 2 chs, shell in next ch, sk 2 chs, sc in next ch; rep from * across, changing to color B in last st; with color B, ch 3, turn.

Row 2: With color B, dc in base of ch; *ch 1, sc in center dc of next shell, ch 1, dc in last dc of next shell, ch 1; working in front of dc just made, dc in last dc of prev shell; rep from * across to last shell, ch 1, sc in center dc of last shell, ch 1, 2 dc in sc of prev row; ch 3, turn.

Row 3: Work 2 dc in base of ch; *sc in next sc, work shell in ch-1 sp between next 2 crossed dc sts; rep from * across, ending last rep with sc in last sc, 3 dc in top of turning ch, changing to color C in last st; with color C, ch 1, turn.

Row 4: With color C, sc in first dc; *ch 1, dc in last dc of next shell, ch 1; working in front of dc just made, dc in last dc of prev shell, ch 1, sc in center dc of next shell; rep from * across, ending last rep with ch 1, sc in top of turning ch; ch 1, turn.

Row 5: Sc in first sc; *work shell in ch-1 sp between next 2 crossed dc sts, sc in next sc; rep from * across, changing to color A in last st; with color A, ch 3, turn.

Rep rows 2–5 for patt, alternating two rows of each color.

Two-Tone Squares

Chain multiple: 4 + 3
Two colors: color A and color B

Instructions

Work beg ch with color A.

Row 1: With color A, sc in 2nd ch from hook and in each rem ch; ch 3 (counts as first dc of following row), turn.

Row 2: Dc in next dc; *ch 2, sk 2 sc, dc in next 2 sc; rep from * across; ch 1, turn.

Row 3: Sc in first 2 dc; *ch 2, sc in next 2 dc; rep from * across, ending last rep with sc in last dc, sc in top of turning ch; change to color B, ch 3, turn.

Row 4: With color B, dc in next sc; *ch 2, dc in next 2 sc; rep from * across; ch 1, turn.

Row 5: With color B, rep row 3, changing to color A at end of row.

Rep rows 4 and 5 for patt, alternating 2 rows of color A with 2 rows of color B.

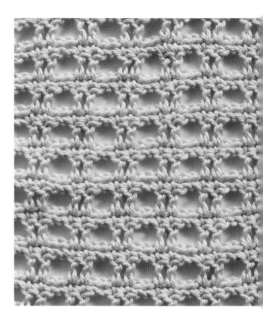

Accent on Shells

Chain multiple: 8 + 2

Two Colors: color A and color B

Stitch Guide

Shell: In specified st work (dc, ch 1) twice, dc in same st: shell made.

Instructions

Work beg ch with color A.

Row 1: With color A, sc in 2nd ch from hook and in each rem ch; ch 1, turn.

Row 2 (RS): Sc in first sc; *ch 1, sk 3 sc, shell in next sc; ch 1, sk 3 sc, sc in next sc; rep from * across; at end of row, drop color A, but do not ch or turn.

Row 3 (RS): With right side facing you, join color B with sc at beg of prev row; *ch 7, sc in next sc; rep from * across; at end of row cut color B, pick up color A and ch 5, turn.

Row 4 (WS): With color A, dc in base of ch; *ch 1, working over ch-7 lp, sc in center dc of next shell, ch 1, shell in next sc; rep from * across to last shell; working over ch-7 lp, sc in center dc of last shell, ch 1, (dc, ch 1, dc) in last sc; drop color A, do not turn.

Row 5 (RS): Join color B at beg of prev row in base of turning ch; ch 4, sc in 4th ch of ch-5 sp of prev row, ch 3, sc in next sc; *ch 7, sc in next sc; rep from * across, ending last rep with ch 3, sc in last dc, cut color B; pick up color A and ch 2, turn.

Row 6 (WS): With color A, sc in first sc; *ch 1, shell in next sc, ch 1; working over ch-7 lp, sc in center dc of next shell of prev row, ch 1, shell in next sc; rep from * across, ending with ch 1, sc in last sc; drop color A but do not turn.

Rep rows 3–6 for patt.

Pumpkin Faces

Chain multiple: 5 + 3
Two colors: color A and color B

Instructions

Work beg ch with color A.

Row 1: With color A, sc in 2nd ch from hook and in each rem ch; ch 1, turn.

Row 2: Sc in each sc across, changing to color B in last st; with color B, ch 1, turn.

Row 3: With color B, sc in each of first 2 sc; *ch 6, sk 3 sc, sc in next 2 sc; rep from * across; ch 3 (counts as first dc of following row), turn.

Row 4: Dc in next sc; *ch 4, dc in next 2 sc; rep from * across; ch 3, turn.

Row 5: Dc in next dc; *ch 3, hdc over next ch-4 sp and over ch-6 sp 2 rows below, ch 3, dc in each of next 2 dc; rep from * across, changing to color A in last st; with color A, ch 1, turn.

Row 6: *With color A, sc in next 2 dc, ch 3; rep from * across, ending last rep with sc in last dc and in top of turning ch; ch 1, turn.

Row 7: Sc in first 2 sc; *3 sc in next ch-3 sp, sc in next 2 sc; rep from * across, changing to color B in last st; with color B, ch 1, turn.

Rep rows 3–7 for patt.

Shells and Picots

Chain multiple: 6 + 2
Two colors: color A and color B

Stitch Guide

Picot: Ch 3, sl st in base of ch: picot made.

Shell: In specified st work (2 dc, picot, 2 dc): shell made.

Instructions

Work beg ch with color A. All rows are worked on the right side; finish off at the end of each row. Do not turn. With right side facing you, join new color yarn in first st at right.

Row 1: With color A, sc in 2nd ch from hook; *ch 9, sk 5 chs, sc in next ch; rep from * across; finish off color A.

Row 2: Join color B in first sc at right; ch 4, 2 dc in base of ch; *ch 1, sc in next ch-9 sp, ch 1**, shell in next sc; rep from * across, ending last rep at **; 3 dc in last sc, finish off color B.

Row 3: Join color A in top of turning ch at right; ch 8 (counts as a tr and ch-4 sp), sc in next sc; *ch 9, sc in next sc; rep from * across, ending last rep with ch 4, tr in last dc; finish off color A.

Row 4: Join color B with sc in 4th ch of turning ch, ch 1; *shell in next sc, ch 1, sc in next ch-9 sp, ch 1; rep from * across, ending last rep with sc in tr; finish off color B.

Row 5: Join color A with sc in sc at right; *ch 9, sc in next sc; rep from * across; finish off color A.

Rep rows 2–5 for patt.

Colored Lanterns

Chain multiple: 8 + 4
Two colors: color A and color B.

Stitch Guide

Cluster (CL): YO, insert hook in specified st and draw up a lp to height of a dc, YO and draw through 2 lps; (YO, insert hook in next st and draw up a lp to height of a dc, YO and draw through 2 lps) 3 times; YO and draw through 5 lps: CL made.

Instructions

Work beg ch with color A.

Row 1 (RS): With color A, work 4 dc in 8th ch from hook; *ch 1, sk 3 chs, dc in next ch, ch 1, sk 3 chs, 4 dc in next ch; rep from * across to last 4 chs, ch 1, sk 3 chs, dc in last ch; ch 5 (counts as a dc and ch-2 sp), turn.

Row 2: *CL over next 4 dc, ch 3**, dc in next dc, ch 2; rep from * across, ending last rep at **; sk top ch of turning ch, dc in next ch; finish off color A, turn.

Row 3: With right side facing you, join color B with a sl st in top of dc, ch 4 (counts as a dc and ch-1 sp); *4 dc in top of CL, ch 1, dc in next dc, ch 1; rep from * across, ending last rep with dc in 3rd ch of turning ch; ch 5, turn.

Rep rows 2 and 3 for patt, alternating 2 rows of each color. End after working a row 2.

All Tied Up

Chain multiple: 6 + 2
Two colors: color A and color B.

Instructions

Work beg ch with color A.

Row 1: With color A, sc in 2nd ch from hook, ch 2, sk 2 chs, sc in next ch; *ch 5, sk 5 chs, sc in next ch; rep from * across to last 3 chs, ch 2, sk 2 chs, sc in last ch; ch 6, turn.

Row 2: Sc in next sc; *ch 7, sc in next sc; rep from * across, ending last rep with ch 3, dc in last sc; ch 1, turn.

Row 3: Sc in first dc, ch 3, sc in next sc; *ch 7, sc in next sc; rep from * across, ending last rep with ch 3, sc in 3rd ch of turning ch, changing to color B in last st; with color B, ch 1, turn.

Row 4: With color B, sc in first sc; *ch 5, hdc over the two ch-7 lps directly below; rep from * across, ending last rep with ch 5, sc in last sc; ch 1, turn.

Row 5: Sc in first sc; *ch 5, sc in next hdc; rep from * across, ending last rep with ch 5, sc in last sc; ch 1, turn.

Row 6: Sc in first sc; *ch 7, sc in next sc; rep from * across; ch 1, turn.

Row 7: Rep row 6, changing to color A in last st.

Row 8: With color A, sc in first sc, ch 3, hdc over 2 ch-7 lps below; *ch 5, hdc over next 2 ch-7 lps; rep from * across, ending last rep with ch 3, sc in last sc; ch 1, turn.

Row 9: Sc in first sc, ch 3, sc in next hdc; *ch 5, sc in next hdc; rep from * across, ending last rep with ch 3, sc in last sc, ch 1, turn.

Row 10: Sc in first sc, ch 5, sc in next sc; *ch 7, sc in next sc; rep from * across, ending last rep with ch 5, sc in last sc; ch 1, turn.

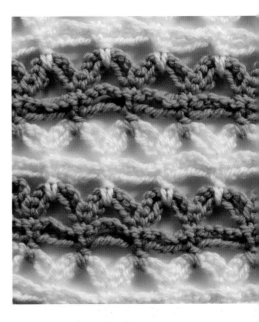

Row 11: Rep row 10, changing to color B in last st.

Rep rows 4–11 for patt, alternating four rows of color A with four rows of color B.

Trident Clusters

Chain multiple: 8 + 1
Two colors: color A and color B

Stitch Guide

Cluster (CL): *YO, insert hook in specified st or ch and draw up a lp to height of a dc; YO and draw through 2 lps; rep from * once in same st, YO and draw through 3 lps: CL made.

Shell: (CL, ch 2) twice in specified st, CL again in same st: shell made.

Instructions

Work beg ch with color A. Carry color not in use loosely up side of work.

Row 1: With color A, sc in 2nd ch from hook; *sk 3 chs, shell in next ch, sk 3 chs, sc in next ch; rep from * across, changing to color B in last st; with color B, ch 6 (counts as a dc and ch-3 sp of following row), turn.

Row 2: With color B, *sc in center CL of next shell, ch 3, dc in next sc, ch 3; rep from * across, ending last rep with dc in last sc; ch 3, turn.

Row 3: Work (CL, ch 2, CL) in first dc; *sc in next sc, shell in next dc; rep from * across to ch-6 turning ch, work (CL, ch 2, CL) in 3rd ch of turning ch, changing to color A in last st; with color A, ch 1, turn.

Row 4: Sc in top of first CL; *ch 3, dc in next sc, ch 3, sc in center CL of next shell; rep from * across, ending last rep with sc in top of last CL; do not work in turning ch, ch 1, turn.

Row 5: Sc in first sc; *shell in next dc, sc in next sc; rep from * across, changing to color B in last st; with color B, ch 6, turn.

Rep rows 2–5 for patt.

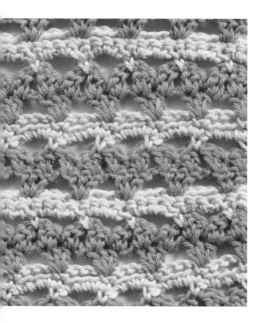

Happy Hearts

Chain multiple: 4 + 2
Two colors: color A and color B

Instructions

Work beg ch with color A.

Row 1: Sc in 2nd ch from hook and in each rem ch; ch 1, turn.

Row 2: Sc in first sc; *ch 3, sk 3 sc, sc in next sc; rep from * across, changing to color B in last st; with color B, ch 6 (counts as a dc and ch-3 sp), turn.

Row 3: With color B, 3 dc in next sc, *ch 3, 3 dc in next sc; rep from * across, ending last rep with ch 3, dc in last sc; ch 5 (counts as a dc and ch-2 sp), turn.

Row 4: *2 dc in next dc, sl st in next dc, 2 dc in next dc, ch 1; rep from * across, ending last rep with dc in 3rd ch of turning ch, changing to color A in last st; ch 1, turn.

Row 5: Sc in dc; *ch 4, sc in next ch-1 sp between hearts; rep from * across, ending last rep with sc in turning ch-5 sp; ch 4, sc in 2nd ch of turning ch, ch 1, turn.

Row 6: Sc in first sc; *3 sc in ch-4 sp, sc in sc; rep from * across, ch 1, turn.

Rep rows 2–6 for patt. End by working a row 6.

Rickrack

Chain multiple: 10 + 2
Two colors: color A and color B

Stitch Guide

Shell: In specified st work (dc, ch 1) 4 times, dc in same st: shell made.

Cluster (CL): *YO, insert hook in specified sp and draw up a lp to height of a dc, YO and draw through 2 lps; rep from * 2 times more in same sp, YO and draw through 4 lps: CL made.

Instructions

Work beg ch with color A.

Row 1: With color A, sc in 2nd ch from hook; *ch 1, sk 4 chs, shell in next ch, ch 1, sk 4 chs, sc in next ch; rep from * across, changing to color B in last sc; with color B, ch 4, turn.

Row 2: With color B, CL in first ch-1 sp of next shell, ch 2, sc in next ch-1 sp, ch 1, sc in next ch-1 sp, ch 2, CL in next ch-1 sp; *ch 1, CL in first ch-1 sp of next shell, ch 2, sc in next ch-1 sp, ch 1, sc in next ch-1 sp, ch 2, CL in next ch-1 sp; rep from * across, ending last rep with tr in last sc; ch 4, turn.

Row 3: (Dc, ch 1, dc) in base of ch; ch 1; *sc in next ch-1 sp, ch 1, shell in next ch-1 sp, ch 1; rep from * across, ending last rep with sc in last ch-1 sp, ch 1, (dc, ch 1) twice in top of turning ch, dc in same place, change to color A; with color A, ch 1, turn.

Row 4: With color A, sc in first dc and in first ch-1 sp, ch 2; *CL in next ch-1 sp, ch 1, CL in first ch-1 sp of next shell, ch 2**; sc in next ch-1 sp, ch 1, sc in next ch-1 sp, ch 2; rep from * across, ending last rep at **; sc in 4th and 3rd chs of turning ch; ch 1, turn.

Row 5: Sc in first sc; *ch 1, shell in next ch-1 sp, ch 1**; sc in next ch-1 sp; rep from * across, ending last rep at **, sc in last sc, change to

color B in last st; with color B, ch 4, turn.

Rep rows 2–5 for patt, alternating two rows of each color.

Pretty Fans

Chain multiple: 6 + 4
Two colors: color A and color B

Stitch Guide

V-stitch (V-st): Work (dc, ch 2, dc) all in same st: V-st made.

Shell: Work 7 dc all in same st: shell made.

Instructions

Work beg ch with color A.

Row 1: With color A, dc in 5th ch from hook; *ch 2, sk 5 chs, V-st in next ch; rep from * across to last 5 chs, sk 4 chs, work (dc, ch 1, dc) in last ch, changing to color B in last st; with color B, ch 3, turn.

Row 2 (RS): With color B, work 3 dc in first ch-1 sp; *work shell in ch-2 sp of next V-st; rep from * across, ending last rep with 4 dc in turning ch-sp, changing to color A in last st; with color A, ch 4, turn.

Row 3: With color A, dc in base of ch; *ch 2, V-st in center dc of next shell; rep from * across, ending last rep with ch 2, (dc, ch 1, dc) in top of turning ch, changing to color B in last st; with color B, ch 3, turn.

Rep rows 2 and 3 for patt.

Leaf Stitch

Chain multiple: 10 + 7

Stitch Guide

Picot: Ch 3, sl st in 3rd ch from hook: picot made.

Instructions

Row 1 (RS): Dc in 4th ch from hook and in next 3 chs; *work picot, sk next ch, (dc in next ch, work picot, sk next ch) twice, dc in next 5 chs; rep from * across; ch 3 (counts as first dc of following row), turn.

Row 2: Dc in next 4 dc; *work picot, (dc in next dc, work picot) 2 times, dc in next 5 dc; rep from * across; ch 3, turn.

Rep row 2 for patt.

Final row: Dc in next 4 dc; *ch 1, (dc in next dc, ch 1) 2 times, dc in next 5 dc; rep from * across.

Peeking Picots

Chain multiple: 8 + 5

Stitch Guide

Picot shell: In specified sp work (sl st, ch 4) 3 times, sl st in same sp: picot shell made.

Instructions

Row 1: Dc in 4th ch from hook and in each rem ch; ch 3 (counts as first dc of row throughout), turn.

Row 2: Dc in next 2 dc; *ch 2, YO, insert hook in next dc and draw up a lp to height of a dc, YO and draw through 2 lps; sk 3 dc, YO, insert hook in next dc and draw up a lp to height of a dc, YO and draw through 2 lps; YO and draw through all 3 lps on hook; work picot shell in sp between last 2 sts; ch 2, dc in next 3 dc; rep from * across, ch 3, turn.

Row 3: Dc in next 2 dc; *ch 2, sc in 2nd ch-3 sp of next picot shell, ch 2, dc in next 3 dc; rep from * across, ch 3, turn.

Row 4: Dc in next 2 dc; *2 dc in ch-2 sp, dc in sc, 2 dc in ch-2 sp, dc in 3 dc; rep from * across; ch 3, turn.

Rep rows 2–4 for patt.

Prancing Picots

Stitch multiple: 8 + 1

Stitch Guide

Picot: Sc in specified st, ch 3, sl st in first ch worked: picot made.

Instructions

Row 1 (RS): Sc in 2nd ch from hook and in each rem ch; ch 6 (counts as a dc and ch-3 lp), turn.

Row 2: Sk next 3 sc, dc in next sc; *ch 3, sk 3 sc, dc in next sc; rep from * across, ch 5 (counts as a dc and ch-2 sp), turn.

Row 3: *3 dc in next dc, ch 2, dc in next dc, ch 2; rep from * across, end dc in 3rd ch of turning ch; ch 4, turn.

Row 4: *2 dc in next dc, dc in next dc, 2 dc in next dc; ch 1, dc in next dc, ch 1; rep from * across, end dc in 3rd ch of turning ch; ch 1, turn.

Row 5: Sc in first dc, sc in ch-1 sp; *work picot in each of next 2 dc, sc in next dc, work picot in each of next 2 dc; sc in next ch-1 sp, in next dc, and in next ch-1 sp; rep from * across, end last rep with sc in next 2 chs of turning ch; ch 6 (counts as a dc and ch-3 sp), turn.

Note: In following row, work all chs loosely.

Row 6: *Sk 2 picots, dc in next sc, ch 3, sk 2 picots, dc in center sc of next 3-sc group, ch 3; rep from * across, end dc in last sc; ch 6, turn.

Rep rows 3–6 for patt.

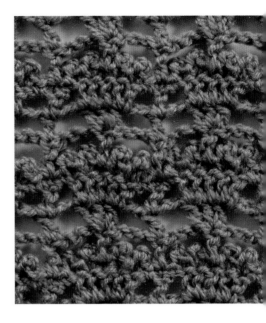

Open Fan

Chain multiple: 12 + 2

Stitch Guide

Picot: Ch 3, sl st in first ch of ch-3 just made: picot made.

Instructions

Row 1: Sc in 2nd ch from hook and in each rem ch; ch 1, turn.

Row 2: Sc in first sc; *ch 5, sk 3 sc, sc in next sc; rep from * across; ch 5 (counts as a dc and ch-2 sp), turn.

Row 3 (RS): *Sc in next ch-5 lp, 8 dc in next ch-5 lp, ch 5; rep from * across; end last rep with sc in last ch-5 lp, ch 2, dc in turning ch-1; ch 1, turn.

Row 4: *(Dc in next dc, work picot) 7 times, dc in next dc, sc in next ch-5 lp; rep from * across to last 8-dc group; (dc in next dc, work picot) 7 times, dc in next dc, sc in 3rd ch of turning ch-5; ch 8 (counts as a dc and ch-5 lp), turn.

Row 5: *Sk 2 picots, sc in 3rd picot, ch 5, sk 1 picot, sc in next picot, ch 5, sk 2 picots, dc in next sc, ch 5; rep from * across; end last rep with dc in turning ch-1; ch 5 (counts as a dc and ch-2 sp), turn.

Row 6: *Sc in ch-5 lp, 8 dc in next ch-5 lp, sc in next ch-5 lp, ch 5; rep from * across; end last rep with sc in last ch-5 lp, ch 2, dc in 3rd ch of turning ch-8; ch 1, turn.

Rep rows 4–6 for patt. End last rep after working row 5.

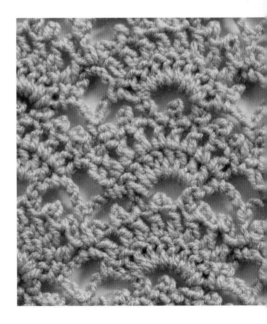

Picot Mesh

Chain multiple: 4 + 2

Stitch Guide

Picot: Ch 3, sl st in 3rd ch from hook: picot made.

Instructions

Row 1: Sc in 2nd ch from hook; *ch 5, sk 3 chs, sc in next ch**, work picot; rep from * across, ending final rep at **; ch 6, turn.

Row 2: Sc in first ch-5 lp, work picot; *ch 5, sc in next ch-5 lp, work picot; rep from * across; ch 2, tr in last sc; ch 1, turn.

Row 3: Sc in tr; *ch 5, sc in next ch-5 lp, work picot; rep from * across; ch 5, sc in turning ch-6 lp; ch 6, turn.

Rep rows 2 and 3 for patt.

A Touch of Picot

Chain multiple: 5 + 4

Stitch Guide

Shell: Work (2 dc, ch 1, 2 dc) all in same st: shell made.

Double triple crochet (dtr): YO 3 times; insert hook in specified st and draw up a lp; (YO and draw through 2 lps) 4 times: dtr made.

Picot: Ch 3, dc in base of ch: picot made.

Instructions

Row 1: Sc in 2nd ch from hook and in each rem ch; ch 3, turn.

Row 2 (RS): Sk 2 sc, shell in next sc; *sk 4 sc, shell in next sc; rep from * across to last 3 sts, sk 2 sc, dc in last sc; ch 1, turn.

Row 3: Sc in first dc; *ch 3, dc in ch-1 sp of next shell, work picot, ch 3, sc in sp between shells; rep from * across, ending last rep with sc in top of turning ch; ch 5, turn.

Row 4: *Shell in center of next picot; rep from * across, ending last rep with dtr in last sc; ch 1, turn.

Rep rows 3 and 4 for patt.

Simply Shells

Chain multiple: 5 + 2

Stitch Guide

Picot: Ch 3, sl st in base of ch: picot made.

Shell: In specified st or sp work (3 dc, picot, 2 dc): shell made.

Instructions

Row 1: Sc in 2nd ch from hook and in each rem ch; ch 3 (counts as a dc throughout), turn.

Row 2: Work 2 dc in base of ch (half shell made); *sk 4 sc, shell in next sc; rep from * across to last 5 sts, sk 4 sc, 3 dc in last sc (half shell made); ch 4, turn.

Row 3: (Dc, ch 2, dc) in sp between half shell and next shell; *ch 2, (dc, ch 2, dc) in sp between next 2 shells; rep from * across to last half shell, (dc, ch 2, dc) between last shell and last half shell, ch 1, dc in top of turning ch; ch 3, turn.

Row 4: *Shell in center ch-2 sp of next (dc, ch 2, dc) group; rep from * across, ending last rep with dc in 3rd ch of turning ch-4; ch 5, turn.

Row 5: Dc in base of ch-5; *ch 2, (dc, ch 2, dc) in sp between next 2 shells; rep from * across, ending with ch 2, (dc, ch 2, dc) in top of turning ch; ch 3, turn.

Row 6: 2 dc in first ch-2 sp; *shell in center of next (dc, ch 2, dc) group; rep from * across, ending last rep with 2 dc in turning ch-sp, dc in 3rd ch of turning ch; ch 5, turn.

Rep rows 3–6 for patt.

Picot Rows

Chain multiple: 6 + 3

Stitch Guide

Picot: (Sl st, ch 4, sl st) all in same sp: picot made.

Instructions

Row 1: Dc in 4th ch from hook and in each rem ch; ch 8 (counts as a dc and ch-5 lp), turn.

Row 2: *Sk next 5 dc, dc in next dc, ch 5; rep from * across, ending last rep with sk 5 dc, dc in last st; ch 6 (counts as a dc and ch-3 lp), turn.

Row 3 (RS): *Work picot in next ch-5 lp, ch 2, dc in next dc, ch 2; rep from * across, ending last rep with dc in 3rd ch of turning ch; ch 8, turn.

Row 4: Dc in next dc; *ch 5, dc in next dc; rep from * across, ending last rep with dc in 3rd ch of turning ch; ch 3, turn.

Row 5: *5 dc in next ch-5 lp, dc in next dc; rep from * across, ending last rep with dc in 3rd ch of turning ch; ch 8, turn.

Rep rows 2–5 for patt.

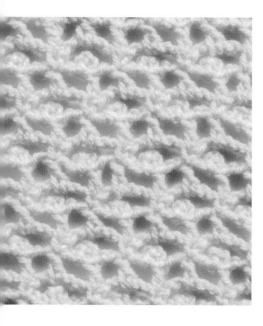

Perfect Picots

Chain multiple: 5 + 2

Stitch Guide

Picot: Ch 3, sl st in dc just made: picot made.

Instructions

Row 1: Sc in 2nd ch from hook and in each rem ch; ch 1, turn.

Row 2: Sc in first sc; *ch 5, sk 4 sc, sc in next sc; rep from * across; ch 5 (counts as a dc and ch-2 sp), turn.

Row 3: *Dc in next ch-5 sp, ch 2, dc in next sc, work picot, ch 2; rep from * across, ending last rep with dc in last ch-5 sp, ch 2, dc in last sc; ch 5 (counts as a dc and ch-2 sp), turn.

Row 4: Sc in next dc; *ch 5, sk picot, sc in next dc; rep from * across, ending last rep with ch 2, dc in 3rd ch of turning ch-5; ch 5, turn.

Row 5: *Dc in next sc, work picot, ch 2**; dc in next ch-5 sp, ch 2; rep from * across, ending last rep at **; dc in 3rd ch of turning ch, ch 1, turn.

Row 6: Sc in first dc, ch 5; *sk picot, sc in next dc, ch 5, rep from * across, ending last rep with ch 2, dc in 3rd ch of turning ch, ch 5, turn.

Rep rows 3–6 for patt. End last rep by working row 4 or row 6.

Little Peaks

Chain multiple: 4

Stitch Guide

Picot: Ch 3, sl st in top of last sc: picot made.

Cluster (CL): YO, insert hook in first specified st and draw up a lp, YO and draw through 2 lps on hook; YO, insert hook in second specified st and draw up a lp, YO and draw through 2 lps on hook; YO and draw through all 3 lps on hook: CL made.

Instructions

Row 1: Sc in 2nd ch from hook; *work picot, sc in next 4 chs; rep from * across to last 2 chs; work picot, sc in last 2 chs; ch 4, turn.

Row 2 (RS): Work CL over first sc (at base of turning ch) and 5th sc (skipping 3 sc in between); *ch 3, CL in same sc as second half of last CL and in 4th sc after same sc (skipping 3 sc in between); rep from * across to last 2 sc; ch 3, CL in same sc as second half of last CL and in last sc; ch 1, turn.

Row 3: Sc in first CL; *work (2 sc, picot, sc) in next ch-3 sp, sc in next CL; rep from * across to turning ch, 2 sc in turning ch; ch 3, turn.

Row 4: Sk first 2 sc, CL in next sc; *ch 3, CL in same sc as last CL and in 4th sc after same sc (skipping 3 sc in between); rep from * across; ch 1, dc in same sc as second half of last CL; ch 1, turn.

Row 5: Sc in turning ch, work picot, sc in next ch-1 sp; *sc in next CL, work (2 sc, picot, sc) in next ch-3 sp; rep from * across to turning ch, sc in turning ch; ch 4, turn.

Rep rows 2–5 for patt.

Trefoil

Chain multiple: 9 + 4

Stitch Guide

Triple cluster (trCL): *YO twice, insert hook in specified st or sp and draw up a lp; (YO and draw through 2 lps on hook) twice; rep from * once more; YO and draw through all 3 lps on hook: trCL made.

Picot: Ch 3, sl st in 3rd ch from hook: picot made.

Instructions

Row 1: Dc in 4th ch from hook (skipped chs count as a dc); *ch 3, sk next 2 chs, sc in next ch, ch 3, sk next ch, sc in next ch, ch 3, sk next 2 chs, dc in next 2 chs; rep from * across; ch 3 (counts as dc of following row throughout), turn.

Row 2: Dc in next dc; *ch 1, sk next ch-3 sp, (trCL, work picot, ch 1) 3 times in next ch-3 sp; dc in next 2 dc; rep from * across; ch 3, turn.

Row 3: Dc in next dc; *ch 3, sk next ch-1 sp, (sc in next ch-1 sp, ch 3) 2 times; dc in next 2 dc; rep from * across; ch 3, turn.

Rep rows 2 and 3 for patt.

Little Squares

Chain multiple: 5 + 2

Stitch Guide

Picot: Ch 3, sl st in 3rd ch from hook: picot made.

Instructions

Row 1: Sc in 2nd ch from hook; *ch 3, work picot, [(dc, work picot) 3 times, dc] in top of last sc made, ch 1, sk next 4 chs, sc in next ch; rep from * across; ch 9, turn.

Row 2: Sk next 3 picots, sc in next picot; *ch 4, sk next 3 picots, sc in next picot; rep from * across; ch 1, turn.

Row 3: Sc in first sc; *ch 3, work picot, [(dc, work picot) 3 times, dc] in top of last sc made, ch 1**, sc in next sc; rep from * across, ending final rep at **; sc in 5th ch of turning ch-9; ch 9, turn.

Rep rows 2 and 3 for patt. End by working a row 2.

Trilogy

Chain multiple: 5 + 1

Stitch Guide

Shell: In specified st or ch work (dc, ch 2) twice, dc in same st or ch: shell made.

Picot: (Sc, ch 3, sc) in specified st: picot made.

Instructions

Row 1: Dc in 6th ch from hook; *sk next 4 chs, shell in next ch; rep from * across to last 5 chs; sk next 4 chs, (dc, ch 3, dc) in last ch; ch 1, turn.

Row 2: Sc in first dc; *ch 4, sk next 2 dc, work picot in center dc of next shell; rep from * across to last 2 dc; ch 4, sk next 2 dc, sc in 3rd ch of turning ch; ch 5, turn.

Row 3: Dc in first sc; *shell in ch-3 sp of next picot; rep from * across to last sc; (dc, ch 2, dc) in last sc; ch 1, turn.

Rep rows 2 and 3 for patt.

Charming Clusters

Chain multiple: 4

Stitch Guide

Picot: Ch 4, sl st in 4th ch from hook: picot made.

Cluster (CL): *YO, insert hook in specified st or sp and draw up a lp, YO and draw through 2 lps on hook; rep from * once more in same st or sp; YO and draw through all 3 lps on hook: CL made.

Instructions

Row 1 (RS): Work picot, sk next 5 chs, (CL, ch 3, CL) in next ch; *work picot, sk next 3 chs, (CL, ch 3, CL) in next ch; rep from * across to last 2 chs; work picot, sk next ch, dc in last ch; ch 4, turn.

Row 2: CL in ch-4 lp of first picot; *work picot, (CL, ch 3, CL) in ch-4 lp of next picot; rep from * across to last picot; work picot, (CL, ch 1, dc) in ch-4 lp of last picot; ch 3, turn.

Row 3: *Work picot, (CL, ch 3, CL) in ch-4 lp of next picot; rep from * across; work picot, tr in turning ch-4 lp; ch 4, turn.

Rep rows 2 and 3 for patt.

Medallions

Chain multiple: 8 + 3

Stitch Guide

Cluster (CL): *YO, insert hook in specified st and draw up a lp, YO and draw through 2 lps; rep from * once in same st, YO and draw through 3 lps: CL made.

Cluster shell (CL shell): In specified st work (CL, ch 3, CL): CL shell made.

Picot group: In specified sp work (sl st, ch 3) twice, sl st in same lp: picot group made.

Instructions

Row 1: Dc in 4th ch from hook and in each rem ch; ch 1, turn.

Row 2: Sc in first dc; *ch 3, sk next 3 dc, CL shell in next dc, ch 3, sk next 3 dc, sc in next dc; rep from * across, ending last rep with sc in 3rd ch of turning ch; ch 4, turn.

Row 3: Dc in ch-3 sp; *ch 3, in next ch-3 sp work picot group; ch 3; (YO, insert hook in next ch-3 sp and draw up a lp, YO and draw through 2 lps) twice, YO and draw through 3 lps; joined dc made; rep from * across, ending last rep with YO, insert hook in next ch-3 sp and draw up a lp, YO and draw through 2 lps; YO twice, insert hook in last sc and draw up a lp, (YO and draw through 2 lps) twice, YO and draw through 3 lps; ch 3, turn.

Row 4: Work 2 dc in base of ch; *ch 1, YO, insert hook in first picot and draw up a lp; YO and draw through 2 lps; YO, insert hook in next picot and draw up a lp, YO and draw through 2 lps; YO and draw through 3 lps, ch 1**; 5 dc in next joined dc; rep from * across, ending last rep at **; 3 dc in last dc; ch 3, turn.

Row 5: Dc in each st and in each sp across, ending dc in top of turning ch; ch 1, turn.

Rep rows 2–5 for patt.

Picot Party

Chain multiple: 8 + 3

Stitch Guide

Picot: Ch 3, sl st in base of ch: picot made.

Picot shell: In specified st work (dc, ch 2, work picot, ch 1, dc): picot shell made.

V-stitch (V-st): Work (dc, ch 1, dc) in specified st: V-st made.

Instructions

Row 1: Dc in 4th ch from hook and in next ch, *ch 2, sk next ch, sc in next ch, ch 2, sk next ch, dc in each of next 5 chs; rep from * across, ending with dc in last 3 chs (instead of 5), ch 1, turn.

Row 2: Sc in base of turning ch; *ch 1, picot shell in next sc; ch 1, sc in center dc of next 5-dc group; rep from * across, ending last rep with ch 1, sc in top of turning ch; ch 3, turn.

Row 3: Dc in base of ch; *ch 3, sc in next picot, ch 3, V-st in next sc; rep from * across, ending last rep with 2 dc in last sc; ch 3, turn.

Row 4: Dc in base of turning ch, dc in next dc, ch 2, sc in next sc; *ch 2, 2 dc in ch-3 sp, dc in ch-1 sp of V-st, 2 dc in ch-3 sp, ch 2, sc in next sc; rep from * across, ending last rep with ch 2, dc in next dc, 2 dc in top of turning ch; ch 1, turn.

Rep rows 2–4 for patt.

Picot Lace

Chain multiple: 7 + 3

Stitch Guide

Picot: Ch 3, sl st in 3rd ch from hook: picot made.

Instructions

Row 1: Hdc in 3rd ch from hook (skipped chs count as a hdc); *ch 3, sk next 2 chs, sc in next ch, ch 3, sk next 2 chs, hdc in next 2 chs; rep from * across; ch 2 (counts as first hdc of following row throughout), turn.

Row 2: Hdc in next hdc; *ch 3, (hdc, work picot, hdc) in next sc, ch 3, hdc in next 2 hdc; rep from * across; ch 1, turn.

Row 3: Sc in first 2 hdc; *sc in next ch-3 sp, ch 5, sc in next ch-3 sp, sc in next 2 hdc; rep from * across; ch 1, turn.

Row 4: Sc in first 2 sc; *sk next sc, 7 sc in next ch-5 sp, sk next sc, sc in next 2 sc; rep from * across; ch 2, turn.

Row 5: Hdc in next sc; *ch 3, sk next 3 sc, sc in next sc, ch 3, sk next 3 sc, hdc in next 2 sc; rep from * across, ending with final sc in turning ch; ch 2, turn.

Rep rows 2–5 for patt.

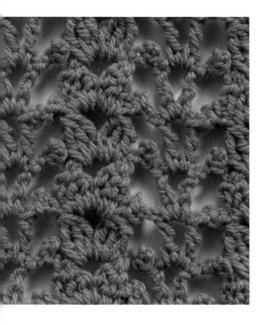

Lacy Love

Chain multiple: 12 + 2

Stitch Guide

Cluster (CL): *YO twice; insert hook in specified st and draw up a lp to height of a tr, (YO and draw through 2 lps) twice; rep from * two more times in same st, YO and draw through 4 lps: CL made.

Shell: Work (CL, ch 3, CL) in specified st: shell made.

Picot: Ch 4, sl st in base of ch.

V-stitch (V-st): Work (tr, ch 2, tr) all in same st or sp: V-st made.

Instructions

Row 1: Tr in 7th ch from hook, ch 1, work picot, ch 1; *sk 4 chs, shell in next ch; ch 1, work picot, ch 1, sk 4 chs**; V-st in next ch; ch 1, work picot, ch 1; rep from * across, ending last rep at **; tr in next ch, ch 1, sk next ch, tr in last ch; ch 5, turn.

Row 2: Tr in next ch-1 sp; *ch 1, work picot, ch 1; shell in next ch-3 sp, ch 1, work picot, ch 1, V-st in next ch-2 sp; rep from * across, ending last rep with (tr, ch 1, tr) in turning ch-sp; ch 5, turn.

Rep row 2 for patt.

Fancy Fun

Chain multiple: 6 + 2

Stitch Guide

Shell: In same st work (dc, ch 1) 3 times, dc in same st: shell made.

Cluster (CL): *YO, insert hook in specified sp and draw up a lp to height of a dc, YO and draw through 2 lps; rep from * once in same sp, YO and draw through 3 lps: CL made.

Picot: Ch 3, sl st in first ch worked: picot made.

Instructions

Row 1: Sc in 2nd ch from hook and in each rem ch; ch 3 (counts as first dc of following row), turn.

Row 2: Sk 2 sc, shell in next sc; *sk 5 sc, shell in next sc; rep from * across to last 3 sc, sk 2 sc, dc in last sc; ch 3, turn.

Row 3 (RS): *(CL, ch 3, CL) in center ch-1 sp of next shell; rep from * across, ending last rep with dc in top of turning ch; ch 1, turn.

Row 4: Sc in first dc; *ch 3, dc in next ch-3 sp, ch 3**, sc between next 2 CL, work picot; rep from * across, ending last rep at **; sc in top of turning ch; ch 3, turn.

Row 5: *Shell in next dc; rep from * across, ending last rep with dc in last sc; ch 3, turn.

Rep rows 3–5 for patt.

Pops and Picots

Chain multiple: 14 + 5

Stitch Guide

Picot: Ch 3, sl st in base of ch: picot made.

Shell: In same st or sp work (dc, picot, 2 dc, ch 2, dc): shell made.

Popcorn stitch (PC): Work 4 dc in specified st; drop lp from hook, insert hook from front to back in top of first dc made, hook dropped lp and draw through: PC made.

Instructions

Row 1 (RS): Dc in 7th ch from hook; *ch 1, sk 4 chs, shell in next ch; ch 1, sk 4 chs**, dc in next ch, ch 1, sk next ch; PC in next ch, ch 1, sk next ch, dc in next ch; rep from * across, ending last rep at **; dc in next ch, ch 1, sk next ch, dc in last ch; ch 4 (counts as a dc and ch-1 sp of following row), turn.

Row 2: Dc in next dc; *ch 1, shell in ch-2 sp of next shell, ch 1**, dc in next dc; ch 1, dc in PC, ch 1, dc in next dc; rep from * across, ending last rep at **; dc in next dc, ch 1, dc in 3rd ch of turning ch; ch 4, turn.

Row 3: Dc in next dc; *ch 1, shell in ch-2 sp of next shell, ch 1, dc in next dc; ch 1**, PC in next dc, ch 1, dc in next dc; rep from * across, ending last rep at **; dc in last dc, ch 1, dc in 3rd ch of turning ch; ch 4, turn.

Rep rows 2 and 3 for patt.

Serenity

Chain multiple: 7 + 2

Stitch Guide

Picot: Ch 3, sl st in first ch made: picot made.

Cluster (CL): *YO, insert hook in specified st and draw up a lp to height of a dc, YO and draw through 2 lps; rep from * 2 more times in same st, YO and draw through 4 lps, ch 1: CL made.

Instructions

Row 1: Sc in 2nd ch from hook and in next ch; *ch 7, sk 4 chs, sc in next ch; ch 1, sk next ch, sc in next ch; rep from * across to last 6 chs, ch 7, sk 4 chs, sc in last 2 chs; ch 6, turn.

Row 2 (RS): *Sc in next ch-7 lp, work picot, ch 3, CL in next ch-1 sp, ch 3; rep from * across to last ch-7 lp, sc in last lp, work picot, ch 3, dc in last sc; ch 1, turn.

Row 3: Sc in dc, sc in ch-3 sp; *ch 7, sc in next ch-3 sp, ch 1, sk CL, sc in next ch-3 sp; rep from * across, ending last rep with sc in 3rd and 4th chs of turning ch; ch 6, turn.

Rep rows 2 and 3 for patt.

Picot Shells

Chain multiple: 12 + 6

Stitch Guide

Picot: Ch 3, sl st in first ch made: picot made.

Picot shell: In specified ch or sp work (2 dc, picot, 2 dc, ch 2, dc): picot shell made.

Instructions

Row 1: Dc in 5th ch from hook, dc in next ch; *ch 1, sk 4 chs, work picot shell in next ch, ch 1, sk 4 chs, dc in each of next 3 chs; rep from * across, ch 3 (counts as a dc of following row), turn.

Row 2: Dc in next 2 dc; *ch 1, work picot shell in ch-2 sp of next picot shell, ch 1, dc in each of next 3 dc; rep from * across, ending last rep with dc in last 2 dc, dc in top of turning ch; ch 3, turn.

Rep row 2 for patt.

Bumps in the Snow

Chain multiple: 8 + 2

Stitch Guide

Popcorn stitch (PC): 3 hdc in next st; remove hook from lp, insert hook from front to back in top of first hdc of group, insert hook into dropped lp and draw through: PC made.

Instructions

Row 1: Sc in 2nd ch from hook and in each rem ch; ch 2 (counts as first hdc of following row), turn.

Row 2 (RS): Hdc in next 2 sc; *ch 1, sk 1 sc, PC in next sc, ch 1, sk next sc, hdc in next 5 sc; rep from * across; end last rep with hdc in last 3 (instead of 5) sc; ch 2 (counts as first hdc of following row), turn.

Row 3: Hdc in next 2 sts; * PC in next ch-1 sp, ch 1, sk next PC, PC in next ch-1 sp; hdc in next 5 sts; rep from * across; end last rep with hdc in last 3 (instead of 5) sts; ch 2, turn.

Row 4: Hdc in next 2 sts; *ch 1, sk next PC, PC in next ch-1 sp, ch 1, sk next PC; hdc in next 5 sts; rep from * across; end last rep with hdc in last 3 (instead of 5) sts; ch 2, turn.

Rep rows 3 and 4 for patt.

Poppers

Chain multiple: 6 + 2

Stitch Guide

Front popcorn stitch (FPC): 4 sc in specified st; remove hook from lp and insert it from front to back in first sc of 4-sc group just made; insert hook in dropped lp and draw through lp on hook, ch 1: FPC made.

Back popcorn stitch (BPC): 4 sc in specified st, remove hook from lp and insert it from back to front in first sc of 4-sc group just made; insert hook in dropped lp and draw through lp on hook, ch 1: BPC made.

Shell: Work 5 dc in specified st.

Instructions

Row 1: Sc in 2nd ch from hook and in each rem ch; ch 3, turn.

Row 2: 2 dc in base of ch, sk 2 sc, FPC in next sc; *sk next 2 sc, 5 dc in next sc: shell made; sk 2 sc, FPC in next sc; rep from * to last 3 sc, sk next 2 sc, 3 dc in last sc; ch 1, turn.

Row 3: Sc in first dc, shell in ch-1 at top of next FPC; *BPC in center dc of next shell; shell in ch-1 at top of next FPC; rep from * to last 3 sts, sk 2 dc, sc in top of ch-3; ch 3, turn.

Row 4: 2 dc in base of ch; FPC in center dc of next shell; *shell in ch-1 at top of next BPC, FPC in center dc of next shell; rep from * across to last sc, 3 dc in last sc; ch 1, turn.

Rep rows 3 and 4 for patt.

Brambles

Chain multiple: 6 + 2

Stitch Guide

Popcorn stitch (PC): 4 dc in specified st; drop lp from hook, insert hook from front to back in first dc of 4-dc group, insert hook in dropped lp and draw through, ch 1: PC made.

Shell: In specified st work (dc, ch 1, dc, ch 1, dc): shell made.

Instructions

Row 1: Sc in 2nd ch from hook and in each rem ch; ch 1, turn.

Row 2: Sc in first sc; *ch 1, sk 2 sc, shell in next sc, ch 1, sk 2 sc, sc in next sc; rep from * across; ch 6 (counts as a dc and ch-3 sp), turn.

Row 3 (RS): *Sc in center dc of next shell, ch 3, PC in next sc, ch 3; rep from * across to last shell, sc in center dc of last shell, ch 3, dc in last sc; ch 1, turn.

Row 4: Sc in first dc; *ch 1, shell in next sc, ch 1, sc in ch-1 sp of next PC; rep from * across to last sc, ch 1, shell in last sc, ch 1, sc in 3rd ch of turning ch-6; ch 6, turn.

Rep rows 3 and 4 for patt.

Diamond Puffs

Chain multiple: 4 + 2

Stitch Guide

Popcorn stitch (PC): 4 sc in specified st or sp; drop lp from hook, insert hook in first sc of 4-sc group, hook dropped lp and draw through lp on hook, ch 1: PC made.

Instructions

Row 1: Sc in 2nd ch from hook and in each rem ch; ch 1, turn.

Row 2 (RS): Sc in first sc; *ch 1, sk next sc, PC in next sc, sk next sc, sc in next sc; rep from * across; ch 1, turn.

Row 3: Sc in first sc and in next ch-1 sp; *ch 1, sc in next ch-1 sp; rep from * across; sc in last sc; ch 1, turn.

Row 4: Sc in first sc, ch 1, sc in next ch-1 sp, ch 1; *PC in next ch-1 sp, sc in next ch-1 sp, ch 1; rep from * to last 2 sc, sk next sc, sc in last sc; ch 1, turn.

Row 5: Sc in first sc and in next ch-1 sp; *ch 1, sc in next ch-1 sp; rep from * to last sc, sc in last sc; ch 1, turn.

Row 6: Sc in first sc, ch 1, PC in next ch-1 sp; *sc in next ch-1 sp, ch 1, PC in next ch-1 sp; rep from * to last 2 sc, sk next sc, sc in last sc; ch 1, turn.

Rep rows 3–6 for patt.

Textured Balls

Chain multiple: 5 + 3

Stitch Guide

Popcorn stitch (PC): Work 5 tr in specified st; drop lp from hook, insert hook from front to back in top of first tr of group, insert hook in dropped lp and draw through, ch 1: PC made.

Instructions

Row 1: Sc in 2nd ch from hook and in each rem ch; ch 4 (counts as first tr of following row), turn.

Row 2 (RS): Tr in next st; *ch 1, sk next st, PC in next st, ch 1, sk next st, tr in each of next 2 sts; rep from * across, ch 1, turn. (**Note:** Push all PC to right side.)

Row 3: Sc in each tr, in each ch-1 sp, and in ch-1 at top of each PC; ch 4, turn.

Rep rows 2 and 3 for patt.

Pops and Posts

Chain multiple: 6 + 1

Stitch Guide

Popcorn stitch (PC): 5 dc in specified st; drop lp from hook, insert hook from front to back through top of first dc made, insert hook in dropped lp and draw through lp on hook: PC made.

Instructions

Row 1: Sc in 2nd ch from hook and in each rem ch; ch 3 (counts as first dc of following row), turn.

Row 2: Dc in next dc; *ch 2, sk 2 sc, dc in next sc; rep from * across to last sc, end dc in last sc; ch 3 (counts as first dc of following row), turn.

Row 3 (RS): PC in next dc; *ch 2, dc in next dc, ch 2, PC in next dc; rep from * across; end last rep with dc in last dc, dc in 3rd ch of turning ch-3; ch 3, turn.

Row 4: Dc in next dc; *ch 2, dc in next PC, ch 2, dc in next dc; rep from * across; end last rep with dc in last PC, dc in 3rd ch of turning ch; ch 3, turn.

Row 5: Dc in next dc; *ch 2, PC in next dc, ch 2, dc in next dc; rep from * across; end last rep with PC in last dc, dc in top of turning ch; ch 3, turn.

Row 6: *Dc in PC, ch 2, dc in next dc, ch 2; rep from * across; end last rep with dc in last dc, dc in top of turning ch; ch 3, turn.

Rep rows 3–6 for patt.

V-Twin Popcorn Stitch

Chain multiple: 10 + 4

Stitch Guide

Popcorn stitch (PC): Work 5 dc all in specified st; drop lp from hook; insert hook from front to back in top of first dc worked; insert hook in dropped lp and draw lp through: PC made.

Front-post triple crochet (FPtr): YO twice; insert hook from front to back to front around post (vertical bar) of specified st; (YO and draw through 2 lps) 3 times: FPtr made.

Back-post triple crochet (BPtr): YO twice; insert hook from back to front to back around post (vertical bar) of specified st; (YO and draw through 2 lps) 3 times: BPtr made.

Instructions

Row 1: Sc in 2nd ch from hook and in each rem ch; ch 3 (counts as first dc of following row), turn.

Row 2 (RS): Dc in next 2 sc; *ch 2, sk 3 sc, (PC in next sc, ch 1) twice; sk 2 sc, dc in each of next 3 sc; rep from * across; ch 3, turn.

Row 3: BPtr around next st, dc in next st; *ch 3, sk 1 ch and 1 PC, 2 sc in next ch-1 sp; ch 3, sk PC and ch-2 sp, dc in next st, BPtr around next st, dc in next st; rep from * across, ending last rep with dc in top of turning ch; ch 3, turn.

Row 4: FPtr around next st, dc in next st; *ch 2, sk 3 chs, PC in next sc; ch 1, PC in next sc, ch 1, sk 3 chs, dc in next st, FPtr around next st, dc in next st; rep from * across, ending last rep in top of turning ch; ch 3, turn.

Rep rows 3 and 4 for patt.

Shells and Popcorns

Chain multiple: 6 + 2

Stitch Guide

Shell: Work 5 dc in specified st: shell made.

Popcorn stitch (PC): Work 5 dc in specified st; drop lp from hook, insert hook from front to back in top of first dc of 5-dc group; insert hook in dropped lp and draw lp through, ch 1: PC made.

Instructions

Row 1: Sc in 2nd ch from hook and in each rem ch; ch 1, turn.

Row 2: Sc in first sc; *sk 2 sc, shell in next sc, sk 2 sc, PC in next sc; rep from * to last 6 sts, sk 2 sc, shell in next sc, sk 2 sc, dc in last sc; ch 3, turn.

Row 3: *Sc in center dc of next shell, ch 2, sc in next PC, ch 2; rep from * across, ending with sc in center dc of last shell, ch 2, dc in last sc; ch 3, turn.

Row 4: *Shell in next sc, PC in next sc; rep from * across, ending shell in last sc, dc in turning ch; ch 3, turn.

Row 5: Rep row 3, ending with dc in top of turning ch; ch 3, turn.

Rep rows 4 and 5 for patt. End last rep by working row 4.

Popcorn Balls

Chain multiple: 16 + 8

Stitch Guide

Front popcorn stitch (FPC): Work 5 dc in specified st or sp; remove hook from lp and insert hook from front to back in top of first dc of group; insert hook in dropped lp and draw through: FPC made.

Back popcorn stitch (BPC): Work 5 dc in specified st or sp; remove hook from lp and insert hook from back to front in top of first dc of group; insert hook in dropped lp and draw through: BPC made.

Instructions

Row 1: Dc in 6th ch from hook (counts as a dc, ch-1 sp and dc); *ch 1, sk 1 ch, 1 dc in next ch; rep from * across; ch 4 (counts as a dc and ch-1 sp of following row), turn.

Row 2 (RS): Dc in next dc, ch 1, dc in next dc, *ch 5, sk next 2 dc, FPC in next dc; ch 5, sk next 2 dc, dc in next dc; (ch 1, dc in next dc) twice; rep from * across; end last rep with dc in top of turning ch; ch 4, turn.

Row 3: Dc in next dc, ch 1, dc in next dc; *ch 4, sc in ch-5 sp, sk FPC, sc into next ch-5 sp, ch 4, dc in next dc; (ch 1, sk 1 ch, dc in next st) twice; rep from * across, end last rep with dc in top of turning ch; ch 4, turn.

Row 4: Dc in next dc, ch 1, dc in next dc; *ch 4, sc in ch-4 sp, sc between next 2 sc, sc in ch-4 sp; ch 4, dc in next dc; (ch 1, sk 1 ch, dc in next st) twice; rep from * across; end last rep with dc in top of turning ch, ch 4, turn.

Row 5: Dc in next dc, ch 1, dc in next dc; *ch 5, BPC in 2nd of 3 sc, ch 5, dc in next dc; (ch 1, dc in next st) twice; rep from * across, end last rep with dc in top of turning ch; ch 4, turn.

Row 6: Dc in next dc, *ch 1, sk 1 ch, dc in next st; rep from * across; end last rep with dc in top of turning ch; ch 4, turn.

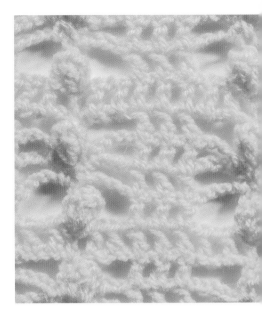

Note: At end of row 6, count to be sure you have the same number of chs and dc sts as in row 2.

Rep rows 2–6 for patt, alternating FPCs and BPCs as needed to maintain patt.

Popcorn Crosses

Chain multiple: 3

Stitch Guide

Popcorn stitch (PC): Work 5 dc in specified st; drop lp from hook, insert hook from front to back in top of first dc worked, insert hook in dropped lp and draw lp through: PC made.

Instructions

Row 1: Sc in 2nd ch from hook and in each rem ch; ch 3 (counts as first dc of following row throughout), turn.

Row 2 (RS): Dc in next st; PC in next st, *sk next st, dc in next st, dc in skipped st, PC in next st; rep from * across to last 2 sts, dc in last 2 sts; ch 3, turn.

Row 3: Dc in next dc and in PC; *sk next dc, dc in next dc, dc in skipped dc, dc in next PC; rep from * across to last 2 sts, dc in last 2 sts; ch 3, turn.

Repeat rows 2 and 3 for patt.

Alternating Shells and Popcorns

Chain multiple: 6 + 1

Stitch Guide

Shell: Work 5 dc in specified st: shell made.

Popcorn stitch (PC): Work 5 dc in specified st; drop lp from hook, insert hook from front to back in top of first of 5-dc group, insert hook in dropped lp and pull through, ch 1: PC made.

Instructions

Row 1: Sc in 2nd ch from hook and in each rem ch; ch 3 (counts as a dc of following row throughout), turn.

Row 2 (RS): Sk 2 sc; *shell in next sc, sk 2 sc, PC in next sc, sk 2 sc; rep from * across to last 4 sc, shell in next sc, sk 2 sc, dc in last sc; ch 3, turn.

Row 3: *Sc in center sc of next shell, ch 2, sc in next PC, ch 2; rep from * across, ending last rep with sc in center dc of last shell, ch 2, sc in top of turning ch; ch 3, turn.

Row 4: *PC in next sc, shell in next sc; rep from * across, ending last rep with PC in next sc, ch 2, dc in base of turning ch; ch 3, turn.

Row 5: *Sc in next PC, ch 2, sc in center dc of next shell, ch 2; rep from * across, ending last rep with sc in last PC, ch 2, dc in top of turning ch; ch 3, turn.

Row 6: Shell in next sc; *PC in next sc, shell in next sc; rep from * across, ending with dc in base of turning ch; ch 3, turn.

Rep rows 3–6 for patt.

Chic Shells

Chain multiple: 8 + 2

Stitch Guide

Shell: Work (2 dc, ch 1, 2 dc) all in same st: shell made.

Popcorn stitch (PC): Work 4 dc in same st; drop lp from hook, insert hook from front to back in top of first dc made, pick up dropped lp and draw through: PC made.

Instructions

Row 1 (RS): Sc in 2nd ch from hook; *ch 2, sk 3 chs, shell in next ch, ch 2, sk 3 chs, sc in next ch; rep from * across; ch 3, turn.

Row 2: Dc in first sc; *ch 3, sc in center ch-1 sp of next shell, ch 3**, work PC in next sc; rep from * across, ending last rep at **; dc in last sc, ch 1, turn.

Row 3: Sc in top of first dc; *ch 2, shell in next sc, ch 2, sc in next PC; rep from * across, ending last rep with shell in last sc, ch 2, sc in last dc; do not work in turning ch; ch 3, turn.

Rep rows 2 and 3 for patt.

Popcorn Diamonds

Chain multiple: 10 + 2

Stitch Guide

Popcorn stitch (PC): 5 dc in specified st; drop lp from hook, insert hook from front to back in top of first dc made, insert hook in dropped lp and draw through, ch 1: PC made.

Instructions

Row 1: Sc in 2nd ch from hook and in each rem ch; ch 1, turn.

Row 2 (RS): Sc in next 5 sc, *PC in next sc, sc in next 9 sts; rep from * across, end last rep with sc in last 5 (instead of 9) sts; ch 1, turn.

Row 3: Sc in next 5 sc; *ch 1, sk next sc, sc in next 9 sc; rep from * across, end last rep with sc in last 5 sts; ch 1, turn.

Row 4: Sc in next 4 sts; *PC in next st, sc in ch-1 sp, PC in next st, sc in next 7 sts; rep from * across, end last rep with sc in last 4 (instead of 7) sts; ch 1, turn.

Row 5: Sc in next 4 sc; *ch 1, sk next PC, sc in next st, ch 1, sk next PC, sc in next 7 sc; rep from * across, end last rep sc in last 4 sts; ch 1, turn.

Row 6: Sc in next 3 sts; *PC in next st, sc in ch-1 sp, PC in next sc, sc in ch-1 sp; PC in next sc, sc in next 5 sts; rep from * across, end last rep with sc in last 3 (instead of 5) sts; ch 1, turn.

Row 7: Sc in next 3 sc; *ch 1, sk next PC, sc in next st, ch 1, sk next PC, sc in next st, ch 1, sk next PC, sc in next 5 sts; rep from * across, end last rep with sc in last 3 (instead of 5) sts; ch 1, turn.

Row 8: Rep row 4.

Row 9: Rep row 5.

Rep rows 2–9 for patt. End last rep by working row 3.

Color Play

Chain multiple: 3 + 2
Two colors: color A and color B

Stitch Guide

Popcorn stitch (PC): Work 5 dc in specified st; drop lp from hook, insert hook from front to back in top of first dc worked, insert hook in dropped lp and draw through, ch 1; PC made.

Instructions

Work beg ch with color A.

Row 1 (RS): With color A, sc in 2nd ch from hook and in each rem ch; ch 4 (counts as first tr of following row), turn.

Row 2: Tr in next sc; *ch 1, sk 1 sc, tr in each of next 2 sc; rep from * across, ch 1, turn.

Row 3 (RS): Sc in each tr and ch-1 sp across; finish off color A. Do not turn.

Row 4 (RS): With right side facing you, join color B with sc in first sc at right; sc in next st; *PC in next st, sc in each of next 2 sts; rep from * across. Finish off color B. Do not turn.

Row 5 (RS): Join color A with sc in first sc at right, sc in next st; *ch 1, sk PC, sc in each of next 2 sts; rep from * across; ch 4, turn.

Row 6: Tr in next sc; *ch 1, sk ch-1 over next PC, tr in each of next 2 sts; rep from * across, ch 1, turn.

Row 7 (RS): Sc in each st and in each ch-1 sp across. Finish off color A. Do not turn.

Rep rows 4–7 for patt.

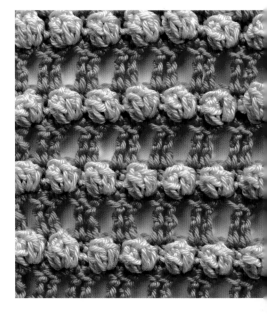

Popcorn Time

Chain multiple: 12 + 4

Stitch Guide

Front popcorn stitch (FPC): Work 4 dc in specified st or sp; drop lp from hook, insert hook from front to back through top of first dc made, insert hook in dropped lp and draw it through lp on hook: FPC made.

Back popcorn stitch (BPC): Work 4 dc in specified ch or sp; drop lp from hook, insert hook from back to front through top of first dc made, insert hook in dropped lp and draw it through lp on hook: BPC made.

Front popcorn stitch shell (FPC shell): Work (FPC, ch 3, FPC) in specified st or sp: FPC shell made.

Back popcorn stitch shell (BPC shell): Work (BPC, ch 3, BPC) in specified st or sp: BPC shell made.

Instructions

Row 1 (RS): In 5th ch from hook work FPC; *ch 3, sk 4 chs, sc in next ch, ch 3, sk next ch, sc in next ch; ch 3 **, sk 4 chs, FPC shell in next ch; rep from * across, ending last rep at **; (FPC, h 1, dc) in last ch; ch 3, turn.

Row 2: Sc in ch-1 sp; *ch 3, sk next ch-3 sp, work BPC shell in next ch-3 sp, ch 3**; work (sc, ch 3, sc) in center ch-3 sp of shell; rep from * across, ending last rep at **; sc in turning ch-sp, ch 1, hdc in 3rd ch of turning ch; ch 4, turn.

Row 3: Work FPC in ch-1 sp; *ch 3, work (sc, ch 3, sc) in ch-3 sp of next shell, ch 3**, sk next ch-3 sp, work FPC shell in next ch-3 sp; rep from * across, ending last rep at **; work (FPC, ch 1, dc) in turning ch-sp; ch 3, turn.

Rep rows 2 and 3 for patt.

Bitty Buttons

Chain multiple: 6

Stitch Guide

Popcorn stitch (PC): Work 4 dc all in same st; drop lp from hook, insert hook from front to back in top of first dc made, insert hook in dropped lp and draw through: PC made.

Shell: Work 5 dc all in same st: shell made.

Instructions

Row 1 (RS): Work PC in 9th ch from hook; *ch 2, sk 2 chs, dc in next ch**, ch 2, sk 2 chs, PC in next ch; rep from * across, ending last rep at **; ch 5 (counts as a dc and ch-2 sp on following row), turn.

Row 2: Dc in next PC, ch 2; *dc in next dc, ch 2, dc in next PC, ch 2; rep from * across; sk next 2 chs of turning ch, dc in next ch of turning ch; ch 1, turn.

Row 3: Sc in first dc; *shell in next dc, sc in next dc; rep from * across, ending last rep with sc in 3rd ch of turning ch; ch 5, turn.

Row 4: Sc in center dc of next shell, ch 2, dc in next sc; *ch 2, sc in center dc of next shell, ch 2, dc in next sc; rep from * across; ch 5, turn.

Row 5: Work PC in next sc, ch 2, dc in next dc; *ch 2, PC in next sc, ch 2, dc in next dc; rep from * across, ending last rep with dc in 3rd ch of turning ch; ch 5, turn.

Rep rows 2–5 for patt.

Popcorns on Popcorns

Chain multiple: 6 + 2

Stitch Guide

Front popcorn stitch (FPC): Work 4 dc in specified st or lp; drop lp from hook, insert hook from front to back in top of first dc of group, insert hook in dropped lp and draw through: FPC made.

Back popcorn stitch (BPC): Work 4 dc in specified st or lp; drop lp from hook, insert hook from back to front in top of first dc of group, insert hook in dropped lp and draw through: BPC made.

Front-post double crochet (FPdc): YO, insert hook from front to back to front around post (vertical bar) of specified st, YO and draw up a lp; (YO and draw through 2 lps) twice: FPdc made.

Back-post double crochet (BPdc): YO, insert hook from front to back to front around post (vertical bar) of specified st, YO and draw up a lp; (YO and draw through 2 lps) twice: BPdc made.

Instructions

Row 1: Sc in 2nd ch from hook and in each rem ch; ch 5 (counts as a dc and ch-2 sp throughout), turn.

Row 2 (RS): *Sk next 2 sts; in next st work (FPC, ch 2, FPC, ch 2, FPC); ch 2, sk 2 sts, dc in next st, ch 2; rep from * across, ch 5, turn.

Row 3: Sk first ch-2 sp; *BPC in next ch-2 sp, ch 3, BPC in next ch-2 sp; ch 2, BPdc around next dc, ch 2; rep from * across, ending last rep with dc in 3rd ch of turning ch-5; ch 5, turn.

Row 4: *In next ch-3 sp work (FPC, ch 2, FPC, ch 2, FPC); ch 2, FPdc around next BPdc, ch 2; rep from * across, ending last rep with dc in 3rd ch of turning ch-5; ch 5, turn.

Repeat rows 3 and 4 for patt. End last rep by working row 4.

Looped Popcorns

Chain multiple: 6 + 1

Stitch Guide

Popcorn stitch (PC): Work 4 dc in specified st; drop lp from hook, insert hook from front to back in top of first dc worked; pick up dropped lp and draw through lp on hook: PC made.

Instructions

Row 1 (RS): Sc in 10th ch from hook; *ch 3, sk 2 chs, PC in next ch, ch 3, sk 2 chs, sc in next ch; rep from * across to last 3 chs, ch 3, sk 2 chs, dc in last ch; ch 3, turn.

Row 2: Dc in ch-3 lp; *ch 3, dc in next ch-3 lp, dc in next PC, dc in next ch-3 lp; rep from *across, ending last rep with ch 3, 2 dc in turning ch-lp; ch 6, turn.

Row 3: Sc in first ch-3 lp; *ch 3, sk next dc, PC in next dc, ch 3, sc in next ch-3 lp; rep from * across, ending last rep with ch 3, dc in top of turning ch; ch 3, turn.

Rep rows 2 and 3 for patt. End last rep by working row 2.

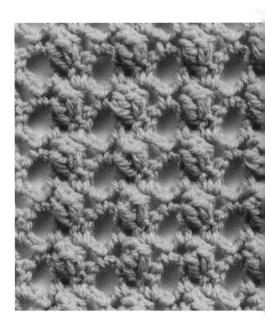

Playful Popcorns

Chain multiple: 16 + 2

Stitch Guide

Popcorn stitch (PC): Work 5 dc in specified st; drop lp from hook, insert hook from front to back to front in top of first dc made, pick up dropped lp and draw lp through; ch 1: PC made.

Instructions

Row 1: Dc in 5th ch from hook and in each of next 3 chs; *ch 2, dc in each of next 2 chs, sk 2 chs; dc in next ch, sk 2 chs, dc in each of next 2 chs**, ch 2, dc in each of next 7 chs; rep from * across, ending last rep at **; ch 2, dc in last ch; ch 5, turn.

Row 2 (RS): Work 2 dc in ch-2 sp; *sk 2 dc, dc in next dc, sk 2 dc, 2 dc in next ch-2 sp**; ch 2; dc in each of next 2 dc, ch 1, sk next dc, PC in next dc, ch 1, sk next dc, dc in each of next 2 dc; ch 2, 2 dc in next ch-2 sp; rep from * across, ending last rep at **; ch 2, dc in next 2 dc, ch 1, PC in next dc, dc in top of turning ch; ch 3, turn.

Row 3: Dc in top of next PC, dc in ch-1 sp, dc in next 2 dc; *ch 2, 2 dc in ch-2 sp, sk next 2 dc, dc in next dc, sk 2 dc, 2 dc in next ch-2 sp, ch 2**; dc in next 2 dc, dc in ch-1 sp, dc in PC, dc in ch-1 sp, dc in next 2 dc; rep from * across, ending last rep at **; dc in 3rd ch of turning ch; ch 5, turn.

Rep rows 2 and 3 for patt.

Deck the Halls

Chain multiple: 4 + 2
Two colors: color A and color B

Stitch Guide

Popcorn stitch (PC): Work 5 dc in specified st; drop lp from hook, insert hook from front to back in top of first dc made, hook dropped lp and draw through: PC made.

Instructions

Work beg ch with color A.

Row 1: With color A, sc in 2nd ch from hook and in each rem ch; ch 4 (counts as a dc and ch-1 sp), turn.

Row 2 (RS): Sk next sc; *PC in next sc, ch 1, sk next sc, dc in next sc, ch 1, sk next sc; rep from * across to last sc, dc in last sc, changing to color B in last st; ch 1, turn.

Row 3: With color B, sc in each st and ch-1 sp across, ending with sc in turning ch-sp and sc in 3rd ch of turning ch; ch 4, turn.

Row 4: With color B, rep row 2, changing to color A in last st; ch 1, turn.

Rep rows 3 and 4 for patt, alternating two rows of each color.

Boxed Pops

Chain multiple: 10 + 2

Stitch Guide

Popcorn stitch (PC): Work 4 dc in same st; drop lp from hook, insert hook from front to back in top of first dc made; pick up dropped lp and draw through lp on hook: PC made.

Instructions

Row 1: Sc in 2nd ch from hook and in each rem ch; ch 1, turn.

Row 2: Sc in first 3 sc; *ch 3, sk 2 sc, PC in next sc, ch 3, sk 2 sc, sc in next 5 sc; rep from * across, ending last rep with sc in last 3 (instead of 5) sc; ch 1, turn.

Row 3: Sc in first 3 sc; *3 sc in ch-3 sp, sc in PC, 3 sc in ch-3 sp, sc in next 5 sc; rep from * across, ending last rep with sc in last 3 (instead of 5) sc; ch 6, turn.

Row 4: Sk in first 4 sc; *sc in each of next 5 sc**, ch 3, sk 3 sc, PC in next sc, ch 3, sk 3 sc; rep from * across, ending last rep at **; ch 3, dc in last sc; ch 1, turn.

Row 5: Sc in dc, 3 sc in ch-3 sp; *sc in next 5 sc, 3 sc in ch-3 sp, sc in PC, 3 sc in ch-3 sp; rep from * across, ending last rep with 3 sc in turning ch-lp, sc in 3rd ch of turning ch-lp; ch 1, turn.

Row 6: Sc in first 3 sc; *ch 3, sk 3 sc, PC in next sc; ch 3, sk 3 sc, sc in next 5 sc; rep from * across, ending last rep with sc in last 3 (instead of 5) sc; ch 1, turn.

Rep rows 3–6 for patt.

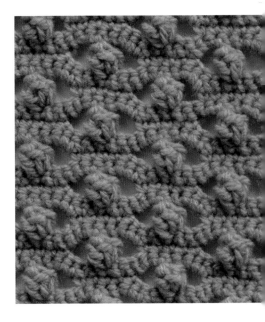

Primarily Popcorns

Chain multiple: 10 + 5

Stitch Guide

Popcorn stitch (PC): Work 4 dc in specified st; drop lp from hook, insert hook from front to back in top of first dc worked; insert hook in dropped lp and draw through lp on hook: PC made.

Instructions

Row 1: Sc in 2nd ch from hook; *ch 3, sk 2 chs, dc in each of next 5 chs; ch 3, sk 2 chs, sc in next ch; rep from * across to last 3 chs, ch 3, sk next 2 chs, dc in last ch; ch 1, turn.

Row 2: Sc in first dc; *ch 2, PC in next sc, ch 2, sc in each of next 5 dc; rep from * across, ending last rep with ch 2, dc in last sc; ch 3, turn.

Row 3: Work 2 dc in ch-2 sp; *ch 3, sk 2 sc, sc in next sc, ch 3, 2 dc in next ch-2 sp, dc in PC, 2 dc in next ch-2 sp; rep from * across, ending last rep with dc in last sc; ch 1, turn.

Row 4: Sc in each of first 6 dc; *ch 2, PC in next sc, ch 2, sc in each of next 5 dc; rep from *across, ending last rep with ch 2, PC in next dc, ch 2, sc in each of next 2 dc and in top of turning ch; ch 1, turn.

Row 5: Sc in first sc; *ch 3, 2 dc in next ch-2 sp, PC in next dc, 2 dc in next ch-2 sp, ch 3, sk 2 sc, sc in next sc; rep from * across, ending last rep with ch 3, dc in last sc; ch 1, turn.

Rep rows 2–5 for patt.

Lacy Look

Chain multiple: 2

Stitch Guide

Puff stitch (Pst): (YO, insert hook in specified st and draw up a lp to height of a dc) 4 times; YO and draw through all 9 lps on hook: Pst made.

Front-post double crochet (FPdc): YO, insert hook from front to back to front around post (vertical bar) of specified st and draw up a lp; (YO and draw through 2 lps on hook) twice: FPdc made.

Back-post double crochet (BPdc): YO, insert hook from back to front to back around post (vertical bar) of specified st and draw up a lp; (YO and draw through 2 lps on hook) twice: BPdc made.

Instructions

Row 1: Sc in 2nd ch from hook and in each rem ch; ch 3 (counts as first dc of following row), turn.

Row 2: Dc in each sc across, ch 3, turn.

Row 3 (RS): *Pst in next dc, FPdc around next dc; rep from * across, dc in last st; ch 3, turn.

Row 4: *Dc in top of next Pst, BPdc around next FPdc; rep from * across, dc in last st; ch 3, turn.

Rep rows 3 and 4 for patt.

All Puffed Up

Chain multiple: 2 + 1

Stitch Guide

Puff stitch (Pst): (YO, insert hook in specified st and draw up a lp to height of a dc) 4 times; YO and draw through all 9 lps on hook: Pst made.

Instructions

Row 1: Sc in 2nd ch from hook and in each rem ch; ch 4 (counts as a dc and ch-1 sp), turn.

Row 2: Sk next st, dc in next st; *ch 1, sk next st, dc in next st; rep from * across, ch 4, turn.

Row 3 (RS): Pst in next dc; *ch 1, dc in next dc, ch 1, Pst in next dc; rep from * across, ch 4, turn. (Push all Pst to right side of work.)

Row 4: *Dc in ch-1 at top of next Pst, ch 1, dc in next dc, ch 1; rep from * across, end dc in last dc; ch 4, turn.

Rep rows 3 and 4 for patt.

Little Balls

Chain multiple: 8 + 3

Stitch Guide

Puff stitch (Pst): YO, insert hook in next sc and draw up a lp to height of a dc, YO and draw through 2 lps; (YO, draw up a lp in same st, YO and draw through 2 lps) 3 times, YO and draw through 5 lps, ch 1: Pst made.

Instructions

Row 1 (RS): Dc in 4th ch from hook and in each rem ch; ch 1, turn.

Row 2: Sc in each st across, ch 1, turn.

Row 3: Sc in 8 sc, Pst in next sc; *sc in next 7 sc, Pst in next sc; rep from * across, end last rep with sc in last 8 sc; ch 1, turn.

Row 4: Sc in each sc and in each Pst, skipping ch-1 sp of each Pst; ch 3, turn.

Row 5: Dc in each st across, ch 1, turn.

Row 6: Rep row 2.

Row 7: Sc in 4 sc, Pst in next sc; *sc in next 7 sc, Pst in next sc; rep from * across, end last rep with sc in last 4 sc; ch 1, turn.

Row 8: Rep row 4.

Row 9: Rep row 5.

Rep rows 2–9 for patt.

Love and Kisses

Chain multiple: 6 + 4

Stitch Guide

Puff stitch (Pst): YO, insert hook in specified st and draw up a lp to height of a dc; (YO, insert hook in same st and draw up a lp to height of a dc) 3 times; YO and draw through all 9 lps on hook, ch 1: Pst made.

Instructions

Row 1: Sc in 2nd ch from hook and in each rem ch; ch 3 (counts as first dc of following row), turn.

Row 2: Dc in each sc, ch 1, turn.

Row 3 (RS): Sc in first 2 dc; *loosely ch 3, sk 2 dc, Pst in next dc; loosely ch 3, sk 2 dc, sc in next dc; rep from * across, sc in 3rd ch of turning ch; ch 5 (counts as a dc and ch-2 sp), turn.

Row 4: 3 sc in ch-1 at top of next Pst; *ch 3, 3 sc in ch-1 at top of next Pst; rep from * to last 2 sc, ch 2, sk next sc, dc in last sc; ch 1, turn.

Row 5: Sc in dc, 2 sc in ch-2 sp; *sc in next 3 sc, 3 sc in next ch-3 sp; rep from * across; end with sc in last 3 sc, 2 sc in next ch-5 sp, sc in 3rd ch of turning ch; ch 3, turn.

Rep rows 2–5 for patt. End by working row 2.

Coronets

Chain multiple: 9 + 2

Stitch Guide

Puff stitch (Pst): YO, insert hook in specified sp, YO and draw up a lp to height of a dc; (YO, insert hook in same sp and draw up a lp) twice, YO and draw through 7 lps on hook: Pst made.

Instructions

Row 1 (RS): Sc in 2nd ch from hook and in next ch, ch 1, sk next ch, sc in next ch; ch 3, sk 2 chs, sc in next ch; *(ch 1, sk next ch, sc in next ch) 3 times; ch 3, sk 2 chs, sc in next ch; rep from * to last 3 chs, ch 1, sk next ch, sc in last 2 chs; ch 1, turn.

Row 2: Sc in first 2 sc, ch 1, Pst in next ch-3 sp; (ch 3, Pst in same sp) twice, ch 2, sk next sc, sc in next sc; *ch 1, sc in next sc, ch 1, Pst in next ch-3 sp, (ch 3, Pst in same sp) twice; ch 2, sk next sc, sc in next sc; rep from * across, sc in last sc; ch 3, turn.

Row 3: Dc in next sc, ch 1, sc in next ch-3 sp, ch 3, sc in next ch-3 sp; *ch 1, (dc in next sc, ch 1) twice, sc in next ch-3 sp, ch 3, sc in next ch-3 sp; rep from * to last 2 sc, ch 1, dc in last 2 sc; ch 1, turn.

Row 4: Sc in first 2 dc, ch 1, Pst in next ch-3 sp; (ch 3, Pst in same sp) twice, ch 2; *(sc in next dc, ch 1) twice, Pst in next ch-3 sp; (ch 3, Pst in same sp) twice, ch 2; rep from * across to last 2 dc, sc in last 2 dc; ch 3, turn.

Rep rows 3 and 4 for patt. End last rep by working row 3.

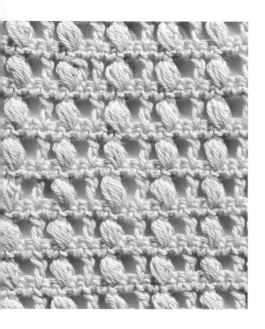

Puff Balls

Chain multiple: 4

Stitch Guide

Puff stitch (Pst): YO; (insert hook in specified st and draw up a lp to height of a dc); (YO, insert hook in same st and draw up a lp to height of a dc) 3 times: YO and draw through all 9 lps on hook: Pst made.

Instructions

Row 1: Sc in 2nd ch from hook and in each rem ch; ch 3, turn.

Row 2: *Dc in next st, ch 1, sk next st, Pst in next st, ch 1, sk next st; rep from * to last 2 sts, dc in last 2 sts; ch 1, turn.

Row 3: Sc in each st and in each ch-1 sp across; ch 3, turn.

Rep rows 2 and 3 for patt.

Puffs and Fans

Chain multiple: 6 + 4

Stitch Guide

Puff stitch (Pst): YO, insert hook in specified ch or st and draw up a lp to height of a dc; (YO and draw up a lp in same st) 3 more times; YO and draw through 9 lps, ch 1: Pst made.

Shell: 7 dc in specified sp: shell made.

Instructions

Row 1: Sc in 2nd ch from hook and in each rem ch; ch 3 (counts as first dc of following row), turn.

Row 2: Dc in next sc; *sk 2 sc, in next sc work (dc, ch 3, dc), sk 2 sc, Pst in next sc; rep from * to last 7 sts, sk 2 sc, in next sc work (dc, ch 3, dc), sk 2 sc, dc in last 2 sts; ch 3, turn.

Row 3 (RS): Dc in next dc; *shell in ch-3 sp, sc in Pst; rep from * across to last ch-3 sp, shell in last sp, dc in last 2 sts; ch 3, turn.

Row 4: Dc in next dc; *in 4th dc of next shell work (dc, ch 3, dc), Pst in next sc; rep from * across to last ch-3 sp, shell in last sp, dc in last 2 dc; ch 3, turn.

Rep rows 3 and 4 for patt. End by working row 3.

Puff Cables

Chain multiple: 4 + 2

Stitch Guide

Puff stitch (Pst): YO, insert hook in specified st and draw up a lp to height of a dc; (YO, insert hook in same st, YO and draw up a lp) two times; YO and draw through all 7 lps on hook; ch 1: Pst made.

Front-post triple crochet (FPtr): YO twice; insert hook from front to back to front around post (vertical bar) of specified st; (YO and draw through 2 lps) 3 times: FPtr made.

Back-post triple crochet (BPtr): YO twice; insert hook from back to front to back around post (vertical bar) of specified st; (YO and draw through 2 lps) 3 times: BPtr made.

Instructions

Row 1: Sc in 2nd ch from hook and in each rem ch; ch 3 (counts as first dc of following row), turn.

Row 2: Dc in each st across; ch 4 (counts as first tr of following row), turn.

Row 3: *BPtr around next st, Pst in next st, BPtr around next st, dc in next st; rep from * across; ch 3, turn.

Row 4 (RS): FPtr around next BPtr, dc in next Pst; *FPtr around next BPtr, dc in next dc, FPtr around next BPtr, dc in next Pst; rep from * across, ending last rep with FPtr around last BPtr, dc in last dc; ch 3, turn.

Rep rows 3 and 4 for patt.

Pretty Puffs

Chain multiple: 3

Stitch Guide

Puff stitch (Pst): (YO, insert hook in specified st and draw up a long lp to height of dc) 3 times in specified st; YO and draw through all 7 lps on hook: Pst made.

Double crochet decrease (dc dec): YO, insert hook in first specified st or sp and draw up a lp, YO and draw through 2 lps on hook; YO, insert hook in second specified st or sp and draw up a lp, YO and draw through 2 lps on hook; YO and draw through all 3 lps on hook: dc dec made.

Instructions

Row 1 (RS): Dc in 6th ch from hook; ch 2, dc dec in same ch as last dc and in 3rd ch (skipping 2 chs in between); *ch 2, dc dec in same ch as 2nd half of last dc dec and in 3rd ch (skipping 2 chs in between); rep from * across; ch 1, dc in same ch as second half of last dc dec; ch 4, turn.

Row 2: Pst in first dc dec; *ch 3, Pst in next dc dec; rep from * across to first dc; ch 3, dc in turning ch; ch 3, turn.

Row 3: Dc in 2nd ch of next ch-3 sp; ch 2, dc dec in same ch as last dc and in 2nd ch of next ch-3 sp; *ch 2, dc dec in same ch as second half of last dc dec and in 2nd ch of next ch-3 sp; rep from * across, working 2nd half of last dc dec in 3rd ch of turning ch-4; ch 1, dc in same ch as 2nd half of last dc dec; ch 4, turn.

Rep rows 2 and 3 for patt.

Pairs of Puffs

Chain multiple: 8 + 5

Stitch Guide

Puff stitch (Pst): *YO, insert hook in specified ch or sp and draw up a lp to height of a dc; rep from * 2 more times in same st, YO and draw through 7 lps: Pst made.

Picot: Ch 3, sl st in base of ch: picot made.

Puff stitch shell (PS): In same ch or sp work (Pst, picot, ch 3, Pst, picot): PS made.

Instructions

Row 1: Work PS in 9th ch from hook; ch 1, sk 3 chs, dc in next ch; *ch 1, sk 3 chs, PS in next ch, ch 1, sk 3 chs, dc in next ch; rep from * across; ch 4 (counts as a dc and ch-1 sp of following row), turn.

Row 2: Work PS in ch-3 sp of next PS, ch 1, dc in next dc; *ch 1, work PS in ch-3 sp of next Pst, ch 1, dc in next dc; rep from * across, ending last rep with dc in 3rd ch of turning ch; ch 4, turn.

Rep row 2 for patt.

Kittens in a Row

Chain multiple: 5 + 4
Two colors: color A and color B

Stitch Guide

Shell: (2 dc, ch 1, 2 dc) in specified st or sp: shell made.

Puff stitch (Pst): (YO, insert hook in sp before first shell in 2nd row below and draw up a lp to height of working row) 4 times: 9 lps on hook; YO and draw through first 8 lps on hook, YO and draw through rem 2 lps: Pst made.

Instructions

Work beg ch with color A.

Row 1 (RS): With color A, dc in 4th ch from hook and in next ch; *sk 2 chs, 2 dc in next ch, ch 1, 2 dc in next ch; rep from * to last 5 chs, sk 2 chs, dc in each of last 3 chs; ch 3 (counts as first dc of following row), turn.

Row 2: Dc in each of next 2 dc; *work shell in next ch-1 sp; rep from * to last 3 sts, dc in last 2 dc, dc in top of turning ch; change to color B, ch 3, turn.

Row 3: Dc in each of next 2 dc, *Pst in sp below, before first shell in 2nd row below; shell in ch-1 sp of next shell, Pst in next sp between shells in 2nd row below; rep from * to last shell, shell in ch-1 sp of last shell, Pst in sp after last shell in 2nd row below; dc in last 2 dc, dc in top of turning ch; ch 3, turn.

Row 4: Dc in each of next 2 dc; *sk next Pst, shell in ch-1 sp of next shell; rep from * to last Pst, sk last Pst, dc in each of last 2 dc, dc in top of turning ch; ch 3, turn.

Row 5: Rep row 2, changing to color A in last dc.

Rows 6 and 7: Rep rows 3 and 4.

Row 8: Dc in each of next 2 dc; *shell in next ch-1 sp; rep from * to last 3 sts, dc in last 2 dc, dc in top of turning ch; change to next color; ch 3, turn.

Rep rows 6–8 for patt.

Puffed Up

Chain multiple: 6 + 4

Stitch Guide

Puff shell (PS): In specified st work hdc; 3 dc, drop lp from hook, insert hook from front to back in first dc, insert hook in dropped lp and draw through, ch 1; hdc: PS made.

Instructions

Row 1: Sc in 2nd ch from hook and in each rem ch; ch 4 (counts as a dc and ch-1 sp throughout), turn.

Row 2 (RS): Sk next sc, dc in next sc; *sk next sc, PS in next sc, sk next sc, dc in next sc; ch 1, sk next sc, dc in next sc; rep from * across; ch 4, turn.

Row 3: Dc in next dc; *ch 1, dc in ch-1 sp of next PS, (ch 1, dc in next dc) twice; rep from * across to turning ch, ch 1, dc in 3rd ch of turning ch; ch 4, turn.

Row 4: Dc in next dc; *ch 1, PS in next dc, (ch 1, dc in next dc) twice; rep from * across to turning ch, dc in 3rd ch of turning ch; ch 1, turn.

Row 5: Sc in first dc; sc in each ch-1 sp and in each dc across, including ch-1 sp of each PS; end last rep with sc in turning ch-sp, and sc in 3rd ch of turning ch; ch 4, turn.

Rep rows 2–5 for patt.

Dancing Puffs

Chain multiple: 12 + 5

Stitch Guide

Puff stitch (Pst): *YO, insert hook in specified st and draw up a lp to height of a dc; rep from * twice more in same st; YO and draw through 7 lps, ch 1: Pst made.

Picot: Ch 3, sl st in base of ch: picot made.

Shell: In specified st work (Pst, picot, ch 5, Pst, picot): shell made.

Double triple crochet (dtr): YO 3 times; (insert hook in specified st and draw up a lp, YO and draw through 2 lps) 4 times: dtr made.

Instructions

Row 1: Sc in 7th ch from hook, *(work picot, ch 3, sk 3 chs, sc in next ch) twice; work picot**; ch 5, sk 3 chs, sc in next ch; rep from * across ending last rep at **; ch 2, sk next ch, dc in last ch; ch 1, turn.

Row 2: Sc in dc, work picot; *ch 3, sk next picot, shell in next picot, ch 3**, sc in next ch-5 sp, work picot; rep from * across, ending last rep at **; sc in turning ch-sp, work picot; ch 7, turn.

Row 3: PS in first picot, work picot; *ch 3, sc in next ch-5 sp, work picot, ch 3**; sk next picot, shell in next picot; rep from * across, ending last rep at **; Pst in last picot, work picot, ch 2, dtr in last sc; ch 1, turn.

Row 4: Sc in dtr, work picot; *ch 3, sk next picot, shell in next picot, ch 3**, sc in next ch-5 sp, work picot; rep from * across, ending last rep at **; sc in turning ch-lp, work picot; ch 7, turn.

Rep rows 3 and 4 for patt.

Perfect Puffs

Chain multiple: any even number

Stitch Guide

Puff stitch (Pst): YO, insert hook in specified st and draw up a lp to height of a dc; (YO, insert hook in same st and draw up a lp to height of a dc) 3 times; YO and draw through 9 lps: Pst made.

Instructions

Row 1: Sc in 2nd ch from hook and in each rem ch; ch 4 (counts as a dc and ch-1 sp of following rows), turn.

Row 2: Sk next sc, dc in next dc; *ch 1, sk 1 sc, dc in next sc; rep from * across; ch 4, turn.

Row 3: *Pst in next ch-1 sp, ch 2; rep from * across to turning ch-sp, Pst in this sp, ch 1, dc in 3rd ch of turning ch; ch 4, turn.

Row 4: *Dc in next ch-2 sp, ch 1; rep from * across, ending last rep with dc in last ch-2 sp, ch 1, dc in 3rd ch of turning ch; ch 4, turn.

Rep rows 3 and 4 for patt.

Fleur-de-Lis

Chain multiple: 6 + 2

Stitch Guide

V-stitch (V-st): In specified st work (dc, ch 2, dc): V-st made.

Puff stitch (Pst): *YO, insert hook in specified sp and draw up a lp to height of a dc; rep from * 2 times more in same lp, YO and draw through 7 lps: Pst made.

Puff stitch shell (PS): In specified sp work (Pst, ch 2) twice, Pst in same sp: PS made.

Instructions

Row 1: Dc in 4th ch from hook and in each rem ch; ch 1, turn.

Row 2: Sc in first dc; *ch 2, sk 2 dc, V-st in next dc, ch 2, sk 2 dc, sc in next dc; rep from * across, ending last rep with sc in top of turning ch; ch 4, turn.

Row 3: *Work PS in ch-2 sp of next V-st, ch 1; rep from * across to last V-st, work PS in last V-st, tr in last sc; ch 4 (counts as a dc and ch-1 sp of following row), turn.

Row 4: *Dc in next ch-2 sp, ch 1, dc in next ch-2 sp, ch 1, dc in next ch-1 sp, ch 1; rep from * across, ending last rep with dc in top of turning ch; ch 3, turn.

Row 5: Dc in each ch-1 sp and in each dc across, ending last rep with dc in turning ch-sp, dc in 3rd ch of turning ch; ch 1, turn.

Rep rows 2–5 for patt.

Puffs and Waves

Chain multiple: 12 + 4

Stitch Guide

Puff stitch (Pst): YO, insert hook in specified ch or st and draw up a lp to height of a dc; (YO, insert hook in same st and draw up a lp to same height) 3 times, YO and draw through all 9 lps on hook, ch 1: Pst made.

Instructions

Row 1: Dc in 6th ch from hook; ch 1, sk next ch, dc in next ch; ch 1, sk next ch, in next ch work (Pst, ch 2, Pst); *(ch 1, sk next ch, dc in next ch) twice; sk 3 chs, (dc in next ch, ch 1, sk next ch) twice, work (Pst, ch 2, Pst) in next ch; rep from * across to last 6 chs, (ch 1, sk next ch, dc in next ch) twice, sk next ch, dc in last ch; ch 3, turn.

Row 2: *(Dc in next ch-1 sp, ch 1) twice, in next ch-2 sp work (Pst, ch 2, Pst); (ch 1, dc in next ch-1 sp) twice; rep from * across, ending last rep with dc in top of turning ch; ch 3, turn.

Rep row 2 for patt.

Soft and Sweet

Chain multiple: 5 + 2

Stitch Guide

Puff stitch (Pst): *YO, insert hook in specified st and draw up a lp to height of a dc; rep from * once in same st, YO and draw through 5 lps: Pst made.

Instructions

Row 1: Sc in 2nd ch from hook; *ch 3, Pst in next ch, ch 3, sk 3 chs, sc in next ch; rep from * across; ch 7, turn.

Row 2: *Sc in top of next Pst, ch 3, Pst in sc just made**, ch 3; rep from * across, ending last rep at **; tr in last sc at base of prev row Pst, ch 1, turn.

Row 3: Sc in tr, sk first Pst; *ch 5, sc in top of next Pst; rep from * across, ending last rep with ch 5, sc in ch-7 lp; ch 1, turn.

Row 4: Hdc in first sc; *work 4 hdc in next ch-5 lp, ch 1; rep from * across to last ch-5 lp, work 4 hdc in last ch-5 lp, hdc in last sc; ch 1, turn.

Row 5: Sc in first hdc; *ch 3, Pst in sc just made; ch 3, sk 4 hdc, sc in next ch-1 sp; rep from * across, ending last rep with sc in last hdc; ch 7, turn.

Rep rows 2–5 for patt. End last rep by working row 4.

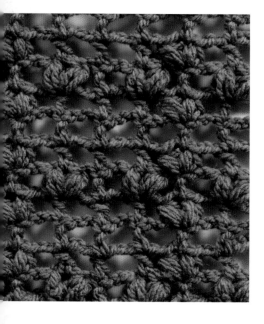

Precious Puffs

Chain multiple: 16 + 5

Stitch Guide

Puff stitch (Pst): *YO, insert hook in specified st and draw up a lp to height of a dc; rep from * in same st 2 more times: 7 lps now on hook; YO and draw through 7 lps, ch 1: Pst made.

Instructions

Row 1: Dc in 9th ch from hook; *ch 3, sk 3 chs, dc in next ch; rep from * across, ch 6 (counts as a dc and ch-3 sp), turn.

Row 2: Dc in next dc; *ch 2, work (Pst, ch 1, Pst) in next dc**; ch 2, dc in next dc, (ch 3, dc in next dc) twice; rep from * across, ending last rep at **; ch 2, dc in next dc, ch 3, dc in 6th ch of turning ch; ch 5, turn.

Row 3: *Work (Pst, ch 1, Pst) in next dc; ch 2, dc in next ch-1 sp, ch 2; rep from * across, ending last rep with dc in 3rd ch of turning ch; ch 6, turn.

Row 4: Dc in next ch-1 sp; *ch 2, work (Pst, ch 1, Pst) in next dc, ch 2, dc in next ch-1 sp**; ch 3, dc in next dc, ch 3, dc in next ch-1 sp; rep from * across, ending last rep at **; ch 3, dc in 3rd ch of turning ch; ch 6, turn.

Row 5: Dc in next dc; *ch 3, dc in next ch-1 sp**, (ch 3, dc in next dc) 3 times; rep from * across, ending last rep at **; ch 3, dc in next dc, dc in 3rd ch of turning ch; ch 6, turn.

Rep rows 2–5 for patt.

Texture Stitch

Chain multiple: 6 + 4

Stitch Guide

Shell: 3 dc in specified st, ch 1; (sc, hdc, dc) around side of last dc made: shell made.

Instructions

Row 1 (RS): 3 dc in 4th ch from hook, sk 2 chs, sc in next ch; *sk 2 chs, shell in next ch; sk 2 chs, sc in next ch; rep from * to last 3 chs, sk 2 chs, 4 dc in last ch; ch 1, turn.

Row 2: Sc in first dc; *sk next 3 dc, shell in next sc, sk 3 sts, sc in next ch-sp; rep from * across; end last rep with sc in top of turning ch, ch 3 (counts as first dc of following row), turn.

Row 3: 3 dc in base of ch, sk 3 sts, sc in next ch sp; *sk 3 sts, shell in next sc, sk 3 sts, sc in next ch-sp; rep from * across; end with sk last 3 sts, 4 dc in turning ch; ch 1, turn.

Rep rows 2 and 3 for patt.

Fences

Chain multiple: any even number

Instructions

When making star sts, draw up each lp to height of a dc.

Row 1 (RS): Insert hook in 2nd ch from hook, YO and draw up a lp; draw up a lp in each of next 3 chs, YO and draw through all 5 lps on hook, ch 1 for "eye" of star: 1 star st made; *draw up a lp in eye of star st just made, draw up a lp only in front and back lps of last lp on same star st, draw up a lp in each of next 2 chs, YO and draw through all 5 lps on hook, ch 1 for eye; rep from * across, dc in last ch; ch 3, turn.

Row 2: Draw up a lp in 2nd ch from hook and a lp in next ch, draw up a lp in dc and a lp in next st and in eye of star, YO and draw through all 5 lps on hook, ch 1; *draw up a lp in eye of star st just made, draw up 1 lp only in front and back lps of last lp on same star, draw up a lp in next st, draw up a lp in next st: eye of star, YO and through all 5 lps on hook, ch 1; rep from * across, dc in last st; ch 3, turn.

Rep row 2 for patt.

Tri Squares

Chain multiple: 6 + 5

Stitch Guide

Front-post double crochet (FPdc):
YO; insert hook from front to back to front around post (vertical bar) of specified st and draw up a lp; (YO and draw through 2 lps) twice: FPdc made.

Back-post double crochet (BPdc):
YO, insert hook from back to front to back around post (vertical bar) of specified st and draw up a lp; (YO and draw through 2 lps) twice: BPdc made.

Instructions

Row 1 (WS): Dc in 4th ch from hook and in each rem ch; ch 3 (counts as first dc of following row), turn.

Row 2: FPdc around each of next 2 dc; *BPdc around each of next 3 dc, FPdc around each of next 3 dc; rep from * across; ch 3, turn.

Rep row 2 for patt.

Tiny Texture

Chain multiple: 2 + 5

Stitch Guide

Front-post double crochet (FPdc):
YO, insert hook from front to back to front around post (vertical bar) of specified st, YO and draw up a lp; (YO and draw through 2 lps) twice: FPdc made.

Back-post double crochet (BPdc):
YO, insert hook from back to front to back around post (vertical bar) of specified st, YO and draw up a lp; (YO and draw through 2 lps) twice: BPdc made.

Instructions

Row 1 (RS): Dc in 4th ch from hook (3 skipped chs count as a dc) and in each rem ch; ch 3 (counts as first dc of following row), turn.

Row 2: FPdc around next st, (BPdc around next st, FPdc around next st) across to last dc, dc in last dc; ch 3, turn.

Rep row 2 for patt.

Posts and Shells

Chain multiple: 7 + 4

Stitch Guide

Front-post double crochet (FPdc):
YO, insert hook from front to back to front around post (vertical bar) of specified dc, YO and draw up a lp; (YO and draw through 2 lps on hook) twice; FPdc made.

Back-post double crochet (BPdc):
YO, insert hook from back to front to back around post (vertical bar) of specified dc, YO and draw up a lp; (YO and draw through 2 lps) twice: BPdc made.

Instructions

Row 1 (RS): Dc in 4th ch from hook and in each rem ch; ch 3, turn.

Row 2: Dc in each dc; ch 3, turn.

Row 3: Dc in next dc; FPdc around next dc; *sc in next dc, hdc in next dc, 3 dc in next dc; hdc in next dc, sc in next dc, FPdc around next dc; rep from * to last 2 dc, dc in last 2 dc; ch 3, turn.

Row 4: Dc in next dc; BPdc around next FPdc; *ch 3, sk next 3 sts, in next st work (sc, ch 3, sc); ch 3, sk next 3 sts, BPdc around next FPdc; rep from * to last 2 sts, dc in last 2 sts; ch 3, turn.

Row 5: Dc in next dc; FPdc around next BPdc; *sk next ch-3 lp, 7 dc in next ch-3 lp: shell made; sk next ch-3 lp, FPdc around next BPdc; rep from * to last 2 dc, dc in last 2 dc; ch 3, turn.

Row 6: Dc in next dc; BPdc around next FPdc, ch 1, sc in front lp only of 4th dc of next shell, ch 1, sk next 3 dc; *in next FPdc work (dc, ch 1, dc); ch 1, sc in front lp only of 4th dc of next shell, ch 1, sk next 3 dc; rep from * to last 3 sts, BPdc around FPdc, dc in last 2 dc; ch 3, turn.

Row 7: Dc in next dc; dc in BPdc, 2 dc in next ch-sp; *dc in sc, dc in ch-sp, (2 dc in next ch-sp) twice; rep from * across, end last rep with dc in sc, 2 dc in next ch-sp, dc in BPdc, dc in last 2 dc; ch 3, turn.

Rep rows 2–7 for patt.

Arrows

Chain multiple: 12 + 4

Stitch Guide

Front-post triple crochet (FPtr):
YO twice, insert hook from front to back to front around post (vertical bar) of specified st, YO and draw up a lp to height of a dc (4 lps on hook); (YO and draw through 2 lps on hook) 3 times: FPtr made.

Instructions

Row 1 (RS): Dc in 4th ch from hook and in next 2 chs; *sk next ch, dc in next 2 chs; working in front of last 2 dc made, dc in skipped ch, sk next 2 chs, dc in next ch; working behind last dc made, dc in each of the 2 skipped chs*, dc in next 6 chs, rep from * to * across, dc in last 4 chs; ch 1, turn.

Row 2: Sc in each st across, ch 3, turn.

Row 3: Dc in next 3 sc; *sk next sc, dc in next 2 sc; working in front of last 2 dc made, FPtr around post of dc one row below skipped sc, sk next 2 sc, FPtr around post of dc below next sc; working behind last FPtr made, dc in each of 2 skipped sc, sk next sc*; dc in next 6 sc; rep from * to * across, dc in last 4 sc; ch 1, turn.

Rep rows 2 and 3 for patt.

Cable Ropes

Chain multiple: 9 + 6

Instructions

Row 1: Sc in 2nd ch from hook and in each rem ch; ch 1, turn.

Row 2 (RS): *Sc in 5 sc, ch 12; sc in next 4 sc, ch 12; rep from * across, end last rep with sc in last 5 sc; ch 1, turn.

Row 3: Holding each ch-12 lp to back of work; sc in each sc across; ch 1, turn.

Rows 4 and 5: Sc in each sc, ch 1, turn.

Rows 6–13: Rep rows 2–5 twice.

Rep rows 2–13 for patt. End last rep with row 12, do not work row 13.

With right side facing you and starting at bottom with first pair of lps at right, pull 2nd lp through bottom lp; cross these lps and then pull next lp above through these lps; continue in this manner to top, repeating for each pair of lp groups across.

Final row: Sc in each sc to first lp, sc in lp and and in sc to secure lp; work in this manner across row.

Braids and Cables

Chain multiple: 8 + 4

Stitch Guide

Front-post triple crochet (FPtr): YO twice; insert hook from front to back to front around post (vertical bar) of specified st and draw up a lp to height of a tr; (YO and draw through 2 lps) 3 times: FPtr made.

Braid (BR): Sk next st; FPtr in each of next 2 sts; working in front of last 2 sts, FPtr in skipped st: BR made.

Instructions

Row 1: Sc in 2nd ch from hook and in each rem ch; ch 3 (counts as first dc of following row), turn.

Row 2 (RS): Dc in each sc, ch 1, turn.

Row 3: Sc in each dc, ch 3, turn.

Row 4: Dc in next 2 sts; *FPtr around next dc in the dc row below, BR over next 3 sts in the dc row below, FPtr around next st in the dc row below, dc in next 3 sts; rep from * across, ch 1, turn.

Row 5: Sc in each st, ch 3, turn.

Row 6: Dc in next 2 sts; *FPtr around next FPtr in the dc row below, BR over next 3 BR sts in dc row below as follows: sk first FPtr, (FPtr over next FPtr) twice, FPtr over skipped FPtr; FPtr around next FPtr in the dc row below; dc in next 3 sts; rep from * across, ch 1, turn.

Rep rows 5 and 6 for patt.

Tracks

Chain multiple: 10 + 7

Stitch Guide

Front-post half double crochet (FPhdc): YO, insert hook from front to back to front around post (vertical bar) of specified st, YO and draw up a lp; YO and draw through rem 3 lps on hook: FPhdc made.

Instructions

Row 1 (RS): Dc in 4th ch from hook and in each rem ch; ch 1, turn.

Row 2: FPhdc around each of first 5 dc; *dc in next dc, (sc in next dc, dc in next dc) 2 times, FPhdc around each of next 5 dc; rep from * across; ch 3, turn.

Row 3: Dc across, ch 1, turn.

Row 4: Sc in first 2 dc, dc in next dc, sc in next dc, dc in next dc; *FPhdc around each of next 5 dc, dc in next dc; (sc in next dc, dc in next dc) 2 times; rep from * across to last 10 dc; FPhdc around each of next 5 dc, dc in next dc, sc in next dc, dc in next dc, sc in last 2 dc; ch 3, turn.

Row 5: Dc across, ch 1, turn.

Rep rows 2–5 for patt.

Filling Stitch

Chain multiple: 2 + 1

Instructions

Row 1 (RS): Dc in 4th ch from hook and in each rem ch; ch 1, turn.

Row 2: Sc in first dc; *sk next dc, (sc, dc) in next dc; rep from * across, ch 3 (counts as first dc on following row), turn.

Row 3: Dc in next dc and in each rem dc and sc across; ch 1, turn.

Rep rows 2 and 3 for patt.

Waffle Stitch

Chain multiple: any even number

Stitch Guide

Front-post double crochet (FPdc): YO, insert hook from front to back to front around post (vertical bar) of specified st, YO and draw up a lp; (YO and draw through 2 lps) twice: FPdc made.

Instructions

Row 1: Dc in 4th ch from hook and in each rem ch; ch 3 (counts as first dc of following row), turn.

Row 2: *FPdc around next dc, dc in next dc; rep from * across, end with dc in 3rd ch of turning ch; ch 3, turn.

Rep row 2 for patt.

Bumpy Road

Chain multiple: 4 + 2

Instructions

Row 1: Sc in 2nd ch from hook and in each rem ch; ch 2, turn.

Row 2: 3 dc in base of ch; *sk next 3 sc, (sc, 3 dc) in next sc; rep from * to last 4 sts, sk 3 sc, sc in last sc; ch 2, turn.

Row 3: 3 dc in base of ch; *sk next 3 dc, (sc, 3 dc) in next sc; rep from * across to last st, sc in 2nd ch of turning ch-2; ch 2, turn.

Rep row 3 for patt.

Interlocked

Chain multiple: 4 + 3

Stitch Guide

Dc2tog (decrease): (YO, insert hook in next dc and draw up a lp, YO and draw through 2 lps on hook) twice; YO and draw through all 3 lps on hook: dc2tog made.

Instructions

Row 1: Sc in 2nd ch from hook and in each rem ch; ch 1, turn.

Row 2: Sc in first sc; *ch 2, 4 dc in sc just made, sk next 3 sc, sc in next sc; rep from * across to last 4 sc, sk next 3 sc, sc in last sc; ch 2, turn.

Row 3: *Sk next dc, dc2tog over next 2 dc, sk next dc, ch 3, sc in top of ch-2; rep from * across; end last rep with sc in top of last ch-2; ch 1, turn.

Row 4: Sc in first sc; *ch 2, 4 dc in sc just made, sk ch-3, sc in next sc; rep from * across; end with sc in top of ch-2; ch 2, turn.

Rep rows 3 and 4 for patt. End last rep by working row 3.

Posted

Chain multiple: any even number

Stitch Guide

Front-post double crochet (FPdc): YO; insert hook from front to back to front around post of specified st and draw up a lp; (YO and draw through 2 lps) twice: FPdc made.

Instructions

Row 1: Dc in 4th ch from hook and in each rem ch; ch 1, turn.

Row 2: Sc in each dc across; ch 3 (counts as first st of following row), turn.

Row 3: *Work FPdc around post of next dc 2 rows below, dc in next sc; rep from * across to last sc, dc in last sc; ch 1, turn.

Row 4: Sc in each st across, ch 3, turn.

Row 5: *Work FPdc around of post of next FPdc 2 rows below, dc in next sc; rep from * across, ending last rep with dc in last sc; ch 1, turn.

Rep rows 4 and 5 for patt.

Checks

Chain multiple: 4 + 2
Two colors: color A and color B

Stitch Guide

Front-post double crochet (FPdc):
YO, insert hook from front to back to front around post (vertical bar) of specified st, YO and draw up a lp; (YO and draw through 2 lps on hook) twice: FPdc made. *Note:* When working FPdc, be sure to draw it up high enough so that it does not pull on the rows below.

Instructions

Work beg ch with color A. All rows are worked on right side.

Row 1 (RS): With color A, sc in 2nd ch from hook and in each rem ch; finish off color A.

Row 2: With right side facing you, join color B in first sc at right edge; ch 3, dc in next 2 sc; *ch 1, sk next st, dc in next 3 sc; rep from * across; end last rep with ch 1, sk next sc, dc in last sc. Finish off color B.

Row 3: With right side facing you, join color A in top of ch-3 at right edge; ch 1, sc in same st; sc in next 2 sts, dc in skipped sc on 2nd row below; *sc in next 3 sts, dc in skipped sc on 2nd row below; rep from * across; end last rep with sc in last st. Finish off color A.

Row 4: Rep row 2.

Row 5: With right side facing you, join color A in top of ch-3 at right edge; ch 1, sc in same st; sc in next 2 dc, FPdc around dc in 2nd row below; *sc in next 3 dc, FPdc around dc in 2nd row below; rep from * across; end last rep with sc in last dc. Finish off color A.

Rep rows 4 and 5 for patt.

Twisty

Chain multiple: 4 + 2

Instructions

Row 1: Sc in 2nd ch from hook and in each rem ch; ch 1, turn.

Row 2: Sc in first sc; *ch 3, sk next 3 sc, sc in next sc; rep from * across; ch 4, turn.

Row 3: *3 tr in first ch-3 sp; YO twice, insert hook in sp at right of 3rd tr from hook and draw up a lp, (YO and draw through 2 lps) 3 times, tr in next sc; rep from * across, ch 1, turn.

Row 4: Sc in first tr; *ch 3, sk next 4 tr, sc in top of tr between groups; rep from * across; end sc in 4th ch of turning ch; ch 4, turn.

Rep rows 3 and 4 for patt.

Arrowheads

Chain multiple: 12 + 4

Instructions

Row 1 (RS): Sc in 2nd ch from hook; *ch 1, sk next ch, sc in next ch; rep from * across; ch 1, turn.

Row 2: Sc in first sc; *ch 1, sc in next sc; rep from * across; ch 1, turn.

Row 3: Sc in first sc, ch 1, sc in next sc; *ch 6, sk next 2 ch-1 sps, sl st in skipped ch of beg ch below next ch-1 sp; ch 6, sk next 2 ch-1 sps, sc in next sc, ch 1, sc in next sc; rep from * across; ch 1, turn.

Row 4: Sc in first sc, ch 1, sc in next sc; *working in front of ch-6 lp, (ch 1, dc in next sc) 4 times, (ch 1, sc in next sc) twice; rep from * across; ch 1, turn.

Row 5: Sc in first sc, ch 1, sc in next sc; *ch 6, sl st in skipped ch one row above prev sl st, ch 6, sk 4 dc, sc in next sc, ch 1, sc in next sc; rep from * across; ch 1, turn.

Row 6: Sc in first sc, ch 1, sc in next sc; *(ch 1, dc in next dc) 4 times, (ch 1, sc in next sc) twice; rep from * across; ch 1, turn.

Rep rows 5 and 6 for patt. End last rep by working row 5.

This Way, That Way

Chain multiple: 4

Instructions

Row 1 (RS): 4 dc in 4th ch from hook, sk 3 chs, sc in next ch; *ch 2, 4 dc in same ch as last sc, sk 3 chs, sc in next ch; rep from * across, ch 5, turn.

Row 2: 4 dc in 4th ch from hook; *sk 4 dc, sc between last dc skipped and next ch-2 sp, ch 2, 4 dc in side of last sc worked; rep from * to last 4 dc, sk 4 dc, sc in ch-2 sp; ch 5, turn.

Rep row 2 for patt.

Crosses and Posts

Chain multiple: 3 + 2

Stitch Guide

Front-post double crochet (FPdc): YO; insert hook from front to back to front around post (vertical bar) of specified st and draw up a lp; (YO and draw through 2 lps on hook) twice: FPdc made.

Back-post double crochet (BPdc): YO; insert hook from back to front to back around post (vertical bar) of specified st and draw up a lp; (YO and draw through 2 lps on hook) twice; BPdc made.

Instructions

Row 1: Sc in 2nd ch from hook and in each rem ch; ch 3 (counts as first dc of following row), turn.

Row 2 (RS): *Sk next st, dc in next st; working in front of dc just made, dc in skipped st; dc in next st; rep from * across; ch 3, turn.

Row 3: *Sk next st, dc in next st, dc in skipped st as before; BPdc around next dc; rep from * across; end last rep with dc in top of turning ch; ch 3, turn.

Row 4: *Sk next st, dc in next st, dc in skipped st as before; FPdc around next BPdc; rep from * across; end last rep with dc in top of turning ch; ch 3, turn.

Rep rows 3 and 4 for patt.

Triple over Triple

Chain multiple: 5 + 3

Stitch Guide

Front-post triple crochet (FPtr): YO twice; insert hook from front to back to front around post (vertical stem) of specified st and draw up a lp; (YO and draw through 2 lps) 3 times: FPtr made.

Instructions

Row 1: Sc in 2nd ch from hook and in each rem ch; ch 4 (counts as first tr of following row), turn.

Row 2: FPtr around next sc; *sk next 2 sc, tr in next sc, ch 1; working in front of tr just made, tr in first skipped sc, FPtr around each of next 2 sc; rep from * across; ch 1, turn.

Row 3: Sc in each st and in each ch-1 sp across; ch 4, turn.

Row 4: FPtr around post of next FPtr 2 rows below; *sk next 2 sc, tr in next sc, ch 1; working in front of tr just made, tr in first skipped sc, FPtr around each of next 2 FPtr 2 rows below; rep from * across; ch 1, turn.

Row 5: Rep row 3

Rep rows 4 and 5 for patt.

Furry Fun

Chain multiple: any even number

Instructions

Row 1: Sc in 2nd ch from hook and in each rem ch; ch 3 (counts as first dc of following row), turn.

Row 2: Dc in next st and in each rem st, ch 1, turn.

Row 3 (WS): *Sl st in back lp of next dc, ch 8; rep from * across to turning ch, sl st in 3rd ch of turning ch; push all chs to back of work, which is the right side; ch 3, turn.

Row 4: Dc in unused lp of each dc across; ch 1, turn.

Rep rows 3 and 4 for patt.

Subtle Chevron

Chain multiple: 20 + 6

Stitch Guide

Front-post double crochet (FPdc): YO, insert hook from front to back to front around post (vertical bar) of specified st and draw up a lp to height of a dc; (YO and draw through 2 lps) twice: FPdc made.

Back-post double crochet (BPdc): YO, insert hook from back to front to back around post (vertical bar) of specified st and draw up a lp to height of a dc; (YO and draw through 2 lps) twice: BPdc made.

Shell: Work (2 dc, ch 2, 2 dc) all in same st: shell made.

Instructions

Row 1 (WS): Work 2 dc in 6th ch from hook; *(ch 1, sk next ch, dc in next ch) 3 times; sk next 2 chs, dc in each of next 2 chs, sk next 2 chs, (dc in next ch, ch 1, sk next ch) 3 times**; 2 dc in next ch, ch 2, 2 dc in next ch; rep from * across, ending last rep at **; 2 dc in next ch, ch 2, dc in last ch, ch 5 (counts as first dc and ch-2 sp on following row), turn.

Row 2 (RS): Work 2 dc in first ch-2 sp, *ch 1, sk next dc, (dc in next dc, ch 1) twice; dc in next dc, sk next dc, FPdc around post of each of next 2 dc, sk next dc, (dc in next dc, ch 1) 3 times**; work shell in next ch-2 sp; rep from * across, ending last rep at **; sk next dc, (2 dc, ch 2, dc) in sp formed by beg 5 skipped chs; ch 5, turn.

Row 3: Work 2 dc in next ch-2 sp, *ch 1, sk next dc, (dc in next dc, ch 1) twice, dc in next dc, sk next dc, BPdc around post of each of next 2 FPdc; sk next dc, (dc in next dc, ch 1) 3 times**; shell in ch-2 sp of next shell; rep from * across, ending last rep at **; 2 dc in turning ch-5 sp, ch 2, dc in 3rd ch of same turning ch-5; ch 5, turn.

Row 4: Work 2 dc in next ch-2 sp, *ch 1, sk next dc, (dc in next dc, ch 1) twice; dc in next dc, sk next dc, FPdc around post of each of next 2 dc, sk next dc, (dc in next dc, ch 1) 3 times**; work shell in next ch-2 sp; rep from * across, ending last rep at **; sk next dc, 2 dc in turning ch-5 sp, ch 2, dc in 3rd ch of same turning ch-5; ch 5, turn.

Row 5: Work 2 dc in next ch-2 sp, *ch 1, sk next dc, (dc in next dc, ch 1) twice, dc next dc; sk next dc, BPdc around post of each of next 2 FPdc; sk next dc, (dc in next dc, ch 1) 3 times**; shell in ch-2 sp of next shell; rep from * across, ending last rep at **; 2 dc in turning ch-5 sp, ch 2, dc in 3rd ch of same turning ch-5; ch 5, turn.

Rep rows 4 and 5 for patt.

Crossing Posts

Chain multiple: 12 + 2

Stitch Guide

Front-post triple crochet (FPtr):
YO 2 times; insert hook from front to back to front around post (vertical stem) of specified st and draw up a lp; (YO and draw through 2 lps) 3 times: FPtr made.

Shell: Work 5 dc in specified st: shell made.

Instructions

Row 1: Sc in 2nd ch from hook and in each rem ch; ch 3 (counts as a dc of following row), turn.

Row 2: Dc in each of next 2 sc; *ch 1, sk next 3 sc, work shell in next sc, ch 1, sk next 3 sc, dc in next 5 sc; rep from * across, ending last rep with dc in last 3 (instead of 5) sc; ch 3, turn.

Row 3: Dc in next 2 dc; *ch 1, dc in first dc of next 5-dc shell, sk next 2 dc of shell, FPtr around next dc of shell, ch 1, crossing in front of FPtr just made, FPtr in 2nd dc of shell, dc in last dc of shell; ch 1, dc in next 5 dc; rep from * across, ending last rep with dc in last 2 dc, dc in top of turning ch; ch 3, turn.

Row 4: Dc in next 2 dc; *ch 1, work 5-dc shell in ch-1 sp between 2 crossed FPtr sts of prev row, ch 1, dc in each of next 5 dc; rep from * across, ending last rep with dc in last 2 dc, dc in top of turning ch; ch 3, turn.

Rep rows 3 and 4 for patt.

Clusters and Posts

Chain multiple: 4 + 2

Stitch Guide

Cluster (CL): YO, insert hook in specified st and draw up a lp, YO and draw through 2 lps; YO, insert hook in same st and draw up a lp, YO and draw through 2 lps; YO and draw through all 3 lps on hook: CL made.

Cluster shell (CL shell): In specified st work (CL, ch 1, CL): CL shell made.

Front-post double crochet (FPdc):
YO, insert hook from front to back to front around post (vertical bar) of specified st and draw up a lp; (YO and draw through 2 lps) twice: FPdc made.

Back-post double crochet (BPdc):
YO, insert hook from back to front to back around post (vertical bar) of specified st and draw up a lp; (YO and draw through 2 lps) twice: BPdc made.

Instructions

Row 1: Sc in 2nd ch from hook and in each rem ch; ch 3 (counts as a dc throughout), turn.

Row 2 (RS): *Sk next sc, CL shell in next sc, sk next sc, dc in next sc; rep from * across; ch 3, turn.

Row 3: *CL shell in ch-1 sp of next CL shell, BPdc around next dc; rep from * across to last st, dc in last st; ch 3, turn.

Row 4: *CL shell in ch-1 sp of next CL shell, FPdc around next BPdc; rep from * across to last dc, dc in last st; ch 3, turn.

Rep rows 3 and 4 for patt.

Post to Post

Chain multiple: 2 + 1

Stitch Guide

Front-post double crochet (FPdc):
YO, insert hook from front to back to front around post (vertical bar) of specified st and draw up a lp; (YO and draw through 2 lps) twice: FPdc made.

Back-post double crochet (BPdc):
YO, insert hook from back to front to back around post (vertical bar) of specified st and draw up a lp; (YO and draw through 2 lps) twice: BPdc made.

Instructions

Row 1: Sc in 2nd ch from hook and in each rem ch; ch 4 (counts as a dc and ch-1 sp), turn.

Row 2: Sk next sc, dc in next dc; *ch 1, sk next sc, dc in next sc; rep from * across, ch 4, turn.

Row 3: *FPdc around next dc, ch 1, BPdc around next dc, ch 1; rep from * across to turning ch, dc in 3rd st of turning ch; ch 4, turn.

Row 4: *BPdc around next BPdc in prev row, ch 1, FPdc around next FPdc in prev row, ch 1; rep from * across to turning ch, dc in 3rd ch of turning ch; ch 4, turn.

Row 5: *FPdc around FPdc in prev row, ch 1, BPdc around BPdc in prev row, ch 1; rep from * across, ending last rep with dc in 3rd ch of turning ch, ch 4, turn.

Rep rows 4 and 5 for patt.

Parade of Shells

Chain multiple: 8 + 2

Stitch Guide

Shell: In specified st work (2 dc, ch 1, dc, ch 1, 2 dc): shell made.

Front-post double crochet (FPdc):
YO, insert hook from front to back to front around post (vertical bar) of specified st and draw up a lp; (YO and draw through 2 lps) twice: FPdc made.

Back-post double crochet (BPdc):
YO, insert hook from back to front to back around post (vertical bar) of specified st and draw up a lp; (YO and draw through 2 lps) twice: BPdc made.

Instructions

Row 1: Sc in 2nd ch from hook and in each rem ch; ch 1, turn.

Row 2: Sc in first sc; *sk 3 sc, shell in next sc, sk 3 sc, dc in next sc; rep from * across to last 4 sts, ending last rep by skipping 3 sc, sc in last sc; ch 3 (counts as a dc of following row throughout), turn.

Row 3 (RS): *Work 2 dc in first ch-1 sp of next shell, ch 1, FPdc around center dc of shell, ch 1, 2 dc in next ch-1 sp of shell, dc in next dc; rep from * across, ending with dc in last sc; ch 3, turn.

Row 4: *Work 2 dc in first ch-1 sp of next shell, ch 1, BPdc around center dc of shell, ch 1, 2 dc in next ch-1 sp of shell, dc in next dc; rep from * across, ending last rep with dc in 3rd ch of turning ch; ch 3, turn.

Row 5: Rep row 3, ending with dc in 3rd ch of turning ch; ch 3, turn.

Rep rows 4 and 5 for patt.

Crossed Posts

Chain multiple: any uneven number

Stitch Guide

Back-post double crochet (BPdc): YO, insert hook from back to front to back around post (vertical bar) of specified st and draw up a lp; (YO and draw through 2 lps on hook) twice: BPdc made.

Instructions

Row 1: Sc in 2nd ch from hook and in each rem ch; ch 3 (counts as first dc of following row throughout), turn.

Row 2: Dc in next sc and in each rem sc across; ch 3, turn.

Row 3 (RS): *Sk next dc, BPdc around post of next dc; working in front of BPdc just made, dc in skipped dc; rep from * across, ending last rep with dc in last st; ch 3, turn.

Row 4: Dc in each st across, ch 3, turn.

Rep rows 3 and 4 for patt.

Squared Off

Chain multiple: 7 + 6

Stitch Guide

Front-post triple crochet (FPtr): YO twice, insert hook from front to back to front around stem (vertical bar) of specified st and draw up a lp to height of a dc; (YO and draw through 2 lps) 3 times: FPtr made.

Instructions

Row 1: Sc in 2nd ch from hook and in each rem ch; ch 1, turn.

Row 2: Sc in first sc; *ch 3, sk 3 sc, sc in next sc; ch 2, sk 2 sc, sc in next sc; rep from * across, ending last rep with ch 3, sk 3 sc, sc in last sc; ch 3, turn.

Row 3 (RS): *3 dc in ch-3 sp, dc in next sc, 2 dc in ch-2 sp, dc in next sc; rep from * across, ending last rep with 3 dc in last ch-3 sp, dc in last sc; ch 1, turn.

Row 4: Sc in first dc; *ch 3, sk 3 dc, sc in next dc; ch 2, sk 2 dc, sc in next dc; rep from * across, ending last rep with ch 3, sk 3 dc, sc in top of turning ch; ch 3, turn.

Row 5: *3 dc in ch-3 sp, FPtr around next dc in 2nd row below, 2 dc in ch-2 sp, FPtr around next dc in 2nd row below; rep from * across, ending last rep with 3 dc in ch-3 sp, dc in last dc; ch 1, turn.

Row 6: Sc in first dc; *ch 3, sk 3 dc, sc in next FPtr; ch 2, sk 2 dc, sc in next FPtr; rep from * across, ending last rep with ch 3, sk 3 dc, sc in top of turning ch; ch 3, turn.

Row 7: *3 dc in ch-3 sp, FPtr around next FPtr in 2nd row below, 2 dc in ch-2 sp, FPtr around next FPtr in 2nd row below; rep from * across, ending last rep with 3 dc in ch-3 sp, dc in last dc; ch 1, turn.

Rep rows 6 and 7 for patt.

Triple Posts

Chain multiple: 8 + 4

Stitch Guide

Front-post double crochet cluster (FPdcCL): *YO, insert hook from front to back to front around post (vertical bar of specified st) and draw up a lp; YO and draw through 2 lps; rep from * two times more, YO and draw through 4 lps: FPdcCL made.

Instructions

Row 1: Dc in 6th ch from hook; *ch 1, sk 1 ch, dc in next ch; rep from * across; ch 4 (counts as a dc and ch-1 sp of following row), turn.

Row 2: Dc in next dc; *ch 1, work FPdcCL around next dc**; (ch 1, dc in next dc) 3 times; rep from * across, ending last rep at **; ch 1, dc in next dc, ch 1, dc in 3rd ch of turning ch; ch 4, turn.

Row 3: Dc in next dc; *ch 1, dc in top of FPdcCL; (ch 1, dc in next dc) 3 times; rep from * across, ending last rep with ch 1, dc in last dc, ch 1, dc in 3rd ch of turning ch; ch 4, turn.

Row 4: Dc in next dc; (ch 1, dc in next dc) twice; *ch 1, work FPdcCL around next dc, (ch 1, dc in next dc) 3 times; rep from * across, ending last rep with ch 1, dc in 3rd ch of turning ch; ch 4, turn.

Row 5: *(Dc in next dc, ch 1) 3 times, dc in top of FPdcCL, ch 1; rep from * across, ending last rep with dc in 3rd ch of turning ch, ch 4, turn.

Rep rows 2–5 for patt.

Small Shells

Chain multiple: 4 + 2

Stitch Guide

Shell: Work 3 dc in specified st: shell made.

Front-post single crochet (FPsc): Insert hook from front to back to front around post (vertical bar) of specified st; YO and draw up a lp, YO and draw through 2 lps: FPsc made.

Instructions

Row 1: Sc in 2nd ch from hook and in each rem ch; ch 1, turn.

Row 2: Sc in first sc; *ch 3, sk 3 sc, sc in next sc; rep from * across; ch 3, turn.

Row 3: Dc in base of turning ch; *sk ch-3 sp, shell in next sc; rep from * across, ending last rep with 2 dc in last sc; ch 1, turn.

Row 4: Sc in first dc, *ch 3, work FPsc around center dc of next shell; rep from * across, ending last rep with ch 3, sc in 3rd ch of turning ch-3; ch 3, turn.

Row 5: Dc in base of turning ch; *sk ch-3 sp, work shell in next FPsc; rep from * across, ending last rep with 2 dc in last sc; ch 1, turn.

Rep rows 4 and 5 for patt.

Shell in the Background

Chain multiple: 4

Instructions

Row 1 (RS): Dc in 4th ch from hook, sk next ch, sc in next ch; *sk next ch, 3 dc in next ch, sk next ch, sc in next ch; rep from * to last 2 chs, sk next ch, 2 dc in last ch; ch 1, turn.

Row 2: Sc in first dc, sk next dc, 3 dc in next sc; *sk next dc, sc in next dc, sk next dc, 3 dc in next sc; rep from * to last 2 sts, sk next dc, sc in top of turning ch; ch 3, turn.

Row 3: Dc in first sc, sk next dc, sc in next dc; *sk next dc, 3 dc in next sc, sk next dc, sc in next dc; rep from * to last 2 sts, sk next dc, 2 dc in last sc; ch 1, turn.

Rep rows 2 and 3 for patt.

Little Shells

Chain multiple: 8 + 3

Stitch Guide

Large shell (LS): (2 dc, ch 3, 2 dc) all in same ch or ch-sp: LS made.

Small shell (SS): (dc, ch 2, dc) all in same ch or ch-sp: SS made.

Instructions

Row 1 (RS): LS in 7th ch from hook; *sk next 3 chs, SS in next ch; sk next 3 chs, LS in next ch; rep from * to last 4 chs, sk 3 chs, dc in last ch; ch 3, turn.

Row 2: LS in ch-3 sp of first LS; *SS in ch-2 space of next SS, LS in ch-3 space of next LS; rep from * across, end dc in top of turning ch; ch 3, turn.

Rep row 2 for patt.

Shell Rows

Chain multiple: 8 + 4

Stitch Guide

Shell: In specified st work (dc, ch 1) 3 times, dc: shell made.

Instructions

Row 1: Sc in 2nd ch from hook and in each rem ch; ch 3 (counts as first dc of following row), turn.

Row 2 (RS): Dc in next 2 sts; *sk 2 sc, shell in next sc, sk 2 sc, dc in next 3 sc; rep from * across, ch 3, turn.

Row 3: Dc in next 2 dc; *ch 2, sc in center ch-1 sp of next shell, ch 2, dc in next 3 dc; rep from * across, ch 3, turn.

Row 4: Dc in next 2 dc; *ch 2, shell in next sc, ch 2, dc in 3 dc; rep from * across, ch 3, turn.

Rep rows 3 and 4 for patt.

Flowerpot

Chain multiple: 3 + 2

Stitch Guide

Shell: (dc, ch 1, dc) all in same ch or ch-1 sp: shell made.

Instructions

Row 1: Dc in 5th ch from hook; *sk next 2 chs, shell in next ch; rep from * across row; ch 3, turn.

Row 2 (RS): 2 dc in first ch-1 sp, 3 dc in each rem ch-1 sp; ch 1, turn.

Row 3: Sc in each of first 2 dc; *ch 3, sk next 2 dc, sc in next dc; rep from * across to last st, sc in turning ch; ch 1, turn.

Row 4: Sc in first sc, ch 3; *sc in next ch-3 sp, ch 3; rep from * across to last 2 sc, sk next sc, sc in last sc; ch 4, turn.

Row 5: Dc in first ch-3 sp, shell in each rem ch-3 sp; ch 3, turn.

Rep rows 2–5 for patt.

Interlocking Shells

Chain multiple: 4 + 2

Stitch Guide

Shell: In specified ch or st work (ch 3, 4 dc): shell made.

Dc2tog (decrease): (YO, draw up a lp in next st, YO and draw through 2 lps) twice, YO and draw through 3 lps: dc2tog made.

Instructions

Row 1 (RS): Sc in 2nd ch from hook, shell in same sc; *sk 3 chs, sc in next ch, shell in same sc; rep from * to last 4 chs, sk 3 chs, sc in last ch; ch 3, turn.

Row 2: *Sk 1 dc of next shell, dc2tog, ch 3, sk 1 dc of shell, sc in 3rd ch of ch-3; rep from * across; ch 1, turn.

Row 3: Sc in first st, shell in same st; *sk 3 chs and next st, sc in next sc, shell in same sc, shell in next sc; rep from * across; end last rep with sk 3 chs and next st, sc in top of turning ch, ch 3, turn.

Rep rows 2 and 3 for patt.

Shells on Parade

Chain multiple: 6 + 2

Stitch Guide

Shell: (2 dc, ch 1, 2 dc) all in same ch or sp: shell made.

Instructions

Row 1 (RS): Sc in 2nd ch from hook; *sk next 2 chs, shell in next ch, sk next 2 chs, sc in next ch; rep from * across; ch 3, turn.

Row 2: 2 dc in both lps of first sc, sc in back lp only of ch-1 sp of next shell; *shell in back lp only of next sc, sc in back lp only of ch-1 sp of next shell; rep from * across, end last rep with 3 dc in both lps of last sc; ch 1, turn.

Row 3: Sc in both lps of first dc; *shell in back lp only of next sc, sc in back lp only of ch-1 sp of next shell; rep from * across, working last sc of last rep in top of turning ch; ch 3, turn.

Rep rows 2 and 3 for patt.

Tipped Blocks

Chain multiple: 8 + 4

Stitch Guide

Shell: Tr in specified st; ch 3, work 3 dc over stem (vertical bar) of tr: shell made.

Instructions

Row 1: Sc in 2nd ch from hook and in each rem ch; ch 3 (counts as first dc of following row throughout), turn.

Row 2 (RS): Dc in next 2 sc; *sk 2 sc, shell in next sc, sk 2 sc, dc in next 3 sc; rep from * across; ch 3, turn.

Row 3: Dc in next 2 dc; *ch 2, sc in top of ch-3 of next shell, ch 2, dc in next 3 dc; rep from * across, ch 3, turn.

Row 4: Dc in next 2 dc; *shell in next sc, dc in next 3 dc; rep from * across; ch 3, turn.

Rep rows 3 and 4 for patt.

Diamond Blocks

Chain multiple: 10 + 7

Stitch Guide

Shell: (dc, ch 5, dc) in specified st or ch: shell made.

Instructions

Row 1: Dc in 4th ch from hook and in next 3 chs; *sk 2 chs, shell in next ch, sk 2 chs, dc in next 5 chs; rep from * across; ch 3 (counts as a dc of following row), turn.

Row 2: Dc in next 4 dc; *ch 2, sc in 3rd ch of shell, ch 2, dc in next 5 dc; rep from * across, ch 3, turn.

Row 3: Sk next dc; *shell in next dc, sk 2 dc, 2 dc in ch-2 sp, dc in sc, 2 dc in ch-2 sp; sk next 2 dc; rep from * across to last 5 dc, sk 2 dc, shell in next dc, sk next dc, dc in turning ch; ch 4 (counts as a dc and ch-1 sp), turn.

Row 4: *Sc in 3rd ch of shell, ch 2, dc in next 5 dc, ch 2; rep from * to last shell, sc in 3rd ch of shell, ch 1, dc in 3rd ch of turning ch; ch 3, turn.

Row 5: Dc in next ch-1 sp and in next sc, 2 dc in ch-2 sp; *sk 2 dc, shell in next dc, sk 2 dc; 2 dc in ch-2 sp, dc in sc, 2 dc in ch-2 sp; rep from * to last ch-2 sp, 2 dc in ch-2 sp, dc in sc, dc in 4th and in 3rd chs of turning ch; ch 3, turn.

Rep rows 2–5 for patt.

Palm Fronds

Chain multiple: 8 + 2

Instructions

Row 1: Sc in 2nd ch from hook and in each rem ch; ch 4 (counts as a tr of following row), turn.

Row 2 (RS): *Sk 3 sc, work 5 tr in next sc, sk 3 sc, tr in next sc; rep from * across, ch 4 (counts as first tr of following row), turn.

Row 3: 2 tr in base of ch, sk 2 tr, tr in next tr; *sk 2 tr, 5 tr in next tr, sk 2 tr, tr in next tr; rep from * to last 3 sts, sk 2 tr, 3 tr in next ch, ch 4, turn.

Row 4: *Sk next 2 tr, 5 tr in next tr, sk 2 tr, tr in next tr; rep from * across, work last tr into 4th ch of turning ch; ch 4, turn.

Rep rows 3 and 4 for patt.

Sea Shells

Chain multiple: 8 + 1

Stitch Guide

Double triple crochet (dtr): YO 3 times; insert hook in specified ch or st and draw up a lp; (YO and draw through 2 lps on hook) 4 times: dtr made.

Instructions

Row 1 (RS): Sc in 2nd ch from hook; *ch 2, sk 3 chs, 4 dtr in next ch, ch 2, sk 3 chs, sc in next ch; rep from * across; end last rep with ch 2, sk 3 chs, sc in last ch; ch 1, turn.

Row 2: Sc in first sc; *ch 3, sk next ch-2 sp and next dtr; sc in next dtr, ch 3; sk next 2 dtr and next ch-2 sp, sc in next sc; rep from * across; end last rep with ch 3, sc in last sc, leave turning ch-1 unworked; ch 3, turn.

Row 3: 2 dtr in first sc; *ch 2, sc in next sc, ch 2, 4 dtr in next sc; rep from * across; end last rep with ch 2, 2 dtr in sc; leave turning ch-3 unworked, ch 1, turn.

Row 4: Sk first dtr, sc in next dtr; *ch 3, sc in next sc, ch 3, sk next ch-2 sp and next 2 dtr; sc in next dtr; rep from * across; end last rep with ch 3, sk ch-2 sp and next dtr, sc in last dtr, sc in top of turning ch; ch 1, turn.

Row 5: Sk first sc, *sc in next sc, ch 2, 4 dtr in next sc, ch 2; rep from * across; end last rep with sc in last dtr; ch 1, turn.

Rep rows 2–5 for patt. End by working a row 2.

Filet Shells

Chain multiple: 6 + 1

Stitch Guide

Shell: (2 dc, ch 1, 2 dc) in specified st: shell made.

Instructions

Row 1: Sc in 2nd ch from hook and in each rem ch; ch 1, turn.

Row 2 (RS): *Sk 2 sc, shell in next sc, sk 2 sc, sc in next sc; rep from * across, ch 5 (counts as a dc and ch-2 sp), turn.

Row 3: *Sc in ch-1 sp of next shell, ch 2, dc in next sc, ch 2; rep from * across, end last rep with dc in last sc; ch 5, turn.

Row 4: *Dc in next sc, ch 2, dc in next dc, ch 2; rep from * across, end dc in 3rd ch of turning ch; ch 5, turn.

Row 5: Dc in next dc; *ch 2, dc in next dc; rep from * across; ch 1, turn.

Row 6: Sc in first dc; *shell in next dc, sc in next dc; rep from * across, end last rep with sc in 3rd ch of turning ch; ch 5, turn.

Rep rows 3–6 for patt.

Offset Shell

Chain multiple: 7 + 3

Stitch Guide

Shell: In specified st work (4 dc, ch 2, dc): shell made.

Instructions

Row 1: Sc in 2nd ch from hook and in each rem ch; ch 3 (counts as first dc of following row), turn.

Row 2 (RS): Sk next 2 sc; shell in next sc; *sk 5 sc, shell in next sc; rep from * to last 3 sc, sk 2 sc, dc in last sc; ch 3, turn.

Row 3: *Shell in ch-2 sp of next shell; rep from * across; end with dc in top of turning ch; ch 3, turn.

Rep row 3 for patt.

Crazy Blocks

Chain multiple: 10 + 9

Stitch Guide

Shell: In same st or sp work (3 dc, ch 2, dc): shell made.

Instructions

Row 1: Sc in 2nd ch from hook and in each rem ch; ch 3 (counts as first dc of following row throughout), turn.

Row 2: Dc in next st; *sk next st; shell in next st, sk 3 sts, dc in each of next 5 sts; rep from * across; end last rep with dc in next 2 (instead of 5) sts; ch 3, turn.

Row 3: Dc in next dc; *shell in ch-2 sp of next shell, dc in each of next 5 dc; rep from * across; end last rep with dc in last dc, dc in top of turning ch; ch 3, turn.

Rep row 3 for patt.

Leaning Shells

Chain multiple: 12 + 4

Stitch Guide

Shell: Work 6 dc in specified ch or st: shell made.

Instructions

Row 1: Dc in 4th ch from hook; *ch 2, sk 2 chs, shell in next ch, sk 4 chs, sc in next ch; ch 2, sk 2 chs, dc in each of next 2 chs; rep from * across; ch 3, turn.

Row 2: Dc in next dc; *ch 2, shell in next sc, sk first 5 dc of next shell, sc in last dc of same shell, ch 2, dc in next 2 dc; rep from * across, end last rep with dc in last dc, dc in top of turning ch; ch 3, turn.

Rep row 2 for patt.

Shell Columns

Chain multiple: 8 + 4

Stitch Guide

Shell: Work (3 dc, ch 1, 3 dc) in same sp: shell made.

Instructions

Row 1: Sc in 2nd ch from hook and in each rem ch; ch 3 (counts as first dc of following row), turn.

Row 2: Dc in next 2 sts, sk 2 sts, (dc, ch 2, dc) in next st, sk 2 sts; *dc in 3 sts, sk 2 sts, (dc, ch 2, dc) in next st, sk 2 sts; rep from * across; end last rep with dc in last 3 sts; ch 3, turn.

Row 3 (RS): Dc in next 2 dc; *shell in next ch-2 sp, dc in next 3 dc; rep from * across, ch 3, turn.

Row 4: Dc in next 2 dc; *ch 1, sk first 3 dc of shell, in ch-1 sp of shell work (dc, ch 2, dc), sk next 3 dc of shell, ch 1, dc in next 3 dc; rep from * across; ch 3, turn.

Row 5: Rep row 3.

Rep rows 4 and 5 for patt.

Slanted Shells

Chain multiple: 4 + 2

Stitch Guide

Shell: In specified st or ch work (sc, ch 3, 3 dc): shell made.

Instructions

Row 1: Sc in 2nd ch from hook and in each rem ch; ch 1, turn.

Row 2 (RS): Shell in first sc; *sk next 3 sc, shell in next sc; rep from * to last 4 sts, sk next 3 sc, dc in last sc; ch 4, turn.

Row 3: Sc in next ch-3 sp; *ch 3, sc in next ch-3 sp; rep from * across, ch 1, turn.

Row 4: Shell in first sc; *shell in next sc; rep from * across, end last rep with dc in last sc of prev row; ch 4, turn.

Row 5: Sc in next ch-3 sp; *ch 3, sc in next ch-3 sp; rep from * across, ch 1, turn.

Rep rows 4 and 5 for patt.

Lattice Shells

Chain multiple: 8 + 4

Stitch Guide

Shell: Work 5 dc in specified st: shell made.

Instructions

Row 1: Sc in 2nd ch from hook and in each rem ch; ch 4 (counts as a dc and ch-1 sp on following row), turn.

Row 2: Sk in next st, dc in next st; *sk 2 sts, shell in next st, sk 2 sts, dc in next st, ch 1, sk next st, dc in next st; rep from * across; ch 4, turn.

Row 3: Dc in next dc; *shell in center dc of next shell, sk next 2 dc on same shell, dc in next dc, ch 1, dc in next dc; rep from * across, end with dc in 3rd ch of turning ch; ch 4, turn.

Rep row 3 for patt.

Fancy Shells

Chain multiple: 8 + 5

Stitch Guide

Shell: Work (dc, ch 2, dc) in specified st: shell made.

Instructions

Row 1: Dc in 5th ch from hook; *ch 2, sk next 3 chs, sc in next ch, ch 2, sk next 3 chs**; shell in next ch; rep from * across, ending final rep at **; (dc, ch 1, dc) in last ch; ch 1, turn.

Row 2 (RS): Sl st in first dc and ch-2 sp, ch 3, 2 dc in same sp; *ch 2, sc in next sc, ch 2**; 5 dc in ch-2 sp of next shell; rep from * across, ending final rep at **; 3 dc in last shell, ch 1, turn.

Row 3: Sc in first 3 dc, ch 7, sk next sc; *sc in next 5 dc, ch 7, sk next sc; rep from * across to last 3 dc; sc in next 2 dc and in 3rd ch of turning ch-3; ch 1, turn.

Row 4: Sc in first 2 sc; *ch 2, shell in 4th ch of next ch-7 lp, ch 2, sk next sc**; sc in next 3 sc; rep from * across, ending final rep at **; sc in last 2 sc; ch 1, turn.

Row 5: Sc in first sc; *ch 2, 5 dc in ch-2 sp of next shell, ch 2, sk next sc, sc in next sc; rep from * across; ch 7 (counts as a tr and ch-3 sp), turn.

Row 6: Sc in next 5 dc; *ch 7, sk next sc, sc in next 5 dc; rep from * across to last sc; ch 3, tr in last sc; ch 4, turn.

Row 7: Dc in base of tr; *ch 2, sk first sc, sc in next 3 sc, ch 2**; shell in 4th ch of next ch-7 lp; rep from * across, ending final rep at **; (dc, ch 1, dc) in 4th ch of turning ch-7; ch 3, turn.

Row 8: Work 2 dc in base of first dc; *ch 2, sk next sc, sc in next sc, ch 2**; 5 dc in ch-2 sp of next shell; rep from * across, ending final rep at **; 3 dc in 3rd ch of turning ch-4; ch 1, turn.

Rep rows 3–8 for patt.

Mesh and Shells

Chain multiple: 5 + 2

Stitch Guide

Shell: Work 5 dc in specified st: shell made.

Instructions

Row 1: Sc in 2nd ch from hook and in each rem ch; ch 1, turn.

Row 2: Sc in first sc; *ch 5, sk 4 sc, sc in next sc; rep from * across; ch 3, turn.

Row 3 (RS): 2 dc in base of ch, sc in next ch-5 lp; *ch 5, sc in next ch-5 lp, shell in next sc, sc in next ch-5 lp; rep from * across, ending last rep with 3 dc in last sc; ch 1, turn.

Row 4: Sc in first dc; *ch 3, sc in next ch-5 lp, ch 3, sc in center dc of next shell; rep from * across, ending last rep with sc in top of turning ch; ch 3, turn.

Row 5: *4 dc in next ch-3 lp; rep from * across, ending last rep with dc in last sc; ch 1, turn.

Row 6: Sc in first dc; *ch 5, sc in last dc of next 4-dc group; rep from * across, ending last rep with sc in top of turning ch, ch 3, turn.

Rep rows 3–6 for patt.

Peacock Tails

Chain multiple: 12 + 8

Stitch Guide

Shell: Work 5 dc in specified ch or st: shell made.

Instructions

Row 1: Sc in 7th ch from hook; *ch 2, sk 3 chs, shell in next ch, ch 2, sk 3 chs, sc in next ch**; ch 5, sk 3 chs, sc in next ch; rep from * across, ending last rep at **; ch 3, sk 3 chs, sc in last ch; ch 1, turn.

Row 2: Sc in base of turning ch; *ch 2, (dc in next dc, ch 1) 4 times, dc in next dc; ch 2, sc in next ch-3 sp; rep from * across, ending last rep with sc in 4th ch of turning ch; ch 3, turn.

Row 3: *(Dc in next dc, ch 2) 4 times, dc in next dc; rep from * across, ending last rep with tr in last sc; ch 4, turn.

Row 4: *Sc in next ch-2 sp, ch 2, sk next dc and ch-2 sp, shell in next dc; ch 2, sk next ch-2 sp and next dc, sc in next ch-2 sp, ch 4; rep from * across, ending last rep with tr in last sc; ch 1, turn.

Rep rows 2–4 for patt.

Shells and Shells

Chain multiple: 4 + 2

Stitch Guide

Shell: Work 5 dc in specified st or sp: shell made.

Instructions

Row 1: Sc in 2nd ch from hook; *ch 5, sk next 3 chs, sc in next ch; rep from * across; ch 4, turn.

Row 2 (RS): *Shell in 3rd ch of next ch-5 lp; rep from * across; tr in last sc; ch 1, turn.

Row 3: Sc in first tr; *ch 5, sk next shell, sc in sp between next 2 shells; rep from * across to last shell; ch 5, sk next shell, sc in 4th ch of turning ch-4; ch 4, turn.

Rep rows 2 and 3 for patt.

Triple Dipper

Chain multiple: 6 + 2

Stitch Guide

Shell: Work 5 tr in specified lp: shell made.

Instructions

Row 1: Sc in 2nd ch from hook and in each rem sc; ch 7 (counts as a tr and ch-3 lp), turn.

Row 2: Sk 2 sc, sc in next sc; *ch 3, sk 2 sc, sc in next sc, ch 7, sk 2 sc, sc in next sc; rep from * to last 5 sc, ch 3, sk 2 sc, sc in next sc, ch 3, sk one sc, tr in last sc; ch 1, turn.

Row 3 (RS): Sc in tr; *shell in next ch-3 lp, sc in next ch-7 lp; rep from * across, ending last rep with shell in last ch-3 lp, sc in turning ch-7 lp; ch 7, turn.

Row 4: Sk first tr in next shell, sc in next tr, ch 3, sk next tr, sc in next tr; *ch 7; sk next tr, next sc, and next tr; sc in next tr, ch 3, sk next tr, sc in next tr; rep from * across, ending last rep with ch 3, tr in last sc; ch 1, turn.

Row 5: Sc in tr; *ch 2, tr in ch-3 lp, ch 2, sc in ch-7 lp; rep from * across, ending last rep with ch 2, tr in last ch-3 lp, ch 2, sc in turning ch-7 lp; ch 7, turn.

Row 6: Sc in first ch-2 sp; *ch 3, sc in next ch-2 sp; ch 7, sc in next ch-2 sp; rep from * across, ending last rep with ch 3, sc in last ch-2 sp, ch 3, tr in last sc; ch 1, turn.

Rep rows 3–6 for patt.

Sweet Little Shells

Chain multiple: 8 + 2

Stitch Guide

Shell: Work (2 dc, ch 1, 2 dc) in specified st: shell made.

Instructions

Row 1: Sc in 2nd ch from hook; *ch 5, sk 3 chs, sc in next ch; rep from * across; ch 6, turn.

Row 2: Sc in first ch-5 lp; *shell in next sc, sc in next ch-5 lp**; ch 5, sc in next ch-5 lp; rep from * across, ending final rep at **; ch 2, tr in last sc; ch 1, turn.

Row 3: Sc in tr; *ch 5, sc in ch-1 sp of next shell, ch 5**; sc in next ch-5 lp; rep from * across, ending final rep at **; sc in turning ch-6 lp; ch 6, turn.

Rep rows 2 and 3 for patt.

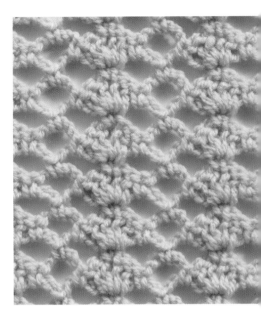

Slanty

Chain multiple: 4 + 2

Stitch Guide

Shell: (Sc, ch 2, 4 dc) in same ch or st: shell made.

Instructions

Row 1: Shell in 2nd ch from hook; *sk next 3 chs, shell in next ch; rep from * across to last 4 chs; sk next 3 chs, sc in last ch; ch 3, turn.

Row 2: 2 dc in first sc; *shell in next ch-2 sp; rep from * across to last ch-2 sp; sc in last ch-2 sp; ch 3, turn.

Row 3: 2 dc in first sc; *shell in next ch-2 sp; rep from * across to turning ch-3; sc in turning ch-3 sp; ch 3, turn.

Rep row 3 for patt.

Fascination

Chain multiple: 8 + 1

Stitch Guide

Shell: Work (3 dc, ch 3, 3 dc) all in same sp: shell made.

Instructions

Row 1: Sc in 2nd ch from hook and in each rem ch; ch 3, turn.

Row 2: Dc in next sc; *ch 1, sk next sc, dc in next sc; rep from * across to last sc, dc in last sc; ch 3 (counts as first dc of following row), turn.

Row 3: Dc in each dc and in each ch-1 sp across; ch 3, turn.

Row 4: Dc in next dc; *ch 1, sk next dc, dc in next dc; rep from * across to last dc, dc in turning ch; ch 3, turn.

Row 5: *Sk next dc, next ch-1 sp, and next dc; shell in next ch-1 sp, sk next dc, next ch-1 sp, and next dc; dc in next ch-1 sp; rep from * across, ending last rep with sk next dc, next ch-1 sp, and next dc; dc in top of turning ch; ch 3, turn.

Row 6: *Shell in ch-3 sp of next shell, dc in next dc; rep from * across, end last rep with dc in top of turning ch; ch 3, turn.

Rows 7 and 8: Rep row 6; at end of row 8, ch 6 (instead of 3), turn.

Row 9: Sc in ch-3 sp of next shell; *ch 3, dc in next dc, ch 3, sc in ch-3 sp of next shell; rep from * across, ending last rep with ch 3, dc in top of turning ch; ch 3, turn.

Row 10: Work (dc, ch 1, dc) in next ch-3 sp; *ch 1, (dc, ch 1, dc) in next ch-3 sp; rep from * across, dc in 3rd ch of turning ch; ch 3, turn.

Rep rows 3–10 for patt; end by working a row 3.

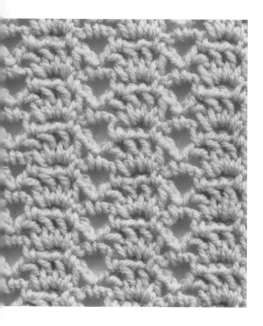

Grouped Shells

Chain multiple: 8 + 3

Stitch Guide

Shell: In specified lp work (dc, ch 1) 3 times, dc in same lp: shell made.

Instructions

Row 1: Sc in 5th ch from hook; *ch 3, sk next 3 chs, sc in next ch; rep from * across to last 2 chs; ch 1, sk next ch, hdc in last ch; ch 1, turn.

Row 2: Sc in first hdc, ch 1; *shell in next ch-3 lp, ch 1**; sc in next ch-3 lp, ch 1; rep from * across, ending last rep at **; sc in last ch-3 lp, ch 4, turn.

Row 3: Sk first ch-1 sp, sc in next ch-1 sp; *ch 3, sk next ch-1 sp, sc in next ch-1 sp**; ch 3, sk next 2 ch-1 sps, sc in next ch-1 sp; rep from * across, ending final rep at **; ch 1, dc in last sc; ch 1, turn.

Row 4: Sc in first dc, ch 1; *shell in next ch-3 sp, ch 1**, sc in next ch-3 sp, ch 1; rep from * across, ending last rep at **; sc in 3rd ch of turning ch-4; ch 4, turn.

Rep rows 3 and 4 for patt.

Single Shells

Chain multiple: 2 + 1

Stitch Guide

Shell: (Sc, ch 3, sc) all in same ch: shell made.

Instructions

Row 1: Dc in 5th ch from hook (skipped chs count as a dc and ch-1 sp); *ch 1, sk next ch, dc in next ch; rep from * across; ch 1, turn.

Row 2: *Sk next dc, shell in next ch-1 sp; rep from * across, end last rep with (sc, ch 1, dc) in turning ch-sp; ch 4, turn.

Row 3: *Dc in ch-3 sp of next shell, ch 1; rep from * across, end last rep with dc in ch-3 sp of last shell; ch 1, turn.

Rep rows 2 and 3 for patt.

Candelabra

Chain multiple: 8 + 2

Stitch Guide

Shell: In specified st work (dc, ch 1) twice, dc in same st: shell made.

Instructions

Row 1: Sc in 2nd ch from hook and in each rem ch; ch 4 (counts as first dc and ch-1 sp of following row throughout), turn.

Row 2: Sk next sc, dc in next sc; *ch 1, sk next sc, dc in next sc; rep from * across; ch 4, turn.

Row 3 (RS): Sk next ch-1 sp; *(dc in next dc and in next ch-1 sp) twice, dc in next dc**; ch 1, dc in next dc, ch 1, sk next ch-1 sp; rep from * across; end last rep at **; ch 1, dc in 3rd ch of turning ch; ch 4, turn.

Row 4: *Sk 2 dc, shell in center dc of next 5-dc group, ch 1, sk 2 dc, dc in next dc, ch 1; rep from * across, end last rep with dc in 3rd ch of turning ch; ch 4, turn.

Row 5: *Dc in each dc and in each ch-1 sp of next shell**; ch 1, dc in next dc, ch 1; rep from * across, ending last rep at **; ch 1, dc in 3rd ch of turning ch; ch 4, turn.

Row 6: *Dc in next dc; (ch 1, sk next dc, dc in next dc) twice, ch 1, dc in next dc, ch 1; rep from * across, ending last rep with dc in 3rd ch of turning ch-4; ch 4, turn.

Rep rows 3–6 for patt.

Lovely Shells

Chain multiple: 8 + 3

Stitch Guide

Shell: Work (dc, ch 1) 3 times in specified st, dc in same st: shell made.

Instructions

Row 1: Dc in 4th ch from hook and in each rem ch; ch 1, turn.

Row 2 (RS): Sc in first dc; *ch 1, sk next 3 dc, shell in next dc, ch 1, sk next 3 dc**, sc in next dc; rep from * across, ending last rep at **; sc in top of turning ch; ch 6, turn.

Row 3: Sc in center ch-1 sp of next shell; *ch 3, dc in next sc**; ch 3, sc in center ch-1 sp of next shell; rep from * across, ending last rep at **; ch 3, turn.

Row 4: *3 dc in next ch-3 sp, dc in next sc**; 3 dc in next ch-3 sp, dc in next dc; rep from * across, ending last rep at **; 3 dc in turning ch-6 lp, dc in 3rd ch of turning ch; ch 1, turn.

Rep rows 2–4 for patt.

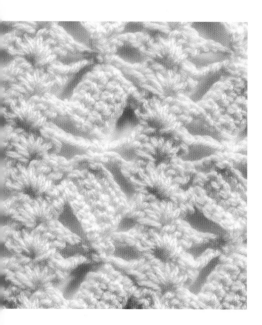

Twisting Blocks

Chain multiple: 12 + 4

Stitch Guide

Shell: Work (3 dc, ch 1, 3 dc) all in same st: shell made.

Instructions

Row 1: Work 2 dc in 4th ch from hook; *ch 3, sk 5 chs, sc in next ch, ch 3, sk 5 chs, shell in next ch; rep from * across, ending last rep with 3 dc (instead of shell) in last ch; ch 3 (counts as a dc of following row), turn.

Row 2: Work 2 dc in base of ch; *ch 3, sc in next sc, ch 3, shell in ch-1 sp of next shell; rep from * across, ending last rep with 3 dc (instead of shell) in top of turning ch; ch 3, turn.

Row 3: Work 2 dc in base of ch; *ch 6 to form base of block; sc in 2nd ch from hook and in each rem ch; ch 1, turn; (sc in each of 5 sc, ch 1, turn) twice; hdc in next sc on prev row, ch 1, turn; sc in each of 5 sc on block, turn; work shell in ch-1 sp of next shell; rep from * across, ending last rep with 3 dc (instead of shell) in top of turning ch; ch 3, turn.

Row 4: Work 2 dc in base of ch; *ch 3, sc in point of block, ch 3, shell in ch-1 sp of next shell; rep from * across, ending last rep with 3 dc in top of turning ch; ch 3, turn.

Row 5: Work 2 dc in base of ch; *ch 3, sc in next sc, ch 3, shell in ch-1 sp of next shell; rep from * across, ending last rep with 3 dc in top of turning ch; ch 3, turn.

Rep rows 3–5 for patt.

Precision

Chain multiple: 8 + 2

Stitch Guide

Shell: Work (2 dc, ch 1, 2 dc) all in same ch or sp: shell made.

Instructions

Row 1: Sc in 2nd ch from hook and in each rem ch; ch 4 (counts as a dc and ch-1 sp of following row), turn.

Row 2: Sk 3 sc; *shell in next sc, ch 1, sk 3 sc, dc in next dc, ch 1, sk 3 sc; rep from * across to last 5 sc, shell in next sc, ch 1, sk 3 sc, dc in last sc; ch 4, turn.

Row 3: *Shell in ch-1 sp of next shell, ch 1, dc in next dc, ch 1; rep from * across, ending last rep with shell in ch-1 sp of last shell, ch 1, dc in 3rd ch of turning ch; ch 4, turn.

Rep row 3 for patt.

Diamond Loops

Chain multiple: 10 + 9

Stitch Guide

Shell: Work 3 dc in specified ch or st: shell made.

Instructions

Row 1: Dc in 4th ch from hook; *ch 3, sk 4 chs, dc in next ch; ch 3, sk 4 chs, 3 dc in next ch; rep from * across to last 5 chs, ch 3, sk 4 chs, dc in last ch; ch 5 (counts as a dc and ch-2 sp), turn.

Row 2: *Work 2 dc in first dc of shell, dc in next dc, 2 dc in next dc; ch 2, dc in next dc, ch 2; rep from * across, ending last rep with 2 dc in last dc, dc in top of turning ch; ch 3 (counts as first dc of following row), turn.

Row 3: Sk next dc, shell in next dc; *ch 3, sk next dc, shell in next dc, ch 1, sk 3 dc, shell in next dc; rep from * across, ending last rep with ch 1, dc in 3rd ch of turning ch 5; ch 6 (counts as a dc and ch-3 sp), turn.

Row 4: Sk first ch-1 sp; *shell in next ch-1 sp, ch 3, dc in next ch-3 sp, ch 3; rep from * across, ending last rep with 2 dc in top of turning ch; ch 6, turn.

Row 5: *Shell in next dc, ch 3, dc in center dc of next shell, ch 3; rep from * across, ending last rep with 2 dc in 3rd ch of turning ch-6; ch 3, turn.

Row 6: 2 dc in next dc; *ch 2, dc in next dc, ch 2, 2 dc in next dc, dc in next dc, 2 dc in next dc; rep from * across, ending with ch 2, dc in 3rd ch of turning ch-6; ch 4, turn.

Row 7: *Shell in next dc, ch 1, sk 3 dc, shell in next dc, ch 3, sk next dc; rep from * across, ending last rep with 3 dc in next dc, ch 1, dc in top of turning ch; ch 3, turn.

Row 8: Dc in base of ch; *ch 3, dc in next ch-3 sp, ch 3, shell in next ch-1 sp; rep from * across, ending last rep with ch 3, dc in 3rd ch of turning ch; ch 3, turn.

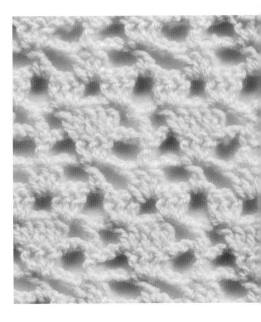

Row 9: Dc in base of ch; *ch 3, dc in center dc of next shell, ch 3, shell in next dc; rep from * across, ending last rep with ch 3, dc in top of turning ch; ch 5, turn.

Rep rows 2–9 for patt.

Boxed In

Chain multiple: 18 + 9

Stitch Guide

Shell: Work (2 dc, ch 2, 2 dc) all in same st: shell made.

Instructions

Row 1 (RS): Work shell in 6th ch from hook, sk 2 chs, dc in next ch; *sk 2 chs, shell in next ch, sk 2 chs, dc in next ch; rep from * across; ch 3, turn.

Row 2: *Shell in ch-2 sp of next shell, dc in next dc; rep from * across, ending last rep with dc in top of turning ch; ch 3, turn.

Row 3: *Shell in ch-2 sp of next shell, (dc in next dc, ch 2, dc in ch-2 sp of next shell, ch 2) twice, dc in next dc; rep from * across, ending last rep with shell in ch-2 sp of last shell, dc in top of turning ch; ch 3, turn.

Rows 4–6: Rep Row 3.

Row 7: Shell in ch-2 sp of next shell; *dc in next dc; (shell in next dc, dc in next dc) twice, shell in ch-2 sp of next shell; rep from * across, ending with dc in top of turning ch; ch 3, turn.

Rep rows 2–7 for patt.

Triangular

Chain multiple: 12 + 2

Stitch Guide

Shell: Work 3 dc in specified ch or st: shell made.

Double triple crochet (dtr): YO 3 times; insert hook in specified st and draw up a lp; (YO and draw through 2 lps) 4 times: dtr made.

Instructions

Row 1: Sc in 2nd ch from hook; *ch 5, sk 5 chs, shell in next ch, ch 5, sk 5 chs, sc in next ch; rep from * across; ch 6, turn.

Row 2: *Shell in next dc, dc in next dc, shell in next dc, ch 3, dc in next sc, ch 3; rep from * across, ending last rep with dc in last sc; ch 5, turn.

Row 3: *Shell in first dc of shell group, dc in each of next 5 dc, shell in next dc**, ch 1; rep from * across, ending last rep at **; dtr in 3rd ch of ch-6 turning ch; ch 3, turn.

Row 4: Dc in dtr; *ch 5, sk 5 dc, sc in next dc, ch 5, 3 dc in next ch-1 sp; rep from * across, ending last rep with ch 5, sk 5 dc, sc in next dc, ch 5, 2 dc in top of turning ch-5; ch 3, turn.

Row 5: 3 dc in next dc; *ch 3, dc in next sc, ch 3, 3 dc in next dc**, dc in next dc, 3 dc in next dc; rep from * across, ending last rep at **, dc in top of turning ch; ch 3, turn.

Row 6: Dc in each of next 2 dc, 3 dc in next dc, ch 1; *3 dc in first dc of next shell group, dc in each of next 5 dc, 3 dc in next dc, ch 1; rep from * across, ending last rep with 3 dc in first dc of shell group, dc in each of next 2 dc, dc in top of turning ch; ch 1, turn.

Row 7: Sc in first dc; *ch 5, 3 dc in next ch-1 sp, ch 5**, sk 5 dc, sc in next dc; rep from * across, ending last rep at **, sc in top of turning ch; ch 6, turn.

Rep rows 2–7 for patt; end by working a row 4 or a row 6.

Shells

Chain multiple: 5 + 3

Stitch Guide

Shell: Work 5 dc all in same st: shell made.

Instructions

Row 1: Dc in 4th ch from hook; *ch 2, sk 2 chs, dc in each of next 3 chs; rep from * across to last 4 chs, ch 2, sk 2 chs, dc in each of last 2 chs; ch 1, turn.

Row 2: Sc in first dc; *shell in next ch-2 sp, sk next dc, sc in next dc, sk next dc; rep from * across, ending last rep with sk last dc, sc in top of turning ch; ch 4, turn.

Row 3: *Sk first dc of shell, dc in each of next 3 dc of shell, sk last dc of shell, ch 2; rep from * across, ending last rep with ch 1 (instead of ch 2), tr in last sc; ch 3, turn.

Row 4: Work 2 dc in base of ch; *sk next dc, sc in next dc**, sk next dc, shell in next ch-2 sp; rep from * across, ending last rep at **; work 3 dc in top of turning ch; ch 3, turn.

Row 5: Sk first dc, dc in next dc, sk next dc; *ch 2, sk next dc of shell, dc in next 3 dc of shell, sk next dc of shell; rep from * across, ending last rep with ch 2, sk next dc, dc in next dc and in top of turning ch; ch 1, turn.

Rep rows 2–5 for patt.

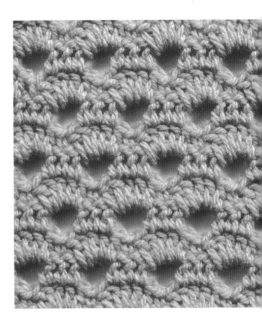

Royal Shells

Chain multiple: 21 + 8

Stitch Guide

Shell: Work (dc, ch 1) 5 times in same st, dc in same st or sp: shell made.

Instructions

Row 1: Sc in 2nd ch from hook and in each rem ch; ch 5 (counts as a dc and ch-2 sp on following row), turn.

Row 2: Sk 2 sc, dc in next sc, ch 2, sk 2 sc, dc in next sc; *ch 4, sk 5 sc, 3 dc in next sc, ch 3, sk 2 sc, 3 dc in next sc, ch 4; sk 5 sc, (dc in next sc, ch 2, sk 2 sc) 2 times, dc in next sc; rep from * across; ch 5, turn.

Row 3: Dc in next dc, ch 2, dc in next dc; *ch 2, shell in next ch-3 sp, ch 2, sk next 3 dc, (dc in next dc, ch 2) twice, dc in next dc; rep from * across, ending last rep with dc in 3rd ch of turning ch, ch 5, turn.

Row 4: Dc in next dc, ch 2, dc in next dc; *(work 3 dc in next ch-1 sp of shell) 5 times; (dc in next dc, ch 2) twice, dc in next dc; rep from * across, ending last rep with dc in 3rd ch of turning ch, ch 5, turn.

Row 5: Dc in next dc, ch 2, dc in next dc; *ch 4, sk next 3-dc group, work 3 dc between next two 3-dc groups; ch 3, work 3 dc between next two 3-dc groups, ch 4, sk last two 3-dc groups; (dc in next dc, ch 2) twice, dc in next dc; rep from * across, ending last rep with dc in 3rd ch of turning ch, ch 5, turn.

Rep rows 3–5 for patt.

Elegant Shells

Chain multiple: 8 + 3

Stitch Guide

Shell: In specified st work (dc, ch 1) 6 times, dc in same st: shell made.

Instructions

Row 1 (RS): Dc in 5th ch from hook; *ch 1, sk next ch, dc in next ch; rep from * across; ch 1, turn.

Row 2: Sc in each dc and in each ch-1 sp across, end with sc in turning ch-sp and sc in top of turning ch; ch 1, turn.

Row 3: Sc in first sc; *sk 3 sc, work shell in next sc, sk 3 sc, sc in next sc; rep from * across; ch 3, turn.

Row 4: *Sk next ch-1 sp of shell, sc in next ch-1 sp, ch 1, sc in next ch-1 sp, ch 3, sc in next ch-1 sp, ch 1, sc in next ch-1 sp**, sk last ch-1 sp of shell, ch 1; rep from * across, ending last rep at **; dc in last sc; ch 1, turn.

Row 5: Sc in dc; *work shell in next ch-3 sp**, sc in ch-1 sp before next shell; rep from * across, ending last rep at **; sc in top of turning ch; ch 3, turn.

Row 6: *Sk next ch-1 sp; (sc in next ch-1 sp, ch 1) 3 times, sc in next ch-1 sp**, ch 1; rep from * across, ending last rep at **; dc in last sc; ch 1, turn.

Row 7: Sc in first dc; sc in each sc and in each ch-1 sp across, ending with sc in top of turning ch; ch 4, turn.

Row 8: Sk first sc, dc in next sc; *ch 1, sk next sc, dc in next dc; rep from * across, ending last rep with dc in last sc; ch 1, turn.

Rep rows 2–8 for patt.

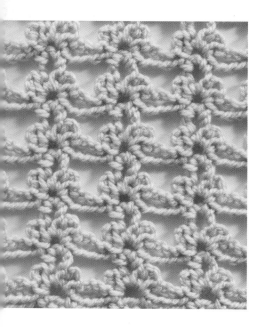

Floral Medley

Chain multiple: 7 + 1

Stitch Guide

Shell: Work (sc, ch 3, sc, ch 5, sc, ch 3, sc) all in same lp: shell made.

Instructions

Row 1: Sc in 2nd ch from hook, ch 1, sk next ch, sc in next ch, ch 3, sk next ch, sc in next ch; *ch 4, sk 4 chs, sc in next ch, ch 3, sk next ch, sc in next ch; rep from * across, ending last rep with ch 1, sk next ch, sc in last ch; ch 1, turn.

Row 2: Sc in first sc, ch 1; *work shell in next ch-3 sp, ch 4; rep from * across, ending last rep with shell in last ch-3 sp, ch 1, sc in last sc; ch 5, turn.

Row 3: *In next ch-5 lp of shell work (sc, ch 3, sc), ch 4; rep from * across, ending last rep with ch 1 (instead of ch 4), tr in last sc; ch 1, turn.

Row 4: Sc in tr, ch 1; *work shell in next ch-3 sp, ch 4; rep from * across, ending last rep with ch 1 (instead of ch 4), sc in 4th ch of turning ch; ch 5, turn.

Rep rows 3 and 4 for patt.

Openwork

Chain multiple: 5 + 1

Stitch Guide

Shell: In same st work (tr, ch 1) twice, tr: shell made.

Instructions

Row 1: Sc in 2nd ch from hook and in each rem ch; ch 7 (counts as a dc and ch-4 sp), turn.

Row 2: *Sk 4 sc, dc in next sc, ch 4; rep from * across, ch 5 (counts as a tr and ch-1 sp), turn.

Row 3: Tr in base of ch; *shell in next dc; rep from * across, ending last rep with (tr, ch 1, tr) in 3rd ch of turning ch; ch 7, turn.

Row 4: Dc in center tr of next shell; *ch 4, dc in center tr of next shell; rep from * across, ending last rep with dc in 4th ch of turning ch; ch 5, turn.

Rep rows 3 and 4 for patt.

Fan Mesh

Chain multiple: 12 + 8

Stitch Guide

Shell: Work 5 dc in specified st: shell made.

Instructions

Row 1: Sc in 8th ch from hook; *ch 5, sk 3 chs, sc in next ch; rep from * across; ch 5, turn.

Row 2: *Sc in next ch-5 lp, ch 5; rep from * across, ending last rep with sc in turning ch-lp; ch 5, turn.

Row 3: Sc in ch-5 lp; *shell in next sc, sc in next ch-5 lp; (ch 5, sc in next ch-5 lp) twice; rep from * across, ending last rep with sc in turning ch-lp; ch 5, turn.

Row 4: Sc in ch-5 lp, ch 5, sc in ch-5 lp; *ch 5, sc in center dc of shell, (ch 5, sc in next ch-5 lp) twice; rep from * across, ending last rep with sc in turning ch-lp; ch 5, turn.

Row 5: Sc in ch-5 lp; *ch 5, sc in next ch-5 lp; rep from * across, ending last rep with sc in turning ch-lp; ch 5, turn.

Rep rows 3–5 for patt.

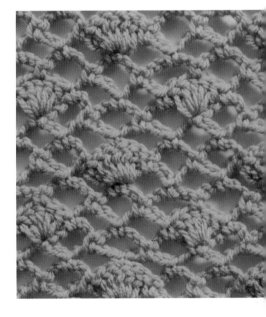

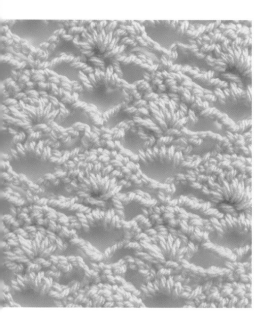

Fanciful Fans

Chain multiple: 10 + 2

Stitch Guide

Shell: In specified st work (dc, ch 1) twice, dc in same st: shell made.

Instructions

Row 1: Sc in 2nd ch from hook and in next ch; *ch 3, sk 3 chs, shell in next ch, ch 3, sk 3 chs, sc in each of next 3 chs; rep from * across, ending last rep with sc in last 2 (instead of 3) chs; ch 1, turn.

Row 2 (RS): Sc in first sc; *ch 3, work 7 dc in center dc of next shell, ch 3, sc in center sc of next 3-sc group; rep from * across, ending last rep with sc in last sc; ch 6, turn.

Row 3: *Sc in each of next 7 dc, ch 5; rep from * across, ending last rep with sc in each of last 7 dc, ch 2, tr in last sc; ch 4, turn.

Row 4: Dc in base of ch; *ch 3, sk 2 sc, sc in each of next 3 sc, ch 3, sk 2 sc, shell in next ch-5 sp; rep from * across, ending last rep with ch 3, (dc, ch 1, dc) in 4th ch of turning ch; ch 3, turn.

Row 5: Work 3 dc in ch-1 sp; *ch 3, sk next sc, sc in next sc, sk next sc, ch 3**, work 7 dc in center dc of next shell; rep from * across, ending last rep at **; work 4 dc in turning ch-sp; ch 1, turn.

Row 6: Sc in each of first 4 dc; *ch 5, sc in each of next 7 dc; rep from * across, ending last rep with sc in last 3 dc, sc in top of turning ch; ch 1, turn.

Row 7: Sc in each of next 2 sc; *ch 3, shell in next ch-5 sp, ch 3, sc in each of center 3 dc of next 7-sc group; rep from * across, ending last rep with sc in each of last 2 sc; ch 1, turn.

Rep rows 2–7 for patt.

Open Shells

Chain multiple: 8 + 2
Two colors: color A and color B

Stitch Guide

Shell: Work (3 dc, ch 5, 3 dc) all in same st: shell made.

Instructions

Work beg ch with color A.

Row 1: With color A, sc in 2nd ch from hook; *sk 3 chs, shell in next ch, sk 3 chs, sc in next ch; rep from * across; ch 4, turn.

Row 2: Sk 2 dc; *dc in next dc; ch 3, sc in ch-5 sp of next shell, ch 3, dc in next dc, sk next 4 dc; rep from * across, ending last rep with tr in sc, changing to color B in last st; with color B, ch 1, turn. Drop color A.

Row 3: With color B, sc in tr; *shell in next sc, sc between next 2 dc; rep from * across, ending last rep with sc in top of turning ch; ch 4, turn.

Row 4: With color B, sk 2 dc; *dc in next dc, ch 3, sc in ch-5 sp of next shell, ch 3, dc in next dc, sk next 4 dc; rep from * across, ending last rep with tr in sc, changing to color A in last st; with color A, ch 1, turn. Drop color B.

Rep rows 3 and 4 for patt, alternating two rows of color A with two rows of color B.

Chain Gang

Chain multiple: 12 + 2

Stitch Guide

Shell: In specified st work (sc, ch 7) 3 times, sc in same st: shell made.

Instructions

Row 1: Sc in 2nd ch from hook and in each rem ch; ch 1, turn.

Row 2: Sc in first sc; *ch 3, sk 3 sc, (sc in next sc, ch 1, sk next sc) twice, sc in next sc; ch 3, sk 3 sc, sc in next sc; rep from * across to last 4 sc, ch 3, sk 3 sc, sc in last sc; ch 8, (counts as a dc and ch-5 lp of following row), turn.

Row 3: *Sk next sc and next ch-1 sp, shell in next sc, ch 5, sk next ch-1 sp and next sc, dc in next sc, ch 5; rep from * across, ending last rep with dc in last sc; ch 1, turn.

Row 4: Sc in first dc; *ch 1, sc in next ch-7 lp, (ch 3, sc in next ch-7 lp) twice, ch 1, sc in next dc; rep from * across, ending last rep with ch 1, sc in 3rd ch of turning ch-8; ch 7, turn.

Row 5: In first sc work (sc, ch 7, sc), ch 5; sk next sc, dc in next sc, ch 5; *sk next sc and ch-1 sp, shell in next sc, ch 5, sk next ch-1 sp and next sc, dc in next sc, ch 5; rep from * across to last sc, in last sc work (sc, ch 7, sc, ch 3, tr); ch 1, turn.

Row 6: Sc in tr, ch 3, sc in ch-7 lp, ch 1, sc in dc; *ch 1, sc in ch-7 lp; (ch 3, sc in next ch-7 lp) twice, ch 1, sc in dc; rep from * across, ending last rep with ch 1, sc in last ch-7 lp, ch 3, sc in turning ch-7 lp; ch 8, turn.

Rep rows 3–6 for patt.

Coral Reef

Chain multiple: 8 + 5

Stitch Guide

Shell: In same st work (sc, ch 5) 3 times, sc: shell made.

V-stitch (V-st): Work (dc, ch 1, dc) in same st: V-st made.

Instructions

Row 1: Dc in 5th ch from hook; *ch 3, sk 3 chs, shell in next ch; ch 3, sk 3 chs, V-st in next ch; rep from * across; ch 6 (counts as a dc and 3 chs of following row), turn.

Row 2: Work (sc, ch 5, sc) in ch-1 sp of V-st; *ch 3, V-st in center ch-5 lp of next shell, ch 3**; work shell in ch-1 sp of next V-st; rep from * across, ending last rep at **; in top of turning ch work (sc, ch 5, dc); ch 4, turn.

Row 3: Dc in dc; *ch 3, shell in ch-1 sp of next V-st, ch 3**, V-st in center ch-5 lp of next shell; rep from * across, ending last rep at **; work V-st in turning ch-sp; ch 6, turn.

Rep rows 2 and 3 for patt.

Crossing Bridges

Chain multiple: 6 + 2

Stitch Guide

Shell: Work (sc, hdc, 5 dc, hdc, sc) in specified lp; shell made.

Instructions

Row 1: Dc in 4th ch from hook and in each rem ch; ch 1, turn.

Row 2: Sc in first dc; *ch 6, sk 5 dc, sc in next dc; rep from * across, working last sc in top of turning ch; ch 1, turn.

Row 3: Sc in first sc; *work shell in next ch-6 sp; rep from * across, ending last rep with sc in last sc; ch 5 (counts as a dc and ch-2 sp), turn.

Row 4: *Sc in center dc of next shell, ch 5; rep from * across, ending last rep with sc in center dc of next shell, ch 2, dc in last sc; ch 3 (counts as a dc of following row), turn.

Row 5: Work 2 dc in ch-2 sp; *dc in next sc, 5 dc in next ch-5 sp; rep from * across, ending last rep with 2 dc in ch-5 sp, dc in 3rd ch of turning ch-5; ch 1, turn.

Rep rows 2–5 for patt.

Stitches in Time

Chain multiple: 10 + 4

Stitch Guide

Shell: In specified sp work (dc, ch 1) twice, dc in same sp: shell made.

Instructions

Row 1: Dc in 5th ch from hook, ch 3, sk 2 chs, sc in next ch; ch 1, sk next ch, sc in next ch; *ch 3, sk 2 chs, dc in next ch, ch 1, sk next ch, dc in next ch; ch 3, sk 2 chs, sc in next ch; ch 1, sk next ch, sc in next ch; rep from * across to last 4 chs, ch 3, sk 2 chs, dc in each of last 2 chs; ch 1, turn.

Row 2: Sc in first dc; *ch 3, shell in next ch-1 sp, ch 3, sc in next ch-1 sp; rep from * across, ending last rep with sc in top of turning ch; ch 1, turn.

Row 3: Sc in first sc and in ch-3 sp; *ch 3, dc in first ch-1 sp of shell, ch 1, dc in 2nd ch-1 sp of shell; ch 3, sc in ch-3 sp, ch 1, sk sc, sc in next ch-3 sp; rep from * across, ending last rep with sc in last sc; ch 4 (counts as a dc and ch-1 sp), turn.

Row 4: Dc in base of ch; *ch 3, sc in ch-1 sp, ch 3, shell in next ch-1 sp; rep from * across, ending last rep with ch 3, sc in ch-1 sp, ch 3, (dc, ch 1, dc) in last sc; ch 3, turn.

Row 5: Dc in first ch-1 sp; *ch 3, sc in ch-3 sp, ch 1, sk next sc, sc in ch-3 sp; ch 3, dc in first ch-1 sp of shell, ch 1, dc in 2nd ch-1 sp of shell; rep from * across, ending last rep with dc in turning ch-sp, dc in 3rd ch of turning ch; ch 1, turn.

Rep rows 2–5 for patt.

Hot Toddy

Chain multiple: 7 + 3

Stitch Guide

Shell: Work (2 dc, ch 2, 2 dc) all in same sp: shell made.

Instructions

Row 1: Sc in 6th ch from hook; *ch 3, sk 2 chs, sc in next ch**; ch 4, sk 3 chs, sc in next ch; rep from * across, ending last rep **; ch 2, dc in last ch; ch 1, turn.

Row 2: Sc in dc; *shell in next ch-3 sp, sc in next ch-4 sp; rep from * across, ending last rep with shell in last ch-3 sp, sc in turning ch-sp; ch 3, turn.

Row 3: Dc in base of ch; *ch 1, work 2 dc in ch-2 sp of next shell, ch 1, 2 dc in next sc; rep from * across; ch 5, turn.

Row 4: Sc in next ch-1 sp; *ch 3, sc in next ch-1 sp**, ch 4, sc in next ch-1 sp; rep from * across, ending last rep at **; ch 2, dc in top of turning ch; ch 1, turn.

Rep rows 2–4 for patt.

Fountains

Chain multiple: 16 + 12

Stitch Guide

Shell: Work 4 dc in specified st: shell made.

Instructions

Row 1: Work 3 dc in 4th ch from hook, sk 7 chs, shell in next ch; *ch 4, sk 3 chs, sc in next ch; ch 4, sk 3 chs, shell in next ch, sk 7 chs, shell in next ch; rep from * across; ch 3, turn.

Row 2: Work 3 dc in base of ch, sk first shell, shell in last dc of next shell; *ch 5, sc in next sc, ch 5, shell in next dc, shell in last dc of next shell; rep from * across, ending last rep with shell in top of turning ch; ch 3, turn.

Row 3: Work 3 dc in base of ch, shell in last dc of next shell; *ch 6, sc in next sc, ch 6, shell in next dc, shell in last dc of next shell; rep from * across, ending last rep with shell in top of turning ch; ch 7, turn.

Row 4: Sc between first 2 shells, ch 4; *shell in last dc of next shell, shell in first dc of next shell, ch 4, sc between next 2 shells, ch 4; rep from * across, ending last rep with dc in top of turning ch; ch 8, turn.

Row 5: Sc in next sc, ch 5; *shell in first dc of next shell, shell in last dc of next shell; ch 5, sc in next sc, ch 5; rep from * across, ending last rep with dc in 3rd ch of turning ch; ch 9, turn.

Row 6: Sc in first sc, ch 6; *shell in first dc of next shell, shell in last dc of next shell; ch 6, sc in next sc, ch 6; rep from * across, ending last rep with dc in 3rd ch of turning ch; ch 3, turn.

Row 7: Work 3 dc in base of ch, shell in first dc of next shell; *ch 3, sc between next 2 shells, ch 3, shell in last dc of next shell**; shell in first dc of next shell; rep from * across, ending last rep at **; work 4 dc in 3rd ch of turning ch; ch 3, turn.

Rep rows 2–7 for patt.

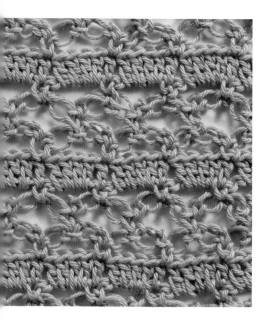

Lover's Knot

Chain multiple: 5 + 3

Instructions

Row 1 (WS): Dc in 4th ch from hook and in each rem ch; ch 1, turn.

Row 2: Sc in first dc; *(draw up lp on hook to measure ½", YO and draw through lp; insert hook between the ½" lp and the single strand behind it and work sc over single strand) twice: knot st made; sk next 4 dc, sk in next dc: knot st lp made; rep from * across working last sc in top of turning ch; ch 3, turn.

Row 3: *Draw up lp on hook to measure ½", YO and draw through lp on hook, insert hook between the lp and the single strand behind it and work sc over single strand as before*, sc in center sc of knot st lp; †rep from * to * twice more, sc in center sc of next knot st lp; rep from † across; end with rep from * to * once, dc in last sc; ch 1, turn.

Row 4: Sc in first dc, ch 4, sk first knot st, sc in center sc of first knot st lp; *ch 4, sc in center sc of next knot st lp; rep from * across, ch 4, sc in top of turning ch; ch 3, turn.

Row 5: *4 dc in ch-4 sp, dc in next sc; rep from * across; ch 1, turn.

Rep rows 2–5 for patt.

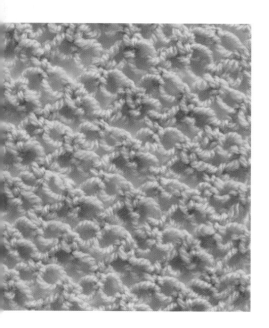

Solomon's Knot

Chain multiple: 5 + 2

Instructions

Row 1 (WS): Sc in 2nd ch from hook; †*draw up lp on hook to measure ½", YO and draw through lp on hook, insert hook between the ½" lp and the single strand behind it and work sc over single strand*: knot st made; rep between * and * once more, sk next 4 chs, sc in next ch: knot st lp made; rep from † across, ch 3, turn.

Row 2: *Draw up lp on hook to measure ½", YO and draw through lp on hook, insert hook between the ½" lp and the single strand behind it and work sc as before*, sc in center sc of knot st lp; †rep between * and * twice, sc in center sc of next knot st lp; rep from † across; rep between * and * once, dc in last sc; ch 1, turn.

Row 3: Sc in first dc; †rep between * and * of row 2 twice, sc in center sc of next knot st lp; rep from † across, end last rep with sc in top of turning ch; ch 3, turn.

Rep rows 2 and 3 for patt.

Fancy Filet

Chain multiple: any even number

Instructions

Row 1 (WS): Dc in 6th ch from hook; *ch 1, sk 1 ch, dc in next ch; rep from * across; ch 3, turn.

Row 2 (star-st row): Draw up a lp in 2nd ch from hook, draw up a lp in next ch, draw up a lp in ch-1 sp, draw up a lp in next dc, YO and draw through all 5 lps on hook, ch 1 for "eye" of star: star st made; *draw up a lp in eye of star just made, draw up a lp in last lp on same star st, draw up a lp in ch-1 sp, draw up a lp in next dc, YO and draw through all 5 lps on hook, ch 1; rep from * across, working last rep until 3 lps on hook, draw up a lp in last sp, sk one st of ch, draw up a lp in next ch, YO and draw through all 5 lps, ch 1; ch 3, turn.

Row 3: Dc in eye of 2nd star; *ch 1, dc in eye of next star; rep from * across, end ch 1, dc in top of last star; ch 3, turn.

Rep rows 2 and 3 for patt.

Crosses and Losses

Chain multiple: 9 + 4

Stitch Guide

Cross stitch (CS): Sk next st, dc in next st; working in front of st just made, dc in skipped st: CS made.

Front-post double crochet (FPdc): YO, insert hook from front to back to front around post (vertical bar) of specified st, YO and draw up a lp; (YO and draw through 2 lps) twice; YO and draw through 3 lps: FPdc made.

Back-post double crochet (BPdc): YO, insert hook from back to front to back around post (vertical bar) of specified st, YO and draw up a lp; (YO and draw through 2 lps) twice; YO and draw through 3 lps: BPdc made.

Instructions

Row 1: Sc in 2nd ch from hook and in each rem ch; ch 3, turn.

Row 2 (RS): Dc in next 3 sts; *(CS over next 2 sts) twice; dc in next 5 sts; rep from * across, end dc in last 4 sts instead of 5; ch 3, turn.

Row 3: Dc in next 2 dc, BPdc around next dc; *(CS over next 2 sts) twice, BPdc around next dc, dc in next 3 dc, BPdc around next dc; rep from * across, end dc in last 3 sts; ch 3, turn.

Row 4: Dc in next 2 dc, FPdc around next dc; *CS over next 2 sts) twice, FPdc around next dc, dc in next 3 dc, FPdc around next dc; rep from * across, end dc in last 3 sts, ch 3, turn.

Rep rows 3 and 4 for patt.

Twist and Turn

Chain multiple: 7 + 4

Instructions

Row 1: Sc in 2nd ch from hook and in each rem ch; ch 3 (counts as first dc of following row throughout), turn.

Row 2 (RS): Dc in next 2 sts; *sk next 2 sts, tr in next 2 sts; working behind 2 tr just made, tr in first skipped st, then tr in next skipped st; dc in next 3 sts; sk next 2 sts, tr in next 2 sts; working in front of 2 tr just made, tr in first skipped st, tr in next skipped st; dc in next 3 sts; rep from * across; ch 1, turn.

Row 3: Sc in each st across, ch 3, turn.

Rep rows 2 and 3 for patt.

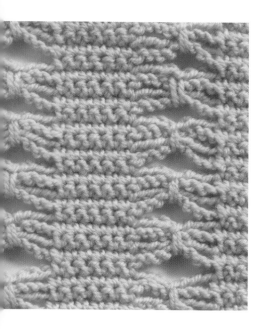

Bow Ties

Chain multiple: 13 + 1

Instructions

Row 1 (RS): Sc in 2nd ch from hook and in each rem ch; ch 1, turn.

Row 2: Sc in first 3 sc; *ch 8, sk next 7 sc, sc in next 6 sc; rep from * to last 3 sc, sc in last 3 sc; ch 1, turn.

Rows 3 and 4: Sc in first 3 sc; *ch 8, sc in next 6 sc; rep from * to last 3 sc, sc in last 3 sc; ch 1, turn.

Row 5: Sc in first 3 sc; *ch 3, sl st around all 3 ch-8 lps below, ch 3, sc in next 6 sc; rep from * to last 3 sc, sc in last 3 sc; ch 1, turn.

Row 6: Sc in first 3 sc, *ch 8, sc in next 6 sc; rep from * to last 3 sts, sc in last 3 sc; ch 1, turn.

Rep rows 3–6 for patt.

Final row: Sc in first 3 sc; *7 sc in ch-8 sp, sc in next 6 sc; rep from * across, sc in last 3 sc.

Hexagons

Chain multiple: 10 + 9

Instructions

Row 1 (RS): Dc in 4th ch from hook and in each of next 4 chs; *ch 5, sk next 5 chs, dc in next 5 chs; rep from * across to last ch, dc in last ch; ch 3 (counts as first dc of following row), turn.

Row 2: Dc in next 5 dc; *ch 5, sk next ch-5 lp, dc in next 5 dc; rep from * to last st, dc in top of turning ch; ch 3, turn.

Row 3: Dc in next 5 dc; *ch 3, insert hook under both ch-5 lps of 2 rows below and work 1 sc, ch 3; dc in each of next 5 dc; rep from * to last st, dc in top of turning ch; ch 3, turn.

Row 4: Dc in next 5 dc; *ch 5, dc in next 5 dc; rep from * across to last st, dc in top of turning ch; ch 3, turn.

Rep rows 2–4 for patt.

Little Baskets

Chain multiple: 4 + 2

Stitch Guide

Basket stitch (BS): Working horizontally around post (vertical bar) of specified dc, work (sc, hdc, 2 dc, tr): BS made.

Instructions

Row 1 (RS): Sc in 2nd ch from hook and in each rem ch; ch 3 (counts as a dc on following rows), turn.

Row 2: Dc in each sc, ch 1, turn.

Row 3: Sc in first dc, BS around next dc, * sk next 2 dc, sc in next dc; BS around post of last dc; rep from * across, ch 3, turn.

Row 4: Dc in each st behind each BS and in each sc; ch 1, turn.

Row 5: Sc in each st across, ch 3, turn.

Rep rows 2–5 for patt.

Puffy Blocks

Chain multiple: 5 + 3

Stitch Guide

Block stitch (BS): Dc in specified st; (YO, insert hook from front to back to front around post [vertical bar] of dc just made and draw up a lp, YO and draw through 2 lps on hook) 4 times; YO and draw through all 5 lps on hook: BS made.

Instructions

Row 1: Sc in 2nd ch from hook and in each rem ch; ch 1, turn.

Row 2: Sc in each sc across, ch 3 (counts as first dc of following row), turn.

Row 3 (RS): Dc in next sc; *ch 1, sk next sc, BS in next sc; ch 1, sk next sc, dc in each of next 2 sc; rep from * across, ch 1, turn.

Row 4: Sc in each dc, each ch-1 sp, and in top of each BS across row; ch 1, turn.

Row 5: Sc in each sc across; ch 1, turn.

Row 6: Sc in each sc across, ch 3, turn.

Rep rows 3–6 for patt.

Diamonds

Chain multiple: 5+1

Stitch Guide

Petal: Work (dc, ch 3, sl st, ch 3, dc) all in specified ch or ch-1 sp: petal made.

Instructions

Row 1 (RS): Dc in 4th ch from hook; *ch 1, sk 4 chs, work petal in next ch; rep from * to last 2 chs, sk next ch, dc in last ch; ch 3, turn.

Row 2: Dc in first dc; *ch 1, work petal in ch-1 sp between next 2 petals; rep from * across, end last rep with petal in last ch-1 sp, sk next dc, dc in top of turning ch; ch 3, turn.

Rep row 2 for patt.

Final row: Sc in first dc; *ch 4, sc in ch-1 sp between petals; rep from * across, end last rep with ch 2, sk next dc, sc in top of turning ch.

Niches

Chain multiple: 11 + 4

Instructions

Row 1: Sc in 2nd ch from hook and in each rem ch; ch 1, turn.

Row 2 (RS): Sc in each sc, ch 1, turn.

Row 3: Sc in each sc, ch 3, turn.

Row 4: Dc in next 2 sc; *sk next 2 sc, tr in next 2 sc; working behind 2 tr just made, tr in 2 skipped sc; sk next 2 sc, tr in next 2 sc; working in front of 2 tr just made, tr in 2 skipped sc; dc in next 3 sc; rep from * across; ch 3, turn.

Row 5: Rep row 4; at end, ch 1 instead of 3, turn.

Rep rows 2–5 for patt.

Slanted Stitch

Chain multiple: 4 + 2

Instructions

Row 1: Sc in 2nd ch from hook and in each rem ch; ch 1, turn.

Row 2 (RS): Sc in each sc, ch 1, turn.

Row 3: Sc in first sc; *ch 4, sk next 3 sc, sc in next sc; rep from * across; ch 4 (counts as first tr of following row), turn.

Row 4: *2 tr in next ch-4 sp; in sp to right of first tr made work 4 dc; rep from * across, end with tr in last sc; ch 4, turn.

Row 5: *Sk next 3 dc and next tr, sc in next tr, ch 4; rep from * across, end with sc in top of turning ch.

Row 6: Work sc in each sc and 3 sc in each ch-4 sp; ch 1, turn.

Row 7: Sc in each sc, ch 1, turn.

Rep rows 2–7 for patt.

Berry Stitch

Chain multiple: any even number

Stitch Guide

Berry stitch (BS): Insert hook in specified sc and draw up a lp; ch 3, draw yarn through both lps on hook: BS made.

Instructions

Row 1: Sc in 2nd ch from hook and in each rem ch; ch 1, turn.

Row 2: Sc in next sc; *BS in next sc, sc in next sc; rep from * across, ch 1, turn.

Row 3: Sc in each sc across, ch 1, turn.

Row 4: *BS in next sc, sc in next sc; rep from * across, end sc in last sc; ch 1, turn.

Row 5: Rep row 3.

Rep rows 2–5 for patt.

Lucky Clovers

Chain multiple: 10 + 2

Instructions

Row 1: Sc in 2nd ch from hook and in each rem ch; ch 3 (counts as first dc of following row), turn.

Row 2: *Dc in next 2 sts, ch 3, sk next 2 sts, sc in next st; ch 3, sk 2 sts, dc in next 3 sts; rep from * across; ch 3, turn.

Row 3: *Dc in next 2 sts, ch 1, sc in next ch-3 sp; ch 3, sc in next ch-3 sp; ch 1, dc in next 3 sts; rep from * across, ch 3, turn.

Row 4: *Dc in next 2 dc; in next ch-3 sp work shell of (2 dc, ch 1, 2 dc); dc in next 3 dc; rep from * across; ch 3, turn.

Row 5: *Dc in next 2 sts, ch 3, sk next 2 sts, sc in next ch-1 sp of shell; ch 3, sk 2 sts, dc in next 3 sts; rep from * across, ch 3, turn.

Rep rows 3–5 for patt.

Bumps on Parade

Chain multiple: any even number

Stitch Guide

Bead stitch (BS): Holding back lp on hook, insert hook in next st, YO and draw up a lp, ch 3 in this lp only, YO and draw through 2 lps on hook: BS made; push all BSs to right side of work.

Instructions

Row 1 (RS): Tr in 5th ch from hook and in each rem ch; ch 1, turn.

Row 2: Sc in each st across, ch 1, turn.

Row 3: Sc in first st, BS in next st; *sc in next st, BS in next st; rep from * across to last st, sc in last st; ch 1, turn.

Row 4: Sc in each st across, ch 1, turn.

Row 5: Rep row 3.

Row 6: Sc in each st across, ch 4, turn.

Row 7: Sk first st, work tr in each st across; ch 1, turn.

Rep rows 2–7 for patt.

Cobblestones

Chain multiple: any uneven number

Stitch Guide

Extended double crochet (Edc): YO, insert hook in specified st and draw up lp; YO and draw through one lp, (YO and draw through 2 lps) twice: Edc made.

Instructions

Row 1: Sc in 2nd ch from hook and in each rem ch; ch 1, turn.

Row 2 (RS): *Sc in next st, Edc in next st; rep from * across ending with sc in last st; ch 2, turn.

Row 3: *Sc in next Edc, Edc in next sc; rep from * across, ending with sc in top of turning ch; ch 2, turn.

Rep row 3 for patt.

Tied Doubles

Chain multiple: 4

Instructions

Row 1 (RS): Sc in 2nd ch from hook and in each rem ch, ch 1, turn.

Row 2: Sc in first 2 sc; *ch 2, sk 2 sc, sc in next 2 sc; rep from * across; ch 3 (counts as first dc of following row), turn.

Row 3: Dc in next sc; *sk next 2 sc, 3 dc in ch-2 sp, dc in 2nd skipped sc; rep from * across; end last rep with dc in last 2 sc; ch 1, turn.

Row 4: Sc in first 2 dc; *ch 2, sk 2 dc, sc in next 2 dc; rep from * across; end last rep with sc in last dc and in top of turning ch; ch 3, turn.

Rep rows 3 and 4 for patt.

Single Crochet Variation

Chain multiple: any number

Stitch Guide

Extended single crochet (esc): Insert hook in specified st and draw up a lp; YO and draw through one lp, YO and draw through 2 lps: esc made.

Instructions

Row 1: Sc in 2nd ch from hook and in each rem sc; ch 1, turn.

Row 2 (RS): Esc in first st and in each rem st; ch 1, turn.

Row 3: Sc in each st across, ch 1, turn.

Rep rows 2 and 3 for patt.

Looped Petals

Chain multiple: 10 + 1

Stitch Guide

Double triple crochet (dtr): YO 3 times; insert hook in specified ch or st and draw up a lp; (YO and draw through 2 lps on hook) 4 times: dtr made.

Instructions

Row 1: Sc in 2nd ch from hook and in each rem ch; ch 4, turn.

Row 2: Dc in 3rd ch from hook; *ch 4, sk 4 sc, in next sc work (sc, ch 7) 3 times, sc in same sc; ch 4, sk 4 sc, dc in next sc; rep from * across to last 4 sc, ch 4, sk 3 sc, dc in last sc; ch 1, turn.

Row 3: *Sc in dc, ch 1, (sc in next ch-7 lp, ch 3) 2 times; sc in next ch-7 lp, ch 1; rep from * across; end with sc in dc, do not work in turning ch; ch 1, turn.

Row 4: (Sc, ch 7) twice in next sc, sc in same sc; *ch 4, sk next (ch-1 sp, sc, and ch-3 lp), dc in next sc; sk next (ch-3, sc, and ch-1 sp), ch 4; in next sc work (sc, ch 7) 3 times, sc in same sc; rep from * across; end last rep with (sc, ch 7, sc, ch 4, dtr) in last sc. Do not work in turning ch; ch 1, turn.

Row 5: Sc in first ch-7 lp, ch 3, sc in next ch-7 lp; *ch 1, sc in next dc, ch 1, (sc in next ch-7 lp, ch 3) 2 times, sc in next ch-7 lp; rep from * across, ending with sc in ch-7 lp, ch 3, sc in last ch-7 sp; ch 2, turn.

Row 6: Dc in first sc, *ch 4, sk (ch 3, sc, ch 1); in next sc work (sc, ch 7) 3 times, sc in same sc; ch 4, sk (ch 1, sc, ch 3), dc in next sc; rep from * across; end last rep with dc in last sc; do not work in turning ch; ch 1, turn.

Rep rows 3–6 for patt. End last rep by working row 3 or row 5.

Crossovers

Chain multiple: 2

Instructions

Row 1: Sc in 2nd ch from hook and in each rem ch; ch 4 (counts as a dc and ch-1 sp of following row), turn.

Row 2: *Sk next sc; dc in next sc; *ch 1, sk next sc, dc in next sc; rep from * across; ch 3, turn.

Row 3 (RS): *Sk next ch-1 sp, dc in next dc, dc in skipped ch-1 sp; rep from * across, ending last rep with dc in 3rd ch of turning ch; ch 4 (counts as a dc and ch-1 sp of following row), turn.

Row 4: *Dc in next dc, ch 1, sk next dc; rep from * across, ending last rep with ch 1, dc in top of turning ch; ch 3, turn.

Rep rows 3 and 4 for patt.

Pyramids

Chain multiple: 4 + 2

Stitch Guide

Extended double crochet (edc):
YO, insert hook in specified st and draw up a lp, YO and draw through one lp on hook, (YO and draw through 2 lps on hook) 2 times: edc made.

Double triple crochet (dtr): YO 3 times, insert hook in specified st and draw up a lp, (YO and draw through 2 lps) 4 times: dtr made.

Instructions

Row 1 (RS): Sc in 2nd ch from hook; *ch 6, sc in 3rd ch from hook, hdc in next ch, dc in next ch, edc in next ch (peak made); sk next 3 chs, sc in next ch; rep from * across; ch 6, turn.

Row 2: Sc in ch-2 sp at top of next peak; *ch 3, sc in ch-2 sp at top of next peak; rep from * across; ch 1, dtr in last sc; ch 10, turn.

Row 3: Sc in first sc; *ch 6, sc in 3rd ch from hook, hdc in next ch, dc in next ch, edc in next ch (peak made); sk next 3 chs, sc in next sc; rep from * across to turning ch-sp; ch 5, dtr in turning ch-sp; ch 1, turn.

Row 4: Sc in first dtr; *ch 3, sc in ch-2 sp at top of next peak; rep from * across, ending with sc in turning ch-sp; ch 1, turn.

Row 5: Sc in first sc; *ch 6, sc in 3rd ch from hook, hdc in next ch, dc in next ch, edc in next ch (peak made); sk next 3 chs, sc in next sc; rep from * across; ch 6, turn.

Rep rows 2–5 for patt. After last rep, end by working row 2.

Peepholes

Chain multiple: 14 + 7

Instructions

Row 1: Dc in 7th ch from hook, ch 1, sk 1 ch, dc in next ch; *ch 3, sk 3 chs, sc in next ch; ch 3, sk 3 chs, dc in next ch**; (ch 1, sk next ch, dc in next ch) 3 times; rep from * across, ending last rep at **; ch 1, sk next ch, dc in next ch; ch 1, sk next ch, dc in last ch; ch 4, (counts as a dc and ch-1 sp of following row throughout), turn.

Row 2: Dc in next dc, ch 1, dc in next dc; *ch 3, sc in next sc, ch 3; dc in next dc**, (ch 1, dc in next dc) 3 times; rep from * across, ending last rep at **; ch 1, dc in next dc, ch 1, dc in 4th ch of turning ch; ch 4, turn.

Row 3: Rep row 2.

Row 4: Dc in next dc, ch 1, dc in next dc; *ch 7, (dc in next dc, ch 1) 3 times, dc in next dc; rep from * across, ending last rep with ch 7, (dc in next dc, ch 1) twice, dc in 3rd ch of turning ch; ch 4, turn.

Row 5: Dc in next dc, ch 1, dc in next dc; *ch 3, sc in ch-7 sp, ch 3**, (dc in next dc, ch 1) 3 times, dc in next dc; rep from * across, ending last rep at **; (dc in next dc, ch 1) twice, dc in top of turning ch; ch 4, turn.

Rep rows 2–5 for patt. End last rep by working row 4.

Clusters Around

Chain multiple: any even number

Stitch Guide

Front-post cluster (FPcl): YO, insert hook from front to back to front around post (vertical bar) of specified st and draw up a lp; YO and draw through 2 lps; YO, insert hook again from front to back to front around post of same st and draw up a lp; YO and draw through 2 lps; YO and draw through 3 lps: FPcl made.

Instructions

Row 1: Sc in 2nd ch from hook and in each rem ch; ch 3 (counts as first dc of following row throughout), turn.

Row 2: Dc in next st and in each rem st across; ch 3, turn.

Row 3 (RS): *FPcl around post of next dc, dc in next dc; rep from * across; ch 3, turn.

Rep rows 2 and 3 for patt.

Pineapple Parade

Chain multiple: 22 + 9

Instructions

Row 1: Sc in 2nd ch from hook and in each rem ch; ch 3 (counts as a dc throughout), turn.

Row 2: Dc in next 2 sc, ch 2, sk 2 sc, dc in next 3 sc; *(ch 1, sk next sc, dc in next sc) 3 times; ch 3, sk 2 sc, dc in next sc; (ch 1, sk next sc, dc in next sc) twice, ch 1, sk next sc, dc in next 3 sc, ch 2, sk 2 chs, dc in last 3 sc; rep from * across, ch 3, turn.

Row 3 (RS): Dc in next 2 dc, ch 2, dc in next 3 dc; *ch 1, in next ch-3 sp work (dc, ch 3) 7 times, dc in same sp; ch 1, dc in next 3 dc, ch 2, dc in next 3 dc; rep from * across; ch 3, turn.

Row 4: Dc in next 2 dc, ch 2, dc in next 3 dc; *ch 2, sc in next ch-3 lp; (ch 3, dc in next ch-3 lp) 6 times, ch 2, dc in next 3 dc, ch 2, dc in next 3 dc; rep from * across; ch 3, turn.

Row 5: Dc in next 2 dc, ch 2, dc in next 3 dc; *(ch 3, sc in next ch-3 lp) 5 times, ch 3, dc in next 3 dc, ch 2, dc in next 3 dc; rep from * across; ch 3, turn.

Row 6: Dc in next 2 dc, ch 2, dc in next 3 dc; *ch 4, (sc in next ch-3 lp, ch 3) 3 times, sc in next ch-3 lp; ch 4, dc in next 3 dc, ch 2, dc in next 3 dc; rep from * across, ch 3, turn.

Row 7: Dc in next 2 dc, ch 2, dc in next 3 dc; *ch 6, (sc in next ch-3 lp, ch 3) twice, sc in next ch-3 lp; ch 6, dc in next 3 dc, ch 2, dc in next 3 dc; rep from * across, ch 3, turn.

Row 8: Dc in next 2 dc, ch 2, dc in next 3 dc; *ch 6, sc in next ch-3 lp, ch 3, sc in next ch-3 lp, ch 6; dc in next 3 dc, ch 2, dc in next 3 dc; rep from * across, ch 3, turn.

Row 9: Dc in next 2 dc, ch 2, dc in next 3 dc; ch 1, in next ch-3 lp work (dc, ch 3) 7 times, dc in same lp; ch 1, dc in next 3 dc, ch 2, dc in next 3 dc; rep from * across, ch 3, turn.

Rep rows 4–9 for patt. End last rep after working row 8.

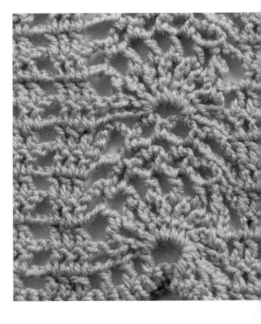

Four-Way Clusters

Chain multiple: 9 + 8

Stitch Guide

Cluster (CL): *YO, insert hook in specified st and draw up a lp to height of a dc; YO and draw through 2 lps; rep from * once more in same st, YO and draw through 3 lps: CL made.

Instructions

Row 1: Dc in 8th ch from hook; *ch 2, sk 2 chs, dc in next ch; rep from * across; ch 5 (counts as a dc and ch-2 sp of following row), turn.

Row 2: Dc in next dc; *ch 2, work CL in same st as last dc made; sk next dc, work CL in next dc; ch 2, dc in same dc as CL just made; ch 2, dc in next dc; rep from * across, ending last rep with dc in 3rd ch of turning ch; ch 5, turn.

Row 3: *Dc in next dc, CL in st between next 2 CL, ch 5, CL between same 2 CL, dc in next dc, ch 2; rep from * across, ending last rep with dc in 3rd ch of turning ch; ch 5, turn.

Row 4: *Dc in next dc, ch 2, dc in ch-5 sp, ch 2, dc in next dc, ch 2; rep from * across, ending last rep with dc in 3rd ch of turning ch; ch 5, turn.

Rep rows 2–4 for patt.

Soaring Arches

Chain multiple: 9 + 3

Instructions

Row 1: Dc in 4th ch from hook, dc in each of next 2 chs; *ch 2, sk 2 chs, dc in each of next 3 chs, ch 1, sk next ch, dc in each of next 3 chs; rep from * across, ending last rep with ch 2, sk 2 chs, dc in each of last 4 chs; ch 3 (counts as first dc of following row), turn.

Row 2: *Dc in each of next 3 dc, ch 5**, dc in each of next 3 dc, ch 1; rep from * across, ending last rep at **; dc in each of last 4 dc; ch 1, turn.

Row 3: *In next ch-5 lp work 12 dc, sc in next ch-1 sp; rep from * across, ending last rep with sc in top of turning ch; ch 6, turn.

Row 4: *Sk 4 dc, sc in each of next 4 dc, ch 2, tr in next sc, ch 2; rep from * across, ending last rep with tr in last sc; ch 3, turn.

Row 5: *Work 2 dc in next ch-2 sp, dc in next sc, ch 2, sk 2 sc, dc in next sc**, 2 dc in next ch-2 sp, ch 1; rep from * across, ending last rep at **; 3 dc in turning ch-lp; ch 3, turn.

Rep rows 2–5 for patt.

Rows of Posies

Chain multiple: 7 + 1

Stitch Guide

Petal: Work (sc, ch 4, tr, ch 4, sc) all in same st: petal made.

Instructions

Row 1: Sc in 2nd ch from hook and in next ch; *ch 1, sk next ch, sc in next ch; rep from * across to last 3 chs, ch 1, sk next ch, sc in each of next 2 chs; ch 4 (counts as a dc and ch-1 sp of following rows), turn.

Row 2: *Sk next sc, dc in next ch-1 sp, ch 1; rep from * across to last 2 sc, ch 1, sk next sc, dc in last sc; ch 1, turn.

Row 3: Sc in first dc; work petal in next ch-1 sp; *(ch 1, sk next dc, sc in next ch-1 sp) twice; ch 1, sk next dc, work petal in next ch-1 sp, ch 1, work petal in next ch-1 sp; rep from * across, ending last rep by working petal in last ch-1 sp, ch 1, sc in turning ch-sp; ch 6, turn.

Row 4: *Sc in tr of each of next 2 petals, ch 4; rep from * across, ending last rep with ch 2, tr in last sc; ch 1, turn.

Row 5: Sc in tr, ch 2; *work petal in each of next 2 sc, ch 4; rep from * across, ending last rep with ch 2 instead of ch 4, sc in turning ch-sp; ch 4, turn.

Row 6: *Sc in tr of next petal, ch 4, sc in tr of next petal**, ch 1; rep from * across, ending last rep at **; ch 1, tr in last sc; ch 1, turn.

Row 7: Sc in tr, ch 1, sc in next sc; *ch 1, sc in next ch-4 sp, ch 1, sc in same ch-4 sp; (ch 1, sc in next sc) twice; rep from * across, ending last rep with sc in last sc, sc in top of turning ch; ch 4, turn.

Row 8: *Sk next sc, dc in next ch-1 sp, ch 1; rep from * across, ending with ch 1, dc in last sc; ch 1, turn.

Row 9: *Sc in dc, ch 1, sc in dc; rep from * across, ending last rep with sc in top of turning ch; ch 4, turn.

Row 10: Rep row 8.

Row 11: Rep row 3.

Rep rows 2–11 for patt. End last rep by working row 9.

Left Slant

Chain multiple: 4 + 3

Instructions

Row 1: Dc in 4th ch from hook and in each rem ch; ch 1, turn.

Row 2: Sc in first dc; *ch 3, sk 3 dc, sc in next dc; rep from * across, ending last rep with sc in top of turning ch; ch 3, turn.

Row 3: *3 dc in sc at base of ch, sc in next sc, ch 3; rep from * across, ending last rep with sc in last sc; ch 6, turn.

Row 4: Sc in top of next ch-3; *ch 3, sc in top of next ch-3; rep from * across; ch 3, turn.

Row 5: Rep row 3, ending last rep with sc in 3rd ch of turning ch; ch 6, turn.

Row 6: Rep row 4.

Row 7: *3 dc in next ch-3 sp, dc in next sc; rep from * across, ending last rep with 3 dc in ch-6 sp, dc in 3rd ch of ch-6 sp; ch 1, turn.

Rep rows 2–7 for patt.

Spikes

Chain multiple: 3 + 2
Two colors: color A and color B

Stitch Guide

Spike stitch (SS): Insert hook in st 2 rows directly below next st and draw up a long lp to height of current row; YO and draw through both lps on hook: SS made.

Instructions

Work beg ch with color A.

Row 1 (RS): With color A, sc in 2nd ch from hook and in each ch across; ch 1, turn.

Row 2: Sc in first sc and in each sc across; ch 1, turn.

Rows 3 and 4: Rep row 2 two times more. Finish off color A.

Row 5 (RS): With right side facing you, join color B with sc in first sc at right, sc in same sc; *sk next 2 sc, work 3 SS in next st; rep from * across to last 3 sc; sk next 2 sc, 2 sc in last sc. Finish off color B. Turn.

Row 6: With wrong side facing you, join in color A with sc in first st, sc in next st and in each st across; ch 1, turn.

Row 7: Sc in first sc and in each sc across; ch 1, turn.

Rep rows 2–7 for patt. After last rep, end by working row 2.

Crosses and Shells

Chain multiple: 9 + 1

Stitch Guide

Shell: Work 5 dc in specified st: shell made.

Cross stitch (CS): Sk next st, dc in next st, dc in skipped st: CS made.

Instructions

Row 1: Sc in 2nd ch from hook and in each rem ch; ch 3 (counts as first dc of following row), turn.

Row 2: Dc in next sc; *ch 1, sk next sc, dc in next 3 sc, ch 1, sk next sc, dc in next sc; work CS over next 2 sc, dc in next sc; rep from * across to last 7 sc, ch 1, sk next sc, dc in next 3 sc, ch 1, sk next sc, dc in last 2 sc; ch 3, turn.

Row 3 (RS): Dc in next dc; *sk ch-1 sp and next dc, shell in next dc; sk next dc and ch-1 sp, dc in next dc; CS over next 2 dc, dc in next dc; rep from * across, ending last rep with sk next dc and ch-1 sp, dc in last 2 dc; ch 3, turn.

Row 4: Dc in next dc; *ch 1, sk first dc of shell, dc in next 3 dc of shell, sk last dc of shell, ch 1; dc in next dc, CS over next 2 dc, dc in next dc; rep from * across, ending with ch 1, dc in last 2 dc.

Rep rows 3 and 4 for patt.

V-Stitch

Chain multiple: 3 + 2

Stitch Guide

V-stitch (V-st): (Dc, ch 1, dc) all in same st or sp: V-st made.

Instructions

Row 1 (RS): Dc in 5th ch from hook (counts as first V-st); *sk 2 chs, V-st in next ch; rep from * across; ch 4 (counts as a dc, ch 1), turn.

Row 2: Dc in first ch-1 sp; *V-st in ch-1 sp of next V-st; rep from * across, end with V-st in last sp; ch 4, turn.

Rep row 2 for patt.

Little Vs

Chain multiple: 2 + 1

Stitch Guide

V-stitch (V-st): (Dc, ch 1, dc) in specified st: V-st made.

Instructions

Row 1: Sc in 2nd ch from hook and in each rem ch; ch 3, turn.

Row 2: *Sk next sc, V-st in next sc; rep from * across to last 2 sc, sk next sc, dc in last sc; ch 3, turn.

Row 3: *V-st in ch-1 sp of next V-st; rep from * to last st, dc in last st; ch 3, turn.

Rep row 3 for patt.

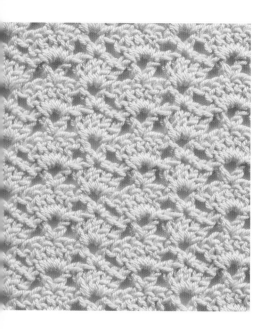

Flower Garden

Chain multiple: 8 + 5

Instructions

Row 1 (RS): Dc in 5th ch from hook; *sk 3 chs, 5 dc in next ch, sk 3 chs, (dc, ch 1, dc) in next ch; rep from * across; ch 3 (counts as first dc of following row), turn.

Row 2: 2 dc in next ch-1 sp, sk 3 dc, (dc, ch 1, dc) in next dc; *5 dc in next ch-1 sp, sk 3 dc, (dc, ch 1, dc) in next dc; rep from * to last sp, 3 dc in last sp; ch 4, turn.

Row 3: Dc in next dc; *5 dc in next ch-1 sp, sk 3 dc, (dc, ch 1, dc) in next dc; rep from * across; ch 3, turn.

Rep rows 2 and 3 for patt.

Floating Shells

Chain multiple: 8 + 2
Two colors: color A and color B

Stitch Guide

V-stitch (V-st): In specified ch or sp work (dc, ch 2, dc): V-st made.

Shell: In specified sp work (3 dc, ch 1, 3 dc): shell made.

Instructions

Work beg ch with color A.

Row 1: With color A, sc in 2nd ch from hook and in each rem ch; ch 6 (counts as first dc and ch-3 sp of following row), turn.

Row 2: *Sk 3 sc, V-st in next sc; ch 3, sk 3 sc, dc in next sc, ch 3; rep from * across, ending with dc in last sc; ch 1, turn.

Row 3: Sc in first dc, ch 1, sc in ch-3 sp; *shell in center ch-2 sp of next V-st, sc in ch-3 lp, ch 2, sc in next ch-3 lp; rep from * across, ending last rep with (sc, ch 1, sc) in ch-6 turning ch-lp, changing to color B in last st; with color B, ch 4, turn.

Row 4: With color B, dc in ch-1 sp; *ch 3, dc in ch-1 sp of next shell, ch 3, V-st in next ch-2 sp; rep from * across to last shell, ch 3, dc in ch-1 sp of last shell, ch 3, dc in ch-1 sp, ch 1, dc in last sc; ch 3, turn.

Row 5: Work 3 dc in ch-1 sp; *sc in ch-3 sp, ch 2, sc in next ch-3 sp, shell in ch-2 sp of next V-st; rep from * across, ending last rep with sc in ch-3 sp, ch 2, sc in ch-3 sp, 4 dc in turning ch-4 sp, changing to color A in last st; with color A, ch 6, turn.

Row 6: With color A, V-st in ch-2 sp; *ch 3, dc in center ch-1 sp of next shell, ch 3, V-st in ch-2 sp; rep from * across, ending with ch 3, dc in top of turning ch; ch 1, turn.

Row 7: Sc in dc, ch 1, sc in ch-3 sp; *shell in center ch-2 sp of next V-st, sc in ch-3 sp, ch 2, sc in next ch-3 lp; rep from * across, ending last rep with sc, ch 1, sc in ch-6 turning ch-lp, changing to color B in last st; with color B, ch 4, turn.

Rep rows 4–7 for patt.

Crazy Vs

Chain multiple: 9 + 2

Stitch Guide

V-stitch (V-st): Work (dc, ch 2, dc) all in same ch or st: V-st made.

Double triple crochet (dtr): YO 3 times, insert hook in specified st or sp and draw up a lp; (YO and draw through first 2 lps on hook) 4 times: dtr made.

Instructions

Row 1 (RS): Sc in 2nd ch from hook; *sk 3 chs, V-st in each of next 2 chs; sk 3 chs, sc in next ch; rep from * across, ch 1, turn.

Row 2: Sc in first sc; *in next ch-2 sp work (dtr, 3 dc); in next ch-2 sp work (3 dc, dtr); sc in next sc; rep from * across; ch 7 (counts as a tr and ch-3 sp on following row), turn.

Row 3: Sk first 4 sts, sc in each of next 2 dc; *ch 7, sk 7 sts, sc in each of next 2 dc; rep from * to last 4 sts, ch 3, sk 3 sts, tr in last sc; ch 1, turn.

Row 4: Sc in first tr; *V-st in each of next 2 sc, sc in ch-7 lp; rep from * across; end with sc in 4th ch of ch-7 turning ch; ch 1, turn.

Rep rows 2–4 for patt. After last rep, end by working row 2.

Victory Stitch 1

Chain multiple: any uneven number

Stitch Guide

V-Stitch (V-st): (tr, ch 1, tr) all in same st: V-st made.

Instructions

Row 1: Sc in 2nd ch from hook and in each rem ch; ch 5 (counts as a tr and ch-1 sp), turn.

Row 2: *Sk next 2 sc, V-st in next sc; rep from * to last 2 sts, sk next st, tr in last st; ch 4, turn.

Row 3 (RS): *V-St in ch-1 sp of next V-st; rep from * across, tr in last st; ch 4, turn.

Rep row 3 for patt.

Easy Pops

Chain multiple: 4 + 2

Stitch Guide

Popcorn stitch (PC): Work 4 dc in specified st; drop lp from hook, insert hook from front to back in top of first dc worked, insert hook in dropped lp and draw through, ch 1: PC made.

V-stitch (V-st): Work (dc, ch 2, dc) in specified st or sp: V-st made.

Instructions

Row 1: Sc in 2nd ch from hook and in each rem ch; ch 3 (counts as first dc of following row), turn.

Row 2 (RS): *Sk next sc, V-st in next sc**, sk next sc, PC in next sc; rep from * across, ending last rep at **; sk next sc, dc in last sc; ch 3, turn.

Row 3: *V-st in ch-2 sp of next V-st**, V-st in top of PC; rep from * across, ending last rep at **; dc in top of turning ch; ch 3, turn.

Row 4: *Vst in ch-2 sp of next Vst**, PC in ch-2 sp of next V-st; rep from * across, ending last rep at **; dc in last dc; ch 3, turn.

Rep rows 3 and 4 for patt.

Triple Loops

Chain multiple: 16 + 12

Stitch Guide

V-stitch (V-st): In specified st work (dc, ch 1, dc): V-st made.

V-stitch in V-stitch (V-st in V-st): Work V-st in ch-1 sp of next V-st: V-st in V-st made.

Cluster (CL): YO, insert hook in next dc and draw up a lp, YO and draw through 2 lps; YO, sk 3 dc, insert hook in next dc and draw up a lp, YO and draw through 2 lps; YO and draw through 3 lps: CL made.

Instructions

Row 1: Sc in 2nd ch from hook and in each rem ch; ch 3 (counts as a dc throughout), turn.

Row 2: *Sk next sc; (V-st in next sc, sk 2 sc) twice, V-st in next sc, sk 1 sc, dc in next 7 sc; rep from * to last 10 sts, sk one st (V-st in next sc, sk 2 sc) twice, V-st in next sc, sk next sc, dc in last sc; ch 3, turn.

Row 3 (RS): *(V-st in V-st) 3 times, dc in next dc; work CL over next 5 dc; sc in sp between the two joined sts of CL, (ch 4, sc in same sp) 3 times, dc in next dc; rep from * across to last 3 V-st, (V-st in V-st) 3 times, dc in top of turning ch; ch 3, turn.

Row 4: *(V-st in V-st) 3 times, dc in next dc; ch 2, sc in center ch-4 lp, ch 2, dc in next dc; rep from * across to last 3 V-st, (V-st in V-st) 3 times, dc in last dc; ch 3, turn.

Row 5: *(V-st in V-st) 3 times, dc in next dc, 2 dc in ch-2 sp, dc in sc, 2 dc in ch-2 sp, dc in next dc; rep from * across to last 3 V-st, (V-st in V-st) 3 times, dc in top of turning ch; ch 3, turn.

Rep rows 3–5 for patt.

Frippery

Chain multiple: 10 + 2

Stitch Guide

Cluster (CL): *YO, insert hook in specified st and draw up a lp to height of a dc; YO and draw through 2 lps; rep from * once more in same st, YO and draw through all 3 lps: CL made.

V-Stitch (V-st): In specified st work (dc, ch 4, dc): V-st made.

Instructions

Row 1: Sc in 2nd ch from hook and in each rem ch; ch 5 (counts as a dc and ch-2 sp on following row), turn.

Row 2: Sk next 4 sc, work V-st in next sc; *ch 2, sk next 4 sc, dc in next sc**, ch 2, sk 4 sc, work V-st in next sc; rep from * across, ending last rep at **; ch 1, turn.

Row 3: *Work 2 sc in next ch-2 sp, sc in first dc of next V-st, 3 sc in ch-4 sp of same V-st, sc in last dc of same V-st**, 2 sc in next ch-2 sp, sk next dc; rep from * across, ending last rep at **; work 2 sc in ch-5 lp, ch 3, turn.

Row 4: *Sk next 2 sc; work CL in each of next 5 sc, sk next 2 sc**, dc in dc in 2nd row below; rep from * across, ending last rep at **; dc in turning ch-1; ch 1, turn.

Row 5: *(Sc in next CL, ch 1) 5 times, ch 1, sk next dc; rep from * across, ending last rep with sc in 3rd ch of turning ch-3; ch 5, turn.

Row 6: *V-st in ch-1 sp above center CL 2 rows below, ch 2, dc in next dc 2 rows below**, ch 2; rep from * across, ending last rep at **; ch 1, turn.

Rep rows 3–6 for patt.

Waves 2

Chain multiple: 8 + 2

Stitch Guide

V-stitch (V-st): In same st work (dc, ch 1, dc): V-st made.

Instructions

Row 1 (RS): Sc in 2nd ch from hook; *ch 2, sk 2 chs, dc in next ch, 3 dc in next ch, dc in next ch, ch 2, sk 2 chs, sc in next ch; rep from * across; ch 4, turn.

Row 2: *Dc in next dc, ch 1, sk next dc, V-st in next dc, ch 1, sk next dc, dc in next dc, ch 2; rep from * across, ending last rep with ch 1 (instead of ch 2), dc in last sc; ch 3, turn.

Row 3: 2 dc in ch-1 sp, ch 2; *sc in ch-1 sp of next V-st, ch 2, 5 dc in next ch-2 sp, ch 2; rep from * across, ending last rep with sc in next ch-1 sp, ch 2, 2 dc in ch-4 sp, dc in 3rd ch of ch-4 sp; ch 3, turn.

Row 4: Dc in base of turning ch, ch 1, sk next dc, dc in next dc; *ch 2, dc in next dc, ch 1, sk next dc, V-st in next dc, ch 1, sk next dc, dc in next dc; rep from * across, ending last rep with ch 2, dc in next dc; ch 1, sk next dc, 2 dc in top of turning ch, ch 1, turn.

Row 5: Sc in base of turning ch; *ch 2, 5 dc in ch-2 sp, ch 2, sc in ch-1 sp of next V-st; rep from across to last ch-2 sp, ch 2, 5 dc in last ch-2 sp, ch 2, sc in top of turning ch; ch 4, turn.

Rep rows 2–5 for patt.

Sophistication

Chain multiple: 6 + 3

Stitch Guide

V-stitch (V-st): (Dc, ch 2, dc) all in same st: V-st made.

Cluster (CL): *YO, insert hook in specified st and draw up a lp; YO and draw through 2 lps; rep from * once in same st, YO and draw through all 3 lps: CL made.

Cluster shell (CL shell): In specified sp work (CL, ch 1) twice, CL in same sp: CL shell made.

Double triple crochet (dtr): YO 3 times; insert hook in specified st and draw up a lp; (YO and draw through 2 lps) 4 times: dtr made.

Instructions

Row 1 (RS): Dc in 4th ch from hook; *ch 1, sk next ch, dc in next ch; rep from * across to last st, dc in last st; ch 1, turn.

Row 2: Sc in first dc; *ch 2, sk next dc and next ch-1 sp, V-st in next dc, ch 2, sk next ch-1 sp and next dc, sc in next ch-1 sp; rep from * across, ending last rep with sc in top of turning ch; ch 4 (counts as a dc and ch-1 sp), turn.

Row 3: *CL shell in ch-2 sp of next V-st, ch 1; rep from * across, dtr in last sc; ch 1, turn.

Row 4: Sc in dtr, sk next ch-1 sp; *ch 1, sc in next ch-1 sp; rep from * across, ending last rep with ch 1, sc in top of turning ch; ch 3, turn.

Row 5: Dc in next ch-1 sp; *ch 1, dc in next ch-1 sp; rep from * to last sc, dc in last sc; ch 1, turn.

Rep rows 2–5 for patt.

Victory Stitch 2

Chain multiple: 3

Stitch Guide

V-stitch (V-st): In specified st work (dc, ch 1, dc): V-st made.

Instructions

Row 1: Sc in 2nd ch from hook, ch 1, sk next ch, sc in next ch; *ch 3, sk 2 chs, sc in next ch; rep from * across to last 2 chs, ch 1, sk next ch, sc in last ch; ch 3 (counts as a dc of following row), turn.

Row 2: *V-st in next sc; rep from * across, ending last rep with dc in last sc; ch 1, turn.

Row 3: Sc in first dc, ch 1; *sc in ch-1 sp of next V-st, ch 3; rep from * across, ending last rep with ch 1 (instead of 3), sc in top of turning ch; ch 3, turn.

Rep rows 2 and 3 for patt.

Pretty Baskets

Chain multiple: 20 + 8

Stitch Guide

V-stitch (V-st): Work (dc, ch 2, dc) all in same st: V-st made.

Picot: Ch 3, sl st in base of ch: picot made.

Instructions

Row 1: Sc in 2nd ch from hook and in each rem ch; ch 5 (counts as a dc and ch-2 sp on following row), turn.

Row 2: Sk next 2 sc, dc in next sc, ch 2, sk 2 sc, dc in next sc; *ch 2, sk 2 sc, sc in next sc, ch 3, sk 3 sc, V-st in next sc; ch 3, sk 3 sc, sc in next sc, (ch 2, sk next 2 sc, dc in next sc) 3 times; rep from * across; ch 5 (counts as a dc and ch-2 sp on following row), turn.

Row 3: Dc in next dc, ch 2, dc in next dc; *5 dc in next ch-3 sp, 5 dc in ch-2 sp of next V-st, 5 dc in next ch-3 sp; dc in next dc, (ch 2, dc in next dc) twice; rep from * across, ending last rep with dc in 3rd ch of turning ch; ch 5, turn.

Row 4: Dc in next dc, ch 2, dc in next dc; *ch 3, sk 4 dc, in next dc work (sc, picot); sc in next dc, ch 5, sk 3 dc, in next dc work (sc, picot), sc in next dc, ch 3, sk 4 dc; (dc in next dc, ch 2) twice, dc in next dc; rep from * across, ending last rep with dc in 3rd ch of turning ch; ch 5, turn.

Row 5: Dc in next dc, ch 2, dc in next dc; *ch 6, sc in ch-5 lp, ch 6, dc in next dc; (ch 2, dc in next dc) twice; rep from * across, ending with dc in top of turning ch; ch 5, turn.

Row 6: Dc in next dc, ch 2, dc in next dc; *ch 2, sc in ch-6 lp, ch 3, V-st in next sc; ch 3, sc in ch-6 lp, ch 2; (dc in next dc, ch 2) twice, dc in next dc; rep from * across, ending last rep with dc in top of turning ch; ch 5, turn.

Rep rows 3–6 for patt.

All Wrapped Up

Chain multiple: 7 + 6

Stitch Guide

Cluster (CL): *YO, insert hook in specified place and draw up a lp to height of a dc; YO and draw through 2 lps; rep from * twice in same place; YO and draw through 4 lps: CL made.

V-stitch (V-st): Work (dc, ch 1, dc) in specified ch or sp: V-st made.

Instructions

Row 1 (RS): Dc in 6th ch from hook and in next 2 chs; work CL around 3-dc group just made (in sp between first dc made and turning ch); *sk 2 chs, V-st in next ch, sk 2 chs, dc in each of next 3 chs, work CL around 3-dc group just made (in sp between first dc of this group and last V-st); rep from * across to last 2 chs, sk next ch, dc in last ch; ch 3 (counts as a dc of following rows), turn.

Row 2: *Dc in top of CL and in each of next 3 dc, V-st in center ch-1 sp of next V-st; rep from * across, ending last rep with dc in last CL, dc in last 3 dc and in top of turning ch; ch 3, turn.

Row 3: *Dc in next 3 dc, work CL as before, V-st in ch-1 sp of next V-st; rep from * across, ending last rep with dc in top of turning ch; ch 3, turn.

Rep rows 2 and 3 for patt.

Delightful Diamonds

Chain multiple: 16 + 10

Stitch Guide

V-stitch (V-st): In specified st work (dc, ch 2, dc): V-st made.

Instructions

Row 1 (RS): Sc in 2nd ch from hook; *ch 5, sk 3 chs, sc in next ch; rep from * across, ch 5, turn.

Row 2: Sc in first ch-5 sp; *ch 1, V-st in next sc, ch 1; (sc in next ch-5 sp, ch 5) 3 times, sc in next ch-5 sp; rep from * across, ending last rep with sc in last ch-5 sp, ch 2, dc in last sc; ch 1, turn.

Row 3: Sc in first dc; *ch 1, V-st in next sc, ch 1, sc in ch-2 sp of next V-st; ch 1, V-st in next sc, ch 1**; (sc in next ch-5 sp, ch 5) twice, sc in next ch-5 sp; rep from * across, ending last rep at **, sc in turning ch-5 sp; ch 1, turn.

Row 4: *Sc in ch-2 sp of next V-st, ch 1, V-st in next sc; ch 1, sc in ch-2 sp of next V-st; (ch 5, sc in next ch-5 sp) twice, ch 5; rep from * across, ending last rep with sc in ch-2 sp of next V-st, ch 2, dc in sc; ch 2, turn.

Row 5: Sc in first dc; *ch 5, sc in ch-2 sp of next V-st**, (ch 5, sc in next ch-5 lp) 3 times; rep from * across, ending last rep at **; ch 5, sc in turning ch-lp, ch 5, turn.

Row 6: *Sc in next ch-5 lp, ch 5; rep from * across, ending last rep with sc in last ch-5 sp, ch 2, dc in last sc; ch 5, turn.

Row 7: Rep row 6, ending last rep with ch 2, dc in next ch-5 lp; ch 5, turn.

Rep rows 2–7 for patt.

Vs in a Row

Chain multiple: 3 + 1

Stitch Guide

V-stitch: (dc, ch 1, dc) all in same st: V-st made.

Instructions

Row 1 (RS): Dc in 4th ch from hook and in each rem ch; ch 3 (counts as first dc of following row), turn.

Row 2: Dc in each dc; ch 3, turn.

Row 3: Rep row 2.

Row 4: Sk next 2 dc, V-st in next dc; *sk next 2 dc, V-st in next dc; rep from * to last 2 sts, sk next dc, dc in last dc; ch 3, turn.

Row 5: Dc in each dc and ch-1 sp across; ch 3, turn.

Rows 6 and 7: Rep row 2.

Rep rows 4–7 for patt.

Floating Chains

Chain multiple: 10 + 2

Stitch Guide

V-stitch (V-st): Work (dc, ch 2, dc) all in same st: V-st made.

Shell: Work 5 dc in same sp: shell made.

Instructions

Row 1: Sc in 2nd ch from hook and in next ch; *ch 3, sk 3 chs, V-st in next ch; ch 3, sk 3 chs, sc in next 3 chs; rep from * across, ending last rep with sc in last 2 chs; ch 1, turn.

Row 2: Sc in first sc; *ch 4, shell in ch-2 sp of next V-st, ch 4, sk next sc, sc in next sc; rep from * across, ending last rep with sk next sc, sc in last sc; ch 7, turn.

Row 3: *Sc in each of next 5 dc, ch 7; rep from * across, ending last rep with ch 4 (instead of 7), tr in last sc; ch 3, turn.

Row 4: Dc in base of ch; *ch 3, sk next sc, sc in each of next 3 sc**, ch 3, V-st in 4th ch of ch-7 lp; rep from * across, ending last rep at **; ch 3, 2 dc in 4th ch of turning ch; ch 3, turn.

Row 5: Work 2 dc in base of ch; *ch 4, sk next sc, sc in next sc, ch 4, shell in ch-2 sp of next V-st; rep from * across, ending last rep with ch 5, sk next sc, sc in next sc, ch 4, 3 dc in top of turning ch; ch 1, turn.

Row 6: Sc in each of first 3 dc; *ch 7, sc in each of next 5 dc; rep from * across, ending last rep with sc in each of last 2 dc, sc in top of turning ch; ch 1, turn.

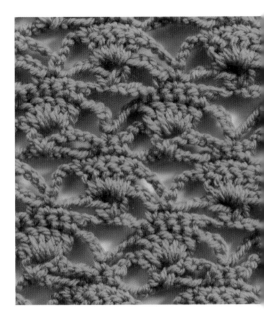

Row 7: Sc in first 2 sc; *ch 3, V-st in 4th ch of ch-7 lp, ch 3, sk next sc, sc in next 3 sc; rep from * across, ending last rep with sc in last 2 sc; ch 1, turn.

Rep rows 2–7 for patt.

Wide Open Spaces

Chain multiple: 14 + 4

Stitch Guide

V-stitch (V-st): Work (dc, ch 2, dc) all in same st: V-st made.

Instructions

Row 1: Sc in 2nd ch from hook and in each rem ch; ch 4 (counts as a dc and ch-1 sp of following row), turn.

Row 2: Sk next sc, dc in next sc, ch 1, sk next sc, dc in next sc; *ch 9, sk 7 sc, (dc in next sc, ch 1, sk next sc) 3 times, dc in next sc; rep from * across to last 5 sc, (dc, ch 1, sk next sc) twice, dc in last sc; ch 4 (counts as a dc and ch-1 sp on following row), turn.

Row 3: Dc in next dc, ch 1, dc in next dc, ch 2; *in next ch-9 sp work (dc, hdc, sc, hdc, dc); ch 2, (dc in next dc, ch 1) 3 times, dc in next dc, ch 2; rep from * across, ending last rep with (dc in next dc, ch 1) twice, dc in 3rd ch of turning ch; ch 4, turn.

Row 4: (Dc in next dc, ch 1) twice; *2 dc in next dc, dc in next hdc, dc in next sc, dc in next hdc, 2 dc in next dc; (ch 1, dc in next dc) 4 times, ch 1; rep from * across, ending last rep with (ch 1, dc in next dc) twice, ch 1, dc in 3rd ch of turning ch; ch 4, turn.

Row 5: Dc in next dc, ch 1, dc in next dc; *ch 2, sk 3 dc, work V-st in next dc, ch 2, sk 3 dc, (dc in next dc, ch 1) 3 times, dc in next dc; rep from * across, ending last rep with (dc in next dc, ch 1) twice, dc in 3rd ch of turning ch; ch 4, turn.

Row 6: Dc in next dc, ch 1, dc in next dc; *ch 9, (dc in next dc, ch 1)

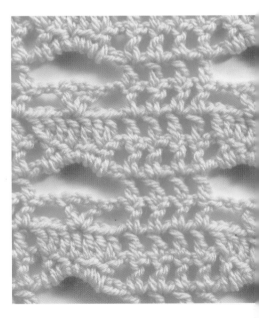

3 times, dc in next dc; rep from * across, ending last rep with (dc in next dc, ch 1) twice, dc in 3rd ch of turning ch; ch 4, turn.

Rep rows 3–6 for patt.

The team of Jean Leinhauser and Rita Weiss has produced projects for knitters and crocheters for many years, but each of these women is well-known and respected in her own right. Both women were among the first elected to the Crochet Guild of America's Hall of Fame. Leinhauser and Weiss are co-owners of Crochet Partners, one of the first crochet internet-discussion groups with thousands of members located all over the world, and of Creative Partners, which specializes in creating needlework books.

Jean Leinhauser was trained as a journalist, and began her professional needlework career as design director for the Boye Needle Company, where she developed new products and publications. She left Boye to start Leisure Arts, which eventually became the country's largest independent needlework book publisher. After leaving Leisure Arts she founded the American School of Needlework (ASN Publishing).

Highly respected by all crochet and knit enthusiasts, Jean served as cochairman of the Standards Committee of the Craft Yarn Council, where she was instrumental in getting all manufacturers and publishers in the United States to work with a standard set of guidelines.

Rita Weiss is an author, designer, and teacher whose name has become a household word in the fields of knitting, crochet, quilting, and stitchery. As founder and head of the Dover Publications needlework division for many years, she became known as an expert in thread crochet.

As executive vice president of the American School of Needlework, Rita produced many books on knitting, crocheting, quilting, embroidery, and other needle arts. She served as president of both the International Quilting Association (IQA) and—a few years later—the Crochet Guild of America (CGOA).

The author of more than 100 books in the needle arts, Rita has taught and lectured in the United States as well as Europe and Australia.

Index